# Meditation
## Science and Practice

*This book is dedicated to my wife,* **Manorama (Pai)**,
*who endured — and endured — and endured*

*and*

*to my eldest daughter-in-law,* **Smita (Ilu)**,
*who served me*
*without expecting any return for her service*

# Meditation

## Science and Practice

*by*

**N.C. Panda**

**D.K. Printworld (P) Ltd.**

**New Delhi**

**Cataloging in Publication Data — DK**
[Courtesy: D.K. Agencies (P) Ltd. <docinfo@dkagencies.com>]

**Panda, N.C. (Nursingh Charan), 1929-**
Meditation.
xvi, 336 p., 23 cm.
Includes bibliographical references (p. )
Includes Index.
ISBN 8124602115

1. Meditation I. Title.

**ISBN 81-246-0211-5** (Hardbound)
**ISBN 81-246-0212-3** (Paperback)


*First published in India* 2003
*Second impression in* 2008



*Printed and published by*:
D.K. Printworld (P) Ltd.
*Regd. office* : *'Sri Kunj'*, F-52, Bali Nagar
Ramesh Nagar Metro Station
New Delhi - 110 015
*Phones* : (011) 2545 3975, 2546 6019
*Fax* : (011) 2546 5926
*E-mail* : dkprintworld@vsnl.net
*Web* : www.dkprintworld.com

# Preface

How old Indian Yoga is has not been accurately determined. Four and a half millennia before Christ may be a roughly estimated date. Patañjali who lived perhaps in the second century BC systematically codified Yoga in aphorisms. In the Indian tradition, the detailed techniques of Yoga were passed on from the preceptor to the disciple through personal coaching and practical demonstration. We get some seminal knowledge on Yoga from the old Indian scriptures, but no old scripture dilates and elucidates the topic exhaustively.

In the twentieth century, a number of books have been written by Indian and foreign authors on Yoga. For many persons, Yoga and *āsana*s (yogic postures) are synonymous. It is very unfortunate that such an erroneous concept has been deep-rooted in the minds of a wider population. Good books have been written on *Haṭha-yoga* with special reference to *āsana*s, *bandha*s, *mudrā*s, *prāṇāyāma* and the six purificatory processes. In contrast, good books on meditation are not many. Some Yoga Schools keep their meditational techniques and the associated *mantra* for initiation secret and occult. A psychology of monopolisation and commercialisation is perhaps operative. Some such occult schools occasionally pass on wrong techniques to their initiated disciples. But no public debate can be made since these techniques do not appear in printed form. Some books on meditation are too much verbose and eulogistic with very little information on the actual methodology. Some modern Yoga Schools use new phraseology to show that their Yoga is a new discovery, not related in any way to the wisdom of ancient Indian seers.

Many modern Yoga Schools do not teach even the ABC of *Pātañjala Yoga-Sūtram* and the other classical Yoga scriptures. It is not our assertion that the classical Yoga cannot be further improved and that the last word has been said in the classical scriptures. But we question the appropriateness of the maintenance of quietude on the wisdom of the ancient seers.

Even in the first half of the twentieth century, Yoga was branded as a cult of superstitions by some Indian (so-called) rationalists whose pseudo-science is claimed to be the only science. Scientific experimentations done by some Western scientists, followed by similar work by a few Indian scientists, lent scientific credence to Yoga. Now it has a firm position in Physiology, Psychology, Therapeutics and Theology. Some authors have made good attempts in scientifically explaining the yogic processes and the benefits that accrue. Still it is felt that the science of meditation needs more vivid clarification. Such an attempt has been made in the third part of this book.

The second part of this book deals with the theory of meditation. Yogic theories and scientific theories have been explained with a holistic and synthetic approach. Any student of Yoga, not interested in yogic theory and scientific explanations, may omit part two and three of this book and may learn the practice of meditation from part one only.

We have not kept any meditational technique secret from our readers. The techniques have been methodically presented. The last three limbs of *Pātañjala Yoga* have been grouped and combinedly named as 'meditation'. In addition, the other limbs of *Pātañjala Yoga* that facilitate meditation have also been presented in a brief manner. Part one of this book is a brief compendium of meditational Yoga. Part two and three of this book are meant for advanced research workers on meditation. If Yoga ever enters into medical curriculum, part three of this book would perhaps provide the basic information.

Any practitioner of medicine, desirous of using *yoga*-therapy as a complementary one or as the main treatment, can use this book as a sample guide.

The theory and practice of Yoga for spiritual uplift, finally leading to liberation, have also been given in this book. After all, Yoga is principally a spiritual subject. And this spiritual aspect has not been ignored.

This author is not only a *yoga*-theorist, but a practitioner since his twenties. It is his firm conviction that *yoga* can improve the quality of life — physical, mental and spiritual. He would be happy if this book helps its readers not only in theoretical knowledge but also in actual practice.

# Acknowledgements

I AM grateful to Dr. Pramod Chandra Samal for his kind help in drawing the figures. I owe to Dr. Bijoy Kumar Sahu and Sri Rabi Narayan Pradhan for their invaluable assistance in the preparation of the manuscript. My sincere thanks are due to Mr. Dhruba Charan Dehury for his secretarial assistance.

I am extremely glad to express my gratitude to Mr. Susheel K. Mittal, Director, D.K. Printworld (P) Ltd., New Delhi, for his kind willingness to publish this book.

I express my hearty thanks to Manorama (wife), Prakash, Bikash and Bibhas (sons), Smita, Snigdha and Arati (daughters-in-law), Shephali (daughter), Sudhir (son-in-law), Nivedita, Madhusmita, Lopamudra, Arpita and Anwesha (granddaughters) and Siddhartha (grandson), whose love and affection have been a constant source of inspiration for me.

*25th Aug. 2002* **Nrusingh Charan Panda**

# Contents

## PART 3

## BENEFITS FROM MEDITATION

# Abbreviations

| | | |
|---|---|---|
| *AL* | : | *Ānandalaharī* |
| *AU* | : | *Aitareya Upaniṣad* |
| *AV* | : | *Atharvaveda* |
| *BG* | : | *Bhagavad Gītā* |
| *Bhā* | : | *Bhāgavatam* |
| *BS* | : | *Brahmasūtram* |
| *BU* | : | *Bṛhadāraṇyaka Upaniṣad* |
| *CU* | : | *Chāndogya Upaniṣad* |
| *DBhā* | : | *Devī-Bhāgavatam* |
| *IU* | : | *Īśopaniṣad* |
| *KTU* | : | *Kaṭhopaniṣad* |
| *MAU* | : | *Māṇḍūkyopaniṣad* |
| *MS* | : | *Manu-smṛti* |
| *MTU* | : | *Maitrī Upaniṣad* |
| *MUU* | : | *Muṇḍaka Upaniṣad* |
| *PU* | : | *Praśna Upaniṣad* |
| *PYD* | : | *Pātañjala Yoga-Darśanam* |
| *ṚV* | : | *Ṛgveda* |
| *ŚB* | : | *Śāṅkara Bhāṣyam* |
| *ŚBrā* | : | *Śatapatha Brāhmaṇa* |
| *SK* | : | *Śāṅkhya Kārikā* |
| *SPS* | : | *Sāṅkhya Pravacana-Sūtram* |
| *ŚU* | : | *Śvetāśvatara Upaniṣad* |

| | | |
|---|---|---|
| *TĀ* | : | *Taittirīya Āraṇyaka* |
| *TU* | : | *Taittirīya Upaniṣad* |
| *VāPu* | : | *Vāyu Purāṇa* |
| *YV* | : | *Yajurveda* |

# List of Figures

# PART 1
# PRACTICE OF MEDITATION

# 1.1

## Preparation for Meditation

We will discuss the topic of the preparation for meditation under two sub-sections, namely, (a) preparation for traditional meditation, and (b) preparation for non-traditional meditation.

### Preparation for traditional meditation

#### THE PLACE OF MEDITATION

If you have a worshipping room in your house, that would be the place of your meditation. You may keep idols, statues, photographs, paintings or pictures of your favourite deities (deity) along with the photograph of your spiritual preceptor (*guru*). Your worshipping rituals are different from your meditation. Both may be done consecutively or separately.

See that you have the least disturbance in your meditation room. The noise of your home T.V. and radio or that of your neighbours should not distract your attention. Your meditation room should be a secluded place as far as practicable. See that discussions in your living room and noises from children disturb you least. Noise from public outside and vehicles on the roads should not create much noise-pollution. If you have facilities and resources, you may make your meditation-room noise-proof.

#### THE TIME OF MEDITATION

You may practise meditation three times, two times or one time a day, in order of preference. The *tri-sandhyā* meditation was the usual practice in the past. The Sanskrit word *sandhyā* means 'junction' or 'juncture' and *tri* means 'three'. For the meditation, the junctions of the four divisions of the day (the day of 24 hours) are known as *sandhyās*. Each division has a duration of six hours. Thus 6 a.m., 12 noon, 6 p.m., and 12-midnight are the four *sandhyās*. The 12-midnight *sandhyā* is not convenient for many persons for meditation due to its being a sleeping hour. Hence meditation three times a day has been more popular than that of four times a day. The exact timings with accuracy of minutes and seconds are not really sacrosanct. The modern man has a busy life. It may not be practicable for him to strictly adhere to these timings. We would recommend ± ( plus minus) one hour for each *sandhyā*.

If you meditate only once a day, you may prefer the morning time. If the morning time is not convenient to you due to some unavoidable reason, the evening time may be adopted. Most meditators meditate twice a day, in the morning and the evening. The noon-time clashes with the office, the farm or the factory hour.

Four-o'clock-morning is the *brāhma-muhūrtta* (the auspicious time for worshipping God or *Brahma;* time for *brahmopāsanā; upāsanā* means 'worshipping'). It is the time in which Nature is in the most peaceful state. At this time Nature is calm and serene. It is the best time for meditation during the day of 24-hours. If it is possible to get up early, meditation may be done during the time from 4 a.m. to 6 a.m.

## THE STATE OF THE G.I. TRACT

The gastro-intestinal (G.I.) tract should be empty during meditation. Any major meal should be avoided during the three hours preceding the actual meditation. One may take a glass of water, a cup of milk, or a cup of soft beverage during the said period. But solid food, intoxicating drinks and the intake of an excessive quantity of fluid should be avoided.

The bowel and the bladder should be evacuated prior to meditation. Retention of excreta and distension of the bowel or the bladder with excreta are factors that distract concentration and pinpointed attention. After attempts for evacuation in the toilet, there may not be real evacuation. In that situation, one may go ahead for meditation.

## BATH PRIOR TO MEDITATION

A bath prior to meditation cools the body and the mind. It has a refreshing effect. It would be advisable to take a bath before meditating. However, it is not a sacrosanct practice which is unavoidable and indispensable. For meditating in the proximity of a deity, it is an unavoidable tradition to purify the body with a bath.

## CLOTHES TO WEAR

New clothes or washed old clothes are put on after taking a bath. The clothes should be clean. According to tradition for worshipping or meditation, one should not use those clothes which had been put on while eating. It is also the tradition that clothes used in the lavatory while defaecating should not be put on for worshipping or meditation. Such used clothes are to be washed and dried before being used for such sacred purposes. Clothes used during urination may not be deemed impure for the purpose of worshipping.

Heavy and tight clothes are to be avoided. Clothes should be light and loose. The weather conditions of the locality and the physical conditions of the room in which meditation is practised are to be considered. A *dhotī* and a shoulder-cloth (*uttarīya*) are the best ones in most places of the tropics. A *kurtā* or a loose tee-shirt may be necessary. An undergarment in the loin may also be necessary. For ladies, a *sāḍī* and a loose blouse or *pāyazāmā*s with *salwār* are recommended. The garments should be such that the person who wears should not perspire, nor should he shiver due to chill. Tightness of garments gives discomfort to the body and makes the mind unsteady.

PUNCTUALITY IN MEDITATION

It would be ideal if the meditator practises meditation at specified time daily. Punctuality conditions the mind and this conditioning immensely helps meditation. On some days, it may not be possible to stick to the exact time of meditation. For such occasions, deviations may be permissible. But such irregularities may be exceptional. However, one should not be regularly irregular.

ĀSANA ON WHICH TO SEAT

Traditional meditation is practised while sitting on the floor. It may be a cement concrete floor, a marble floor, a mosaic floor or a wooden floor. It is essential that the floor-ground is firm. The floor may or may not be carpeted. A small mat may be spread on the floor. A four-folded blanket may be placed on the mat. The blanket may be placed on the floor-carpet directly. The meditator sits on the blanket on which a cotton-sheet may or may not be placed. Specially made carpet *āsana*s are available in the market. Such an *āsana* may be used instead of a blanket.

### Preparation for non-traditional meditation

Most of the items that have already been written for traditional meditation with reference to preparation hold good for non-traditional meditation. Only the exceptions will be mentioned here.

The place of meditation may not be a worshipping room. No idols, pictures and photographs of deities and *guru*s may be placed in the meditation-room. A bath prior to meditation may be dispensed with. Clothes used during meditation should be clean and light; but the restrictions with reference to the non-use of clothes used in toilet and in dining may be ignored. The meditator may preferably sit on the floor for meditation. But he may also sit on a chair. He may use the bed for this purpose. But foam-bed or any other soft-bed should be avoided. A hard-bed may do. The seat should be firm (*sthira*) and comfortable (*sukha*). During meditation, the *yogī* sits upright with his head, neck and torso on a vertical line, perpendicular to the horizontal ground level. The spinal cord inside the vertebral column should be vertically straight.

# 1.2

# Āsanas for Meditation

YOGIC poses (*yogāsanas*) are many. They are practised for the improvement of physical health in normal physiological conditions and the treatment of many diseases. The regular practice of some *āsanas* exerts beneficial effects on mental health also.

Only a small number of *āsanas* are recommended for meditation. They are: *siddhāsana, padmāsana, svastikāsana, vajrāsana* and *sukhāsana*. For the purpose of meditation, the five *āsanas*, just mentioned, are in order of preference. They have been illustrated in *figs*. 1.1, 1.2, 1.3, 1.4 and 1.5, respectively. For *āsanas*, Iyengar's book may be referred to.[1]

## Siddhāsana

Follow the following steps for sitting in *siddhāsana* (accomplished pose). Only men should do this *āsana*. Its substitute for women follows:

1. Sit on the floor with legs extended in front.
2. Bend the left leg at the knee. By holding the left foot with the hands, place the left heel near the perineum. The sole of the left foot should rest against the right thigh.
3. Bend the right leg at the knee. Place the right foot over the left ankle, while keeping the right heel against the pubic bone.

---

1. Iyengar, B.K.S., 1997.

4. Place the right sole between the left thigh and the left calf muscle.
5. Do not rest the body on the heels.
6. Stretch the arms in front. Place the backs of the hand on the respective knees, with palms facing upwards. Join the respective thumbs and the index fingers, keeping the other fingers extended.
7. Keep the back, neck and head erect.
8. Repeat the same procedure for the right leg by placing the right heel near the perineum first and then the left foot over the right ankle.

**Siddha yoni āsana**

This is the female accomplished pose, recommended for females as a substitute for *siddhāsana*. Follow the following steps for sitting in *siddha yoni āsana:*

1. Sit on the floor with legs extended in front of you.
2. Fold the left leg at the knee. Place the sole of the left foot flat against the inner right thigh.
3. Place the left heel inside the labia majora of the vagina. (This *āsana* is best done without underwear.)
4. Fold the right leg at the knee. Place the right foot on the left leg in the space between the calf and the thigh.
5. Make the spine and the head fully erect and straight.
6. Practise this *āsana* in conjunction with *cin-mudrā* or *jñāna-mudrā.*

It may be practised with either leg uppermost.

**Padmāsana**

Follow the following steps for sitting in *padmāsana* (lotus pose):

1. Sit on the floor.

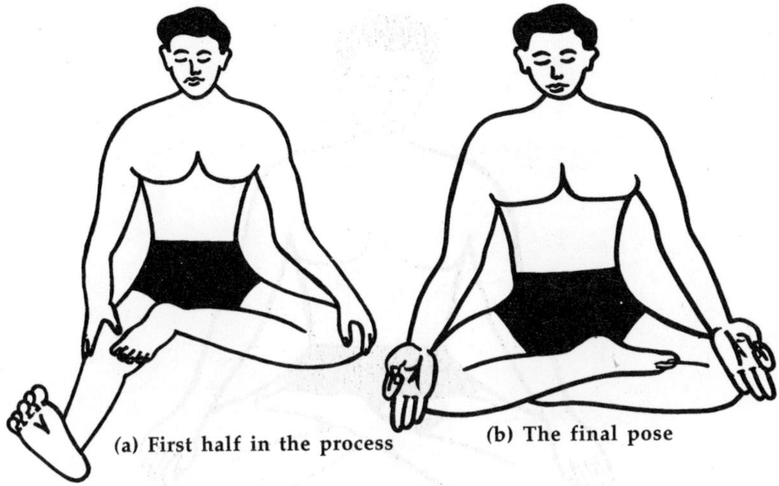


*fig.* **1.1** ***Siddhāsana***

2. Bend the right leg at the knee. Holding the right foot with the hands, place it at the root of the left thigh so as to keep the right heel near the navel.
3. Bend the left leg at the knee. Hold the left foot with the hands and place it over the right foot at the root of the right thigh so as to keep the left heel near the navel. The sole of each foot should be turned up.
4. Keep the back, the neck and the head perpendicularly straight. While stretching the arms, place the backs of the hands on the respective knee, with the palms upwards. Bend the index finger and the thumb of each hand to touch each other. Alternately, place the hands in the middle where the feet cross each other, with palms facing upwards and with the back of the right hand kept upon the left palm. This is the *bhairava-mudrā.*

*fig.* **1.2** ***Padmāsana***

## Svastikāsana

Follow the following steps to sit on *svastikāsana* (the auspicious pose):

1. Sit on the floor. Assume the base position. Fold the left leg and place the left foot near the right thigh muscles.
2. Bend the right leg and place the right foot in the space between the left thigh and calf muscles.
3. Place the toes of both feet between the thighs and calves of the opposite leg.
4. Place the hands on the corresponding knees in *jñāna* or *cin-mudrā* or on the lap, with palms facing upwards and with the back of the right hand kept on the left palm (*bhairava-mudrā*).

**Note:** The final poses of *siddhāsana* and *svastikāsana* look alike. In the former, the heel of the lower leg presses the perineum, wheras in the latter it does not.

*fig.* 1.3 *Svastikāsana*

### Vajrāsana

*Vajra* means 'thunderbolt'. Hence *vajrāsana* is the thunderbolt pose. *Vajra* is the name of a major *nāḍī* (prāṇic channel) in the subtle body. It is directly connected with the genito-urinary system. This *nāḍī* regulates the sexual energy of the body. Sequentially follow the following steps to sit in *vajrāsana:*

1. Sit with both the legs folded at the knees and feet stretched backwards and big toes crossed.
2. Keep the knees together, but the heels apart.
3. Lower the buttocks to place them in between the feet, the bottoms of which face upwards. Keep the heels at the sides of the hips.
4. Place each hand on its respective knee, with palms downwards.

*Vajrāsana* is the only pose that can be practised right after meals to improve digestion. It is the only meditative pose for persons suffering from sciatica and sacral infections.

*fig.* 1.4 *Vajrāsana*

**Sukhāsana**

Follow the following steps to sit on *sukhāsana* (the comfortable pose):

1. Sit on the floor and stretch both the legs in front of the body.
2. Fold the left foot under the right thigh.
3. Fold the right foot under the left thigh.
4. Place the hands on the lap, with palms upwards and with the back of the right hand/palm on the left.
5. Keep the head, neck and back erect.

*Sukhāsana* is the ideal meditative pose for beginners for whom the classical meditative poses are difficult. After mastering any of the classical meditative poses, the meditator should dispense with the *sukhāsana*. A folded blanket at the back below the two buttocks may improve this meditational pose.

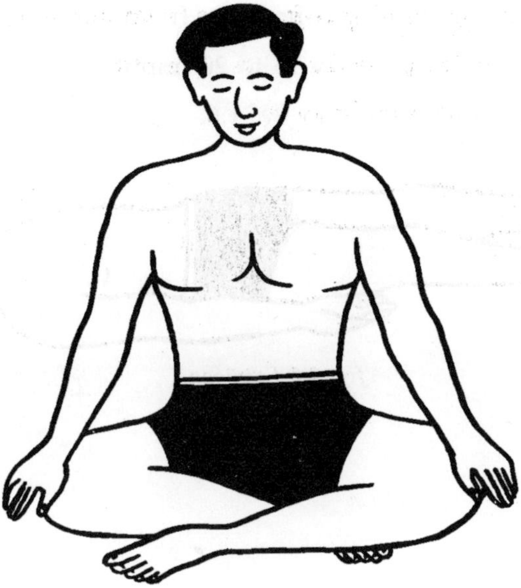

*fig.* **1.5** ***Sukhāsana***

## Śavāsana

The corpse-pose or *śavāsana* is not a meditative pose. Since we recommend *prāṇāyāma* to precede meditation and since every *prāṇāyāma* session is followed by *śavāsana,* we deem it proper to briefly describe this *āsana.* The technique is given below:

1. Lie flat on the back, without any pillow, with hands a little away from the thighs and with palms up.
2. Keep the heels together and the toes apart.
3. Close the eyes.
4. Relax the whole body. All skeletal muscles should be placid. Limbs and joints should not be tense at all. The lower jaw should hang loose. The tongue and the pupils of the eyes should be passive.
5. Breathe slowly and evenly, without jerky movements.

6. Keep the mind passive, free from thought.
7. Stay in the pose for 15 to 20 minutes.

The *śavāsana* is illustrated in *fig*. 1.6.

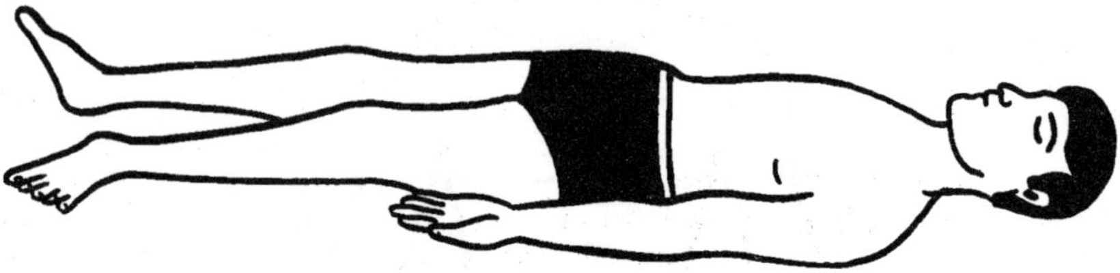

*fig.* **1.6** ***Śavāsana***

# 1.3

# Mudrās and Bandhas for Prāṇāyāma, Pratyāhāra and Meditation

*Mudrās* and *bandhas* are many in *yoga*. They are generally meant for the improvement of physical and mental health. Some of them have positive effects on the improvement of concentration. Some play specific roles in specific yogic practices. Most of the *mudrās* facilitate the process of the withdrawal of senses (*pratyāhāra*). Here we briefly mention those *mudrās* and *bandhas* that have specific functions in *prāṇāyāma* and meditation. For *mudrās* and *bandhas*, reference may be made to the book of Swami Satyananda Saraswati.[2]

## Mudrās

The Sanskrit word *mudrā* means 'a symbolic gesture' which evokes a certain mood or emotion in the inner being. It also means 'a seal or a sealing posture'.

### JÑĀNA-MUDRĀ

Sequentially follow the following steps for doing the *jñāna-mudrā*:

1. Sit in a meditative *āsana*.
2. Fold the index fingers of both hands so that each one touches the ventral (inside) root of each respective thumb. Alternatively, the tips of both the index finger and the thumb should touch.
3. Keep the other fingers extended.

2. Saraswati, Swami Satyananda, 1983.

4. Stretch the arms out straight so that the ventral part of each wrist rests on the respective knee, with the palms downwards and three unbent fingers and the thumb of each hand facing the floor in front of the feet.

The *jñāna-mudrā* is illustrated in *fig*. 1.7.

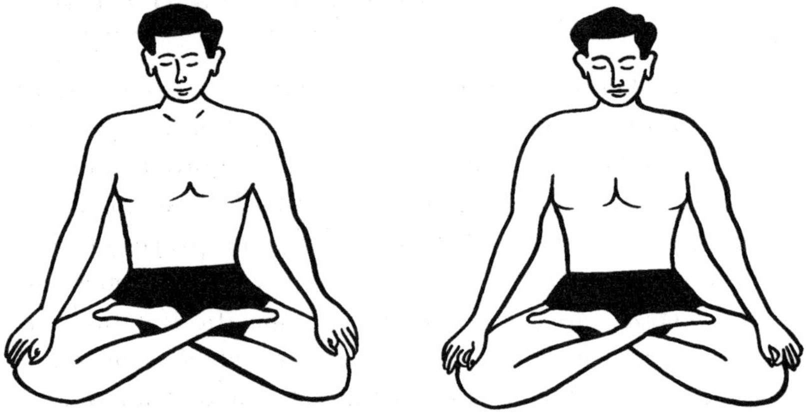

***fig*. 1.7 *Jñāna-mudrā***

CIN-MUDRĀ

*Cin-mudrā* is the psychic gesture of consciousness. It is performed in the same way as *jñāna-mudrā* with the single exception that the palms of both hands face upwards while placed on the knees. The *cin-mudrā* is illustrated in *fig*. 1.8 (a).

While doing *prāṇāyāma*, the right hand remains busy in controlling the intake and outgo of air (with *prāṇa*) through the left and right nostrils. Hence only the left hand remains free for the *cin-mudrā*. The left arm is kept straight, with the back of the left wrist resting on the left knee and the left palm facing upwards. There is a variation of the *cin-mudrā* too. Instead of the bent index finger touching the ventral root of the respective thumb, the tip of the bent forefinger touches the tip of the respective bent thumb. This variation has been illustrated in *fig*. 1.8 (b).

*fig.* **1.8** ***Cinmudrā*** **(a)**

*fig.* **1.8** ***Cinmudrā*** **(b)**

### ŚĀMBHAVĪ-MUDRĀ

By this *mudrā,* gazing is done at the eyebrow centre (*ājñā-cakra*). To perform this *mudrā,* follow the following steps:

1. Sit in any meditative posture. Keep the head, neck and torso erect. Place the hands on the respective knees in *cin-mudrā* or *jñāna-mudrā.*
2. Look at a fixed point in front of you.
3. Without moving the head, look upward as high as possible.
4. Concentrate and focus your eyes on the spot between the two eyebrows.
5. Suspend all thoughts except the *praṇava* (O'Ṁ-AUṀ), on which meditate.

### AGOCARĪ-MUDRĀ

This is the nosetip gazing. In Sanskrit, it is known as *nāsikāgra-dr̥ṣṭi.* To perform this *mudrā,* follow the following steps:

1. Sit in any meditative *āsana,* with the spine and head erect. Keep the hands in *cin-mudrā* or *jñāna-mudrā.*
2. Focus the two eyeballs on the tip of the nose.

In *śāmbhavī-mudrā,* the focus of gazing is the spot at the top of the nose, whereas, in *agocarī-mudrā,* it is the tip of the nose which is at the bottom.

### KĀKĪ- MUDRĀ

The Sanskrit word *kāka* means 'crow' and *kākī* means 'pertaining to the crow'. In this *mudrā,* the lips are pursed so as to resemble a crow's beak. Hence is the name. A crow is said to live long and to live a disease-free life. This *mudrā* bestows longevity and hence is named so. The vibrations of the incoming air stimulate the nerve-endings present in the mucous membrane of the throat. The *viśuddhi-cakra* is activated thereby. Thus the immune system of the body and the purificatory mechanism of the body are strengthened. The nosetip gazing associated with the *kākī-mudrā* fortifies concentration and withdrawal of senses. To perform this *mudrā,* follow the following technique:

1. Sit in any meditative *āsana.*
2. Gaze at the nosetip.
3. Purse the lips so as to make a narrow tube like the crow's beak.
4. Inhale slowly and deeply through the mouth.
5. Close the lips and slowly exhale through the nose.
6. Repeat the processes as long as you can.

TRĀṬAKA

*Trāṭaka* is steady gazing at a particular point without winking. This is one of the six yogic purificatory exercises (*ṣaṭkarma: dhauti, bastī, neti, nauli, trāṭaka* and *kapālabhāti*) of *Haṭha-Yoga.* We consider it as a *mudrā* too. It develops concentration and mental focussing. The technique is given below:

1. Sit in a meditative *āsana* in *jñāna-mudrā* or *cin-mudrā.*
2. Intently gaze on a point or a spot without winking.
3. When the eyes are tired or if they begin to water, close them and relax. Do not move your body. Continue the practice of *trāṭaka* with eyes closed on the mental image of the spot which had been gazed on. As soon as you get relief in your eyes, open them and continue to gaze on the external spot.

The spot on which gazing is focussed may be one of the following:

1. It may be a small circle or a dot drawn on a white paper with black ink. It may be placed at a distance of

30 to 60 cm from the face.

2. It may be a small AUṀ (ॐ) drawn on a white paper with black ink.
3. It may be the white moon on the *Śivaliṅga.*
4. It may be the eyebrow centre of your deity — Gaṇeśa, Viṣṇu, Kṛṣṇa, Durgā, Kālī, Lakṣmī, Sarasvatī or any other you love and adore. Put a round mark with white-sandalwood-paste, red-sandalwood-paste or vermilion at the spot between the eyebrows of the deity. That spot may be used to be gazed upon.
5. It may be the tip of the flame of a lamp (*dīpa*) or a candle.
6. It may be a crystal, preferably a white quartz, placed in front at a distance of 30 to 60 cm. The crystal may be placed in the vicinity of a flame.
7. It may be the moon or a bright star in a clear night-sky. To gaze at the moon or a star, the *yogī* may lie down on his back with face upwards on a lawn or on a roof or terrace. Gazing at the sun may be avoided.

The nosetip-gazing has already been described as a special *mudrā* (*agocarī-mudrā*). It is also a type of *trāṭaka.*

*Trāṭaka* has two varieties, namely, outer (*bahiraṅga*) and inner (*antaraṅga*). The outer variety of *trāṭaka* has been so far described. In the inner variety, internal gazing is done, with the eyes closed. The spot on which the *yogī* gazes is the seed (*bīja*) in the *maṇḍala* of a *cakra.* For this purpose, the meditator must be acquainted with the anatomy of the concerned *cakra* and its colour.

YONI-MUDRĀ

The Sanskrit word *yoni* means 'uterus or womb' or 'vagina' or 'source'. In the present context, it means 'source'. The source of the universe is *Brahman* or Śiva. Through *yoni-mudrā,* the meditator withdraws his senses (*pratyāhāra*) from the external world and concentrates on his primeval source (Śiva). He internally gazes on the *bindu* (point) of the *bindu-visarga* or on the light-point in the *sahasrāra* (thousand-petalled lotus). The light-point is Jyotirliṅga Śiva. The alternative name of *yoni-mudrā* is *ṣaṇmukhī-mudrā.* To perform this *mudrā,* follow the following steps:

1. Sit in any meditative *āsana.*
2. Inhale slowly and deeply. Retain the breath.
3. Close the ears with the respective thumbs, the eyes with the respective index fingers, the nostrils with the respective middle fingers, and place the ring and little fingers on the upper lip and the lower lip, respectively, to close the mouth.
4. While retaining the breath, concentrate on the lighted point in the *sahasrāra.* You may hear the *oṅkāra dhvani* (the sound of *oṁ*), eternally and continuously generated by *Prakṛti* (Nature).
5. After retaining the breath as long as it is comfortable to you, release the pressure on the nostrils exerted by the middle fingers and exhale slowly. Keep the other fingers in their places. Inhale again. At the end of the full inhalation, close the nostrils with the respective middle fingers. Repeat the process as long as you can.

This is really the technique of the *nāda-yoga.*

ĀKĀŚĪ MUDRĀ

While practising this *mudrā,* the *yogī* performs two other *mudrās*, namely, *khecarī-mudrā* and *śāmbhavī-mudrā* and does *ujjayī prāṇāyāma*. Follow the following steps:

1. Sit in any meditative *āsana*.
2. Fold the tongue back against the upper palate (*khecarī-mudrā*).
3. Remain in *śāmbhavī-mudrā*. Gaze at the spot in between the two eyebrows. While gazing at the eyebrow centre, bend the head backward to a slight extent (not to the fullest extent).
4. Practise *ujjayī prāṇāyāma*. Breathe slowly and deeply through both the nostrils.

### KHECARĪ MUDRĀ

The Sanskrit word *kha* means *ākāśa* or space. The verb-root *car* means 'to move'. The word *khecarī* literally means 'one who moves in space'.

The lower tendon of the tongue is to be severed. It is cut by a sharp, sterilised knife little by little every week under the guidance of a *guru*. Salt and turmeric powders are sprinkled on the wound to prevent the rejoining of the cut edges. The cutting of the tendon of the tongue is done once a week and regularly repeated for a period of six months. By applying fresh butter, the tongue may be milked as a milkman manipulates the teats of the udder while milking. By such means, the tongue is to be lengthened so as to reach the roof of the throat-cavity. This is the preliminary step preparatory to the *khecarī-mudrā*. Ordinarily, we do not recommend this preliminary step to the common meditator. He may preferably dispense with it.

To perform the *khecarī-mudrā,* follow the following steps:

1. Sit in any meditative *āsana*.
2. Roll the tongue backward so that its lower surface

touches the upper palate. Take the tip of the tongue as far back as possible without any straining effort.

3. Close the mouth and breathe normally through the nostrils. In due course of time, the respiration rate may be gradually reduced.
4. Perform the tongue-lock as long as possible. When it is uncomfortable to you, relax the tongue for a few seconds and then repeat the *mudrā*.

### AŚVINĪ-MUDRĀ

The Sanskrit word *aśva* means 'horse'. The horse makes a rhythmic movement of its anal region. This *mudrā* simulates the horse's manipulation of the anal sphincters and the anal muscles. Hence is the name of this *mudrā*.

To perform this *mudrā*, proceed with the following steps:

1. Sit in any meditative *āsana*. Relax the body.
2. Contract the sphincter muscles of the anus for a few seconds and then relax them for a few seconds. Repeat this alternate process of contraction and relaxation as many times as possible. There are two anal sphincters — the external and the internal. See that both the sphincters rhythmically contract and relax.
3. Concentrate on the anal region and the *mūlādhāra-cakra* while performing this *mudrā*.

### VIPARĪTA-KARAṆĪ-MUDRĀ

By performing this *mudrā*, the sun (dwelling in the *maṇipūra-cakra* or navel region) is brought upward to the *viśuddhi* and the moon (dwelling in the *bindu-visarga* which is above the *lalana-cakra* and is in between the *ājñā-cakra* and the *sahasrāra*) is carried downward to the *viśuddhi*. Hence is the name, *viparīta-karaṇī*, literally meaning 'reversing'.

For performing the *mudrā*, proceed with the following steps. The posture is illustrated in *fig*. 1.9

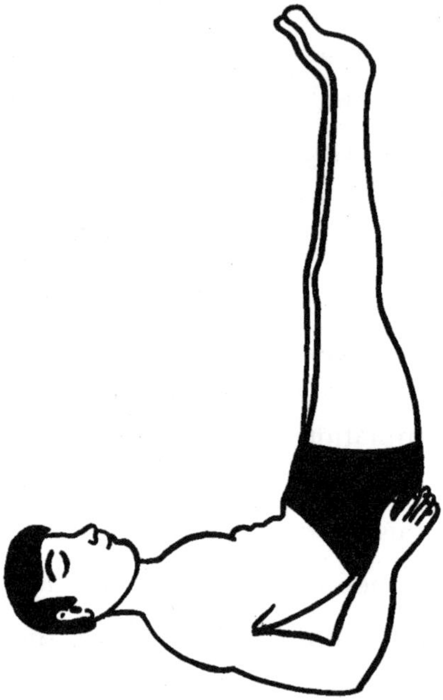

***fig*. 1.9 *Viparīta-karaṇī mudrā***

1. Lie on the floor, with face upward. Relax the body and close the eyes.
2. Raise the legs up and keep them vertically straight.
3. Support the buttocks on both sides by the hands by resting the elbows on the ground. In *sarvāṅgāsana*, the flexure is below the neck whereas in *viparīta-karaṇī-mudrā*, the flexure is below the diaphragm.
4. To start with, the duration may be one minute. The period may gradually be increased up to fifteen minutes or more.
5. You may terminate your *viparīta-karaṇī-mudrā* with step

4. But, preferably, perform this *mudrā* in conjunction with *khecarī-mudrā* and *ujjayī prāṇāyāma.* Shift your awareness too in accordance with steps 6 and 7.
6. As you inhale slowly, gradually shift your consciousness from the *maṇipūra-cakra* to the *bindu.*
7. While exhaling, gradually shift your awareness from the *bindu* to the *viśuddhi* and maintain there.
8. During the repetition of inhalation and exhalation, the shifting of awareness would be as in steps 6 and 7, respectively.

***Caution***: The *viparīta-karaṇī-mudrā* should not be practised by persons with enlarged thyroid, serious hypertension or cardiac problems.

### YOGA-MUDRĀ

*Yoga-mudrā,* traditionally named as a *mudrā,* is really an *āsana.* If practised properly, it can bestow the benefit of a *mudrā.* In section A, we present the technique of the *āsana,* and in section B, the technique of the *mudrā.*

A. 1. Sit in *padmāsana.* Close the eyes.
2. Catch hold of the left wrist behind the back with your right hand.
3. While exhaling slowly, bend forward until your forehead touches the ground.
4. While inhaling slowly, return to the original straight position.
5. If you retain the pose, with the forehead touching the ground, for a long time, breathe slowly and normally.
6. If you cannot maintain the pose as in step 5, repeat the *āsana* a few times.

The *yoga-mudrā āsana* has been illustrated in *fig.*1.10.

*fig.* **1.10** ***Yoga-mudrā***

B.1&2. Perform steps 1 and 2 as in section A above.

3. Exhale slowly (*recaka*). Retain the breath after full exhalation (*bāhya kumbhaka*). Concentrate on the *mūlādhāra-cakra* in the *bāhya kumbhaka.*
4. Inhale slowly (*pūraka*) and feel the breath. In the *pūraka,* gradually shift your awareness from the *mūlādhāra* to the *ājñā-cakra.*
5. Retain the breath for a few seconds (*antara kumbhaka*) while concentrating on the *ājñā-cakra.*
6. Exhale slowly (*recaka*) while you bend forward. Forward bending starts with the beginning of exhalation; air is fully expelled from the lungs by the time the forehead touches the ground.
7. While doing step 6, feel the exhaling breath and gradually shift your awareness from the *ājñā* to the *mūlādhāra-cakra.*
8. Retain the breath after the full exhalation for a few seconds. During this *bāhya kumbhaka,* concentrate on the *mūlādhāra-cakra.*
9. Inhale slowly (*pūraka*) while you raise your trunk to the vertical position. During this *pūraka,* feel the breath and gradually shift your awareness upward from the *mūlādhāra* to the *ājñā-cakra.*

10. Concentrate on the *ājñā-cakra* during the *antara kumbhaka* (while holding the breath after the inhalation), while you are in the upright position.
11. Exhale and bend forward again to repeat the process.

MAHĀ-MUDRĀ

The word *mahā* means 'great'. *Mahā-mudrā* is the most important of all the *mudrās* and hence is the name. It is illustrated in *fig*.1.11. Follow the following technique to perform the *mudrā*:

***fig.* 1.11 Mahāmudrā**

1. Sit on the floor while pressing the anus with the left heel and stretching the right leg straight in front.
2. Bend forward just enough so as to hold the right big toe with the fingers of both the hands.
3. Inhale slowly and deeply (*pūraka*).
4. Retain the breath (*kumbhaka*). During this *kumbhaka*, perform *jālandhara-bandha* (press the chin against the chest firmly) and *mūla-bandha* (a posture where the body, from the anus to the navel, is contracted and lifted up and towards the spine). During this time, fix the gaze on the spot between the two eyebrows

(*bhrūmadhya-dṛṣṭi* or *śāmbhavī-mudrā*).

5. While retaining the breath inside (*kumbhaka*), shift your awareness from *mūlādhāra* to *viśuddhi* and from *viśuddhi* to *ājñā* in repeating pulses (repeat the shifting of awareness in the sequence: *mūlādhāra* → *viśuddhi* → *ājñā*). The awareness may remain in each of these three *cakras* for one to two seconds.
6. Exhale slowly.
7. Retain the forward bent posture as long as you can.
8. Inhale deeply and repeat the whole process. Six repetitions in the morning and six in the evening should be enough.
9. Practise first on the left leg and then on the right leg.

For the *yogī, mahā-mudrā, mahā-bandha* and *mahāvedha* form a good combination.

## Bandhas

The word *bandha* means 'binding', 'bonding', or 'locking'. While doing the *bandhas*, various parts of the body are contracted and tightened.

The *bandhas* may be practised on their own. In addition, they are practised in conjunction with other yogic techniques such as *mudrās* and *prāṇāyāma.*

### THE TRIPLE BANDHAS

The *mūla-bandha,* the *uḍḍīyāna-bandha* and the *jālandhara-bandha* constitute the *bandha-traya* (the triple *bandhas*). In some *prāṇāyāmas,* all these three *bandhas* are practised simultaneously.

#### *Mūla-bandha*

The word *mūla* means 'root' or 'base'. By this *bandha,* the muscles in the region of the perineum are contracted and drawn upwards; concentration is focussed on the *mūlādhāra-*

*cakra;* the *apāna-vāyu* moves upwards and unites with the *prāṇa-vāyu;* the united *prāṇa-apāna-vāyu* enters the *suṣumṇā nāḍī* and thereby facilitates the ascent of Kuṇḍalinī. When *apāna* unites with *prāṇa, anāhata dhvani* (mystical divine sound) is distinctly heard. Follow these steps for performing the *mūla-bandha*:

1. Sit in *siddhāsana* or *siddha-yoni-āsana*. Both the knees should touch the ground. *Padmāsana* may also be used. Place the palms on the respective knees. Close the eyes and relax the body.
2. Inhale deeply; retain the breath; perform *jālandhara-bandha* (chin-lock).
3. Contract the muscles of the perineal region and draw them upward. This step is the proper *mūla-bandha* and the preceding ones are preparatory to it.
4. While retaining the breath, maintain this pose as long as you can do.
5. Release the contraction of the perineum; slowly raise the head (unlock the *jālandhara-bandha*); and slowly exhale.
6. Repeat up to ten times.

### *Uḍḍīyāna-bandha*

The Sanskrit word *uḍḍīyāna* has come from the verb-root *ḍi* with the prefix *ut*. It means 'to fly up'. When this *bandha* is practised, the *prāṇa* flies up through the *suṣumṇā nāḍī*. Hence is the significance of this name. *Uḍḍīyāna-bandha* (the abdominal retraction lock) can be practised in a sitting or a standing posture. It is the first stage of *nauli kriyā* which is generally done in a standing position, with hands on the thighs. In *prāṇayāmas* with retention of breath, *uḍḍīyāna-bandha* is practised in a sitting position. It is practised at the end of *kumbhaka* and the beginning of *recaka*. This *bandha,* in the sitting

*fig.* 1.12. *Uḍḍīyāna bandha* (in sitting position)

*fig.* 1.13 *Uḍḍīyāna bandha* (in standing position)

and the standing position, is illustrated in *fig.* 1.12 and 1.13, respectively. To perform the *bandha,* follow the following technique:

1. Sit in a meditative pose (*siddhāsana, padmāsana* or *svastikāsana;* not *sukhāsana*) so that the knees rest on the floor. Close the eyes. Relax the body.
2. Lean slightly forward. Place your hands on your thighs, above the knees or close to the groin. The weight of the torso must rest on the arms.
3. Empty the lungs by a deep, strong, forceful expiration. You may exhale forcibly through the mouth. Retain the breath outside (*bāhya kumbhaka*).
4. Perform the chin-lock (*jālandhara-bandha*).
5. Contract the abdominal muscles to push them backward (towards the spine) and upward. In the same attempt, the diaphragm is raised up.
6. Hold this abdominal retraction lock as long as you can retain your breath outside.
7. Slowly release the stomach muscles and the *jālandhara-bandha* and inhale.
8. The process may be repeated up to ten times.

While doing the *bandha,* concentration may be fixed on the *maṇipūra-cakra.*

***Caution***: You are to introduce *uḍḍīyāna-bandha* during *bāhya kumbhaka* (the interval between complete exhalation and the start of inhalation), when the lungs are fully empty. Never do *uḍḍīyāna* during *antara kumbhaka* (the holding of breath during the interval between complete inhalation and the start of exhalation). *Uḍḍīyāna* during *antara kumbhaka* strains the heart.

***Special note***: There is a difference between the abdominal grips in *uḍḍīyāna* and in *mūla-bandha.* In the *uḍḍīyāna-bandha,* the entire region from the anus to the diaphragm is pulled back towards the spine and lifted up. In contrast, in the *mūla-bandha,* only the perineal and the lower abdominal area between the anus and the navel is contracted, pulled back to the spine and lifted up towards the diaphragm.

*Jālandhara-bandha*

The Sanskrit word *jāla* means 'net' or 'web'. It is the chin-lock. In this *bandha,* the chin is pressed tightly against the chest (particularly the sternum). This *bandha* is practised at the end of *pūraka* and the beginning of *kumbhaka* and is retained during the entire period of *antara kumbhaka* (while the breath is retained during the interval between complete inhalation and the start of exhalation). This is the recommended *bandha* during *kumbhaka* only. It is illustrated in *fig.* 1.14. To perform the *bandha,* follow the following steps:

1. Sit in *siddhāsana, padmāsana* or *svastikāsana* (not *sukhāsana).* See that the knees are in firm contact with

***fig.* 1.14 *Jālandhara bandha***

the floor. Place the palms on the respective knees. Relax your body and close your eyes.

2. Take a deep inspiration. Retain the breath inside. Bend the head forward and press the chin tightly against the sternum.
3. Straighten the arms and lock them into position. At the same time, hunch the shoulders upward and forward so that the arms stay locked.
4. Stay in the chin-lock position as long as you can retain the breath.
5. Relax the shoulders; bend the arms; slowly release the chin-lock; raise the head; exhale.
6. Repeat up to ten times.

***Precaution***: Do not inhale or exhale until the chin-lock is released and the head is raised to the upright position.

### THE PRACTICE OF THE BANDHA-TRAYA

The *bandha-traya* (the three *bandhas* — *mūla, uḍḍīyāna* and *jālandhara*) may be performed simultaneously to get the maximum benefits. Whenever practised, one important condition is that the lungs must be empty and that this state must be maintained. The three *bandha*s combine in this order: *mūla-bandha, uḍḍīyāna-bandha* and *jālandhara-bandha*.

When these *bandha*s are separately practised, the areas on which to concentrate are different and specific. The muscles which are contracted in a *bandha* are related to the area concentrated upon. For the *mūla-bandha,* it is the perineal and sacral area and also the *mūlādhāra-cakra.* For the *uḍḍīyāna-bandha,* it is the lumbar and abdominal area and also the *maṇipūra-cakra* (the area of the solar plexus). For the *jālandhara-bandha,* it is the area of the neck and the throat and also the *viśuddhi-cakra.*

If and when the three *bandhas* are combined, you should first concentrate on the *mūla-bandha,* then on the *uḍḍīyāna-bandha* and finally on the *jālandhara-bandha.* When the *bandhas* are released, follow the reverse order: first *jālandhara,* then *uḍḍīyāna,* and finally *mūla.* Concentrate on each *bandha* as it relaxes. The simultaneous practice of the *bandha-traya* has been illustrated in *fig.* 1.15.

***fig.* 1.15 *Bandha-traya* (*mūla* + *uḍḍīyāna* + *jālandhara*)**

The *bandha-traya* is also practised in conjunction with some varieties of *prāṇāyāma,* especially with those in which the breath is retained (*kumbhaka*). But the *bandha-traya,* referred to in the foregoing paragraphs, is different from the one which is associated with *prāṇāyāma.* The *mūla-bandha* can be practised in all the three states of *prāṇāyāma,* that is, in *pūraka, kumbhaka* and *recaka.* Both *mūla-bandha* and *jālandhara-bandha* are simultaneously practised in internal retention after inhalation (*antara kumbhaka*). *Uḍḍīyāna-bandha* is contraindicated in any situation in which the lungs are full. *Uḍḍīyāna* is practised when the lungs are empty. Hence, its practice begins at the end of *kumbhaka* and the beginning of *recaka* and is maintained during the whole period of *recaka*. However, both the *mūla-bandha* and the *jālandhara-bandha* can be practised with full lungs and also with empty lungs. Hence, in the practice of the *bandha-traya* without any association of *prāṇāyāma,* all the three *bandha*s are performed after emptying the lungs.

### *Mahā-bandha*

This is the perineum retraction lock. *Mahā-mudrā, mahā-bandha* and *mahā-vedha* make a combination of yogic *kriyā*. *Yogī*s generally practise this triple *krīyā*. *Mahā-mudrā* is the preliminary exercise for the *mahā-bandha*. To perform the *mahā-bandha,* follow the following steps:

1. Sit on the floor. Press the anus with the left heel. Place the right foot upon the left thigh.
2. Contract the anal muscles and muscles of the perineum. Thereby draw the *apāna vāyu* upwards. This step 2 is the *mūla-bandha*.
3. Inhale slowly and retain the breath by *jālandhara-bandha*. Remain in this *bandha* as long as you can.
4. Relax the *mūla-bandha* and the *jālandhara-bandha* and then exhale.
5. Repeat steps 2, 3 and 4 for about ten times.

First practise the *mahā-bandha* on the left side (pressing the anus with the left heel and placing the right foot upon the left thigh) and then on the right side.

# 1.4

# Prāṇāyāma Before Meditation

MEDITATION preceded with *prāṇāyāma* gives better effects. One may directly do meditation without prior *prāṇāyāma* and by doing so one will certainly be benefitted. We, however, recommend *prāṇāyāma* to be followed by meditation for maximising the benefits.

Out of many types of *prāṇāyāma,* we would recommend only two types, namely, *ujjayī* and *nāḍī-śodhana.* The latter has two varieties — without retention of breath (*kumbhaka-rahita*) and with retention of breath (*kumbhaka-sahita*).

## Preliminary notes

*Siddhāsana, padmāsana* and *svastikāsana* are ideal *āsana*s for *prāṇāyāma.* One may or may not use any of these *āsana*s for *ujjayī* which may also be practised while sitting on a hard chair, while standing and walking and while lying down in *śavāsana.*

As *vajrāsana* can be done at any time of the day in full or empty stomach, so is *ujjayī prāṇāyāma* without retention of breath. If retention of breath is introduced in *ujjayī,* it must be done with empty stomach. It is a general recommendation that *prāṇāyāma* may be done three hours after eating a full meal.

Use a four-folded blanket or any such *hard*-cushioning material for sitting in any meditative posture which is also suitable for *prāṇāyāma. Cin-mudrā* or half-*cin-mudrā* (left hand only) is recommended for most *prāṇāyāma*s. *Sukhāsana* is not very suitable for *cin-mudrā.*

As for meditation, the erect position is recommended for *prāṇāyāma.* The head, the neck and the torso should be in a vertical straight line wihout any sagging or bend in any part of the spine.

The eyes should be closed during *prāṇāyāma.* The whole body should be relaxed. There should not be any straining in any part of the body. All skeletal muscles and smooth muscles should be free from tension. The mind also should be relaxed.

Think of the universal Space (*Ākāśa*) filled with *Prāṇa* and you are inside the ocean of *Prāṇa* in the analogy of an aquatic animal inside the ocean. Collect the *Prāṇa* from the ocean; channellise it; regulate it; and store it for your use.

At the outset, a few technical terms with reference to *prāṇāyāma* may be mentioned. The process of filling up the lungs through inhalation is known as *pūraka.* The process of the evacuation of air from the lungs through exhalation is known as *recaka.* The action of retaining the breath inside the lungs is known as *kumbhaka.* It is the interval of time after full inhalation and before the onset of the subsequent exhalation. *Antara kumbhaka* is the suspension of breath after full inhalation whereas *bāhya kumbhaka* is the suspension of breath after full exhalation.

Three *bandha*s, namely, the *mūla-bandha,* the *uḍḍīyāna-bandha* and the *jālandhara-bandha,* are practised in conjunction with *prāṇāyāma.* They have already been described. *Jñāna-mudrā, cin-mudrā* and *khecarī-mudrā* which are also practised in association with *prāṇāyāma* have been described. In *ujjayī prāṇāyāma* in any of the recommended *āsana*s, both the hands are free and hence both of them are placed on the respective knees in *jñāna-mudrā* or *cin-mudrā.* In other *prāṇāyāma*s in which the right hand is busy with closing and opening the nostrils, only the left hand is placed in *cin-mudrā.*

During *prāṇāyāma,* the right-hand fingers do specific jobs. The right thumb is used in closing and opening the right nostril. The little finger and the ring finger of the right hand are used in closing and opening the left nostril. Pressure is applied on the lowermost and lateral soft parts of the nose without distorting the natural shape of the nasal septum. The pressure should be applied less medially and more towards the bottom to avoid the distortion of the natural shape of the nasal septum. The right middle and index fingers should be straight, pointing towards the *ājñā*. Alternatively, they may be bent towards the tip of the nose with the flexure point at the knuckle. During *antara kumbhaka,* only the middle or the index finger remains in the bent position, the other one of these remaining erect upwards by the side of the nose in front of the eye. The finger that remains vertically erect reminds the *yogī* that *recaka* is to be done through the corresponding nostril. The *prāṇāyāma* posture and the position of the hands and fingers have been

***fig.* 1.16 The *prāṇāyāma* posture and the positions of the hands and fingers in the process**

illustrated in *fig*. 1.16. For more details on *prāṇāyāma,* reference may be made to the book of B.K.S. Iyengar[3] and that of K.S. Joshi[4].

During inhalation (*pūraka*), gradually shift your awareness from the nostril through the *ājñā-cakra* and *sahasrāra* down to the *mūlādhāra.* During exhalation (*recaka*), gradually shift your awareness from the *mūlādhāra* through the *ājñā* and the *sahasrāra* to the nostril. The flow of *prāṇa* changes its side (left to right and right to left) from the *ājñā* to the *sahasrāra* by a flexure. When inhalation or exhalation is done through the left or the right nostril, be conscious of the downward flow or the upward flow of *prāṇa* through the *iḍā* or the *piṅgalā nāḍī.* Concentrate on the collection of *Prāṇa* from the universal source and the filling of your body with the Prāṇic energy.

All *prāṇāyāma*s begin with exhalation (*recaka*) and end with inhalation (*pūraka*). These two initial and final steps are not included in the *prāṇāyāma* cycles.

All inhalations are made with a sibilant sound 'ssss' and all exhalations with an aspirate sound 'hhhh'.

Do not produce too much sound while inhaling or exhaling. Breathing should be slow and even. See that the lungs are fully filled in and fully emptied.

*Śavāsana* is recommended at the end of the *prāṇāyāma.* If you practise more than one variety of the *prāṇāyāma* or more than one *prāṇāyāma* in succession, only one *śavāsana* should be enough at the end of the whole *prāṇāyāma* practice.

## NETI (NASAL CLEANSING)

*Neti* is one of the six yogic techniques (*ṣaṭkarma*s) of *Haṭha-Yoga.* It is a process of cleansing and thereby purifying the

---

3. Iyengar, B.K.S., 1981.

4. Joshi, K.S., 1983.

nasal passage. Cleansing may be done with water, ghee or oil. For this purpose, a special vessel called a *neti loṭā* is used. Cleansing the nasal passage is necessary for the efficiency of *prāṇāyāma*. Follow the techniques given below:

1. Fill the vessel with pure lukewarm water, neither too hot nor too cold.
2. Add two teaspoonfuls of salt to one litre of water. Let it be dissolved.
3. Insert the spout of the vessel gently into the left nostril. Slowly tilt the head to the right so that water runs into the left nostril. If the position of the *loṭā* and the tilting angle of the head are correct, and the respiration is through the open mouth, water should flow into the left nostril and pass out of the right nostril (*fig*.1.17).
4. Allow the flow of water through the nostrils for about 20 seconds.
5. Remove the spout of the *loṭā* from the nose. Clean the nose by vigorously blowing out as in *bhastrikā prāṇāyāma*.
6. Repeat the process by tilting the head to the left, pouring water into the right nostril and getting the water out through the left nostril.
7. Repetition of the process should be done four times, by the entry of water two times through the left nostril and two times through the right nostril.
8. Dry the nose by the following technique.

Stand erect with the feet together. Clasp the hands behind the back. Bend forward at the waist so that the head hangs upside down. Remain in this position for 30 seconds. In the bending position, vigorously exhale through the nose five times. Then stand erect.

Close the left nostril. Vigorously inhale and exhale several times in quick succession. Repeat the same process with the right nostril closed. Finally, with both nostrils open, vigorously breathe in and breathe out.

***Caution***: If you suffer from acute or chronic haemorrhage from the mucous membrane of the nose, you may avoid doing *neti*.

*fig.* **1.17** ***Neti*: Nasal cleansing**

SARALA-NĀSĀ-ŚODHANA-KRIYĀ

You may not get time to do *neti* daily. In that case, you may do *sarala-nāsā-śodhana-kriyā* (simple nose-cleansing technique). The technique is as follows:

1. Stand near a water-basin.
2. Close the left nostril.
3. Vigorously breathe in and breathe out through the right nostril. Wash the nose.

4. Close the right nostril.
5. Vigorously breathe in and breathe out through the left nostril. Wash the nose.
6. Repeat the process several times through each nostril until the nasal passages are fully cleared.

With these introductory notes, we shall proceed with the actual steps of *prāṇāyāma.*

## UJJAYĪ PRĀṆĀYĀMA

### *Variety I*

You may do this *prāṇāyāma* while sitting on the floor, sitting on a hard chair, standing, walking, or lying in *śavāsana.*

### ***Technique***

1. Inhale slowly and deeply through both nostrils. The lungs should be full.
2. While inhaling, mentally (silently; not verbally) utter *'so'* (*saḥ*) and shift your awareness from the nostrils through your eyebrow centre and *sahasrāra* down to the *mūlādhāra.*
3. Exhale slowly through both nostrils to evacuate the lungs completely.
4. While exhaling, mentally utter *'haṁ'* (*aham*) and shift your consciousness from the *mūlādhāra* through the *ājñā* up to the *sahasrāra* and then down to the nostrils.

This completes one cycle. Repeat the cycles for 10 to 15 minutes. See that the *prāṇāyāma* is done through pulmonary breathing and not through abdominal breathing.

The *mantra so'ham* is called *ajapā-japa.* The word *japa* means 'repetition of a *mantra*'. When *japa* is unconsciously done without the movement of the lips, it is *ajapā.* Every human being unconsciously does *ajapā-japa* of the *so'ham mantra* 21,600 times daily (within 24 hours). He makes the sound *'so'* when he inhales and the sound *haṁ* when he exhales.

*Prakṛti* (Nature) constantly does *japa* of the one-syllabled *praṇava-mantra AUṀ*. Any person with some practice of meditation can hear this occult sound of Nature. It is called the *anāhata dhvani* (unbeaten sound).

What we do unconsciously is done consciously by the *so'ham prāṇāyāma*. The synchronisation of our inhalation and exhalation with the shifting of our consciousness in accordance with the flow of *prāṇa* in the *suṣumṇā* is important.

No *bandha*s and *mudrā*s are used in this *prāṇāyāma* although one may use *cin-mudrā* and *mūla-bandha* in the sitting posture, if one likes.

*Variety II*

1. Sit in *siddhāsana, padmāsana* or *svastikāsana* with *jālandhara-bandha* and *cin-mudrā*.
2. Inhale and exhale as in Variety I. Listen to the sibilant sound (ssss) during inhalation and the aspirate sound (hhhh) during exhalation.
3. After each inhalation and exhalation, allow a fractional pause. This momentary pause is not the real *kumbhaka*.

*Variety III*

This variety is the same as Variety II except the following:

Remain in *khecarī-mudrā* in addition to *jālandhara-bandha* and *cin-mudrā*.

*Variety IV*

This variety is the same as Variety II except the following:

1. After full inhalation (*pūraka*), hold the breath for two seconds. This is internal retention or *antara kumbhaka*.

Do *mūla-bandha* during *antara kumbhaka.*

2. After full exhalation (*recaka*), pause for two seconds before the next inhalation, that is, retain your breath outside. This external retention is known as *bāhya kumbhaka.* Remain in *uḍḍīyāna-bandha* in *bāhya kumbhaka.*

**Note 1:** Never breathe in while you are in *uḍḍīyāna-bandha.* This would strain your heart. Lift the *uḍḍīyāna-bandha* during *pūraka.* This *bandha* is also contraindicated during *antara kumbhaka.* Its practice is recommended in *recaka* and *bāhya kumbhaka* only.

**Note 2:** *Mūla-bandha* is not contraindicated during any stage of the *prāṇāyāma.* However, both *mūla-bandha* and *jālandhara-bandha* are specifically recommended for *antara kumbhaka.*

**Note 3:** Ordinarily, *jālandhara-bandha* is practised during *antara kumbhaka* and is lifted during *recaka.* It is not usually recommended for *pūraka.* However, *ujjayī prāṇāyāma* is an exception. *Jālandhara-bandha* is recommended for all the three stages (*pūraka, kumbhaka* and *recaka*) of *ujjayī. Jālandhara bandha* may be dispensed with in *ujjayī prāṇāyāma* done in standing and lying postures and also in sitting on a hard chair. (It is not included in the Variety I of *ujjayī prāṇāyāma.*)

*Variety V*

This variety is the same as Variety IV except the following:

Gradually increase the period of *antara kumbhaka* up to 10 to 15 seconds or as long as it is comfortable for you.

Gradually increase the period of *bāhya kumbhaka* up to five seconds.

Very little risk is involved in *ujjayī prāṇāyāma.* It is comparatively easy to practise. It is recommended for all meditators unless someone has some serious health problem like heart disease, asthma and very serious hypertension.

SŪRYABHEDĪ PRĀṆĀYĀMA

The *sūrya-nāḍī* is the *piṅgalā*, the prāṇic channel on the right side of *suṣumṇā*. The verb-root of *bhid* means 'to pierce'. In this *prāṇāyāma, prāṇa* pierces the *sūrya-nāḍī*. All inhalations are done through the right nostril and all exhalations through the left nostril.

*Technique for Variety I*

1. Sit in *siddhāsana, padmāsana* or *svastikāsana* in an erect position.
2. Keep your left palm on your left knee in *cin-mudrā.*
3. Close your eyes.
4. Relax your body and mind.
5. Partially close your right nostril by your right thumb and your left nostril by your right ring and little fingers, without distorting the nasal septum.
6. Exhale through your right nostril after closing the left nostril.
7. Inhale deeply through your right nostril.
8. Exhale fully through your left nostril after closing your right nostril.

This completes a cycle. Repeat the cycles for 10-15 minutes. Finally inhale through both nostrils. Lie in *śavāsana.*

*Technique for Variety II*

This variety is similar to Variety I, with the addition of internal retention.

After deep and full inhalation through the right nostril, block both nostrils and do internal retention with simultaneous *mūla-bandha* and *jālandhara-bandha.* Retain the breath as long as you feel comfortable.

Release the two *bandhas*. Exhale slowly, steadily and deeply through the partially opened left nostril till you feel that the lungs are completely empty.

This completes one cycle. Repeat the cycles as in Variety I.

*Technique for Variety III*

This variety is similar to Variety II, with the addition of external retention.

After exhalation through the left nostril, block both the nostrils, do *uḍḍīyāna-bandha* and external retention to your capacity without strain.

CANDRABHEDĪ PRĀṆĀYĀMA

The *candra-nāḍī* is the *iḍā*, the prāṇic channel on the left side of the *suṣumṇā*. In this *prāṇāyāma, prāṇa* pierces the *candra-nāḍī*. All inhalations are done through the left nostril and all exhalations through the right nostril.

There are also three varieties of this *prāṇāyāma*. The techniques are the same as in the *sūryabhedī prāṇāyāma* except the nostrils used for inhalations and exhalations, already mentioned.

***Special notes***: *Sūryabhedī prāṇāyāma* warms the body and *candrabhedī prāṇāyāma* cools it. Both these *prāṇāyāma*s should not be practised on the same day. They antagonise each other, especially with reference to heat production.

The meditator may proceed for meditation after *ujjayī prāṇāyāma* or *nāḍī-śodhana prāṇāyāma*. Either *sūryabhedī* or *candrabhedī prāṇāyāma* may be necessary in some special situations. In very cold environment, it may be felt to warm up the body before meditation. The nasal passages may partially be blocked due to accumulation of phlegm and nasal catarrh and the nasal mucous membrane may be swollen due to rhinitis. In such situations, *sūryabhedī prāṇāyāma* may be practised. In very hot environment, the meditator may feel uncomfortable and, to cool the body, he may do *candrabhedī prāṇāyāma.* In addition to the heating or the cooling effect, these two *prāṇāyāma*s have also the other beneficial effects of *prāṇāyāma* in general to facilitate meditation.

### NĀḌĪ-ŚODHANA PRĀṆĀYĀMA

A tubular structure is known as *nāḍī.* In the present context, *nāḍī* means 'a subtle (not gross) tubular passage for the flow of *prāṇa*'. It may further be emphasised that *nāḍī* is not a nerve and neither is it a blood vessel (artery or vein). The word *śodhana* means 'purifying' or 'cleansing'. By the *nāḍī-śodhana prāṇāyāma,* the blockages of the subtle prāṇic channels (total number is 72,000; *suṣumṇā* is the central vertical channel; *iḍā* is the channel left of *suṣumṇā; piṅgalā* is the channel right of *suṣumṇā*) of the body are cleared and cleansed.

*A. Technique for nāḍī-śodhana without kumbhaka*

1. Strictly follow the preparatory steps which have already been specified for *prāṇāyāma.* Sit in *ṣiddhāasana, padmāsana* or *svastikāsana. Vajrāsana* may be avoided for this purpose. *Sukhāsana* may be used, but it may be the last resort. Maintain your head, neck and torso in a vertically erect position. Close your eyes. Relax your body and mind. *Prāṇāyāma* should be done after *āsana*s and *mudrā*s and before meditation. Keep your left hand on your left knee in *cin-mudrā.* Your right thumb should be placed on your right nostril and right ring and little fingers on your left nostril. These fingers and thumb should touch the lowermost and lateral side of the nose. Throughout the process of the *prāṇāyāma,* the thumb and the third and fourth fingers of the right hand should remain in contact with the nose. Apply partial pressure so that both the nostrils

are partially closed. Inhalations and exhalations are done in *prāṇāyāma* while the nostrils are partially closed.

2. Exhale through the left nostril. This is preliminary and not included in the *prāṇāyāma* cycle. The cycle begins with step 3.
3. Inhale through the left nostril.
4. Exhale through the right nostril.
5. Inhale through the right nostril.
6. Exhale through the left nostril.

Steps 3 to 6 make a cycle. Repeat the cycles as long as you can. In the beginning, you may do for a couple of minutes. Gradually increase the time to 10 to 15 minutes per sitting. Three sittings at the three *sandhyā*s a day may be ideally done. The second preference is for two sittings, in the morning and evening. The third preference is only one sitting, preferably in the morning. Remember that *nāḍī-śodhana prāṇāyāma* is always done with empty stomach (three hours after taking a full meal).

Inhalations and exhalations should be full so that the lungs are completely filled and completely emptied. They should be slow, steady and deep. See that minimum sound is produced in the inhaling and the exhaling processes.

Inhalation (*śvāsa*) and exhalation (*praśvāsa*) should be of equal duration. Some *yogī*-instructors recommend counting digits or counting *praṇava-japa* (*OṀ*). However, we are not in favour of counting. Counting distracts the mind from the real concentration on the flow of *Prāṇa.* And the concentration on the pervasive nature of *Prāṇa,* its collection from the cosmic source, its regulated flow in the *nāḍī*s, its storage in *cakra*s and the vitalisation of all the cells of the body by the Prāṇic Energy is the most important activity in *prāṇāyāma.* Concentrating on the mechanics of respiration, on the lungs and on counting with or without *praṇava-japa* becomes too much mechanical. In this regard, we have one suggestion, however. The ratio of *pūraka* to *recaka* should be approximately 1:1. This ratio is almost maintained in course of practice and experience. No harmful effects shall be produced if the ratio is not strictly maintained.

This *prāṇāyāma* is practised without *bandhas* (*jālandhara, uḍḍīyāna* and *mūla*). One may remain in *mūla-bandha* if one likes.

No risk is involved in the practice of *nāḍī-śodhana prāṇāyāma* without *kumbhaka,* except for individuals who suffer from serious cardiac ailments, serious asthma or any other complicated diseases.

*B. Technique for nāḍī-śodhana prāṇāyāma with kumbhaka*

Follow steps 1 and 2, as given in A, and then proceed with the following steps:

1. Inhale through the left nostril.
2. Close both nostrils and retain the breath as long as you can without discomfort, straining and struggling.
3. Exhale through the right nostril.
4. Inhale through the right nostril.
5. Close both nostrils and retain the breath as long as you can without discomfort, straining and struggling.
6. Exhale through the left nostril.

Steps 1 to 6 constitute a cycle. Repeat the cycle as long as you can do. You may begin with three cycles and gradually increase through practice. A duration of ten minutes per sitting is an optimum period. The recommendation of three sittings, two sittings or one sitting a day, as given for A, also holds good for this *prāṇāyāma.*

The durations of *pūraka, kumbhaka* and *recaka* should ideally be 1:4:2. Most *gurus* prescribe strict adherence to this proportion by counting digits, by *praṇava-japa,* by *gāyatrī-japa* or other means. However, we are not in favour of the strict observance of this proportion through counting time. We do recommend this proportion of 1:4:2, which may be observed approximately through practice and experience. Our key-recommendation is: Remain in *kumbhaka* as long as it is not uncomfortable for you.

Your inhalation should be slow, steady and deep. Fill the lungs to the brim so that each alveolus of each lung bulges out like a ripe grape from the collapsed state. Maximum oxygenation of the arterial blood cannot occur if the lungs are not fully inflated and aerated. Without the entry of sufficient quantity of oxygen into the lungs, breath cannot be retained for a prolonged period. More entry of air into the lungs increases the intra-pulmonary pressure that leads to enhanced absorption of oxygen into the pulmonary arterioles. The longer the *kumbhaka,* the more the absorption of oxygen into the blood.

In normal circumstances, a person's brain-cells can withstand anoxia (lack of oxygen) for a maximum period of about three minutes, beyond which the brain-cells die permanently. If this happens, nothing can be done subsequently for the revival of the dead brain-cells. Paralysis, loss of memory, coma and death are the outcomes of cerebral anoxia. Hence injudicious retention of breath may prove to be very harmful or fatal. However, controlled, long and safe *kumbhaka* can oxygenate arterial blood in a more efficient way and can infiltrate *Prāṇa* throughout the gross, subtle and causal bodies in a saturated state. That is why a prolonged *antara kumbhaka* (internal retention) which must also be safe is recommended in this *prāṇāyāma.*

It is a general tendency with new learners to expel the pulmonary air in a sudden gush or intermittent spurts. This should be controlled and prevented. Exhalation should be steady and slow. The elimination of carbon dioxide ($CO_2$) from the pulmonary venous blood is better effected if *recaka* is done through a longer period. However, too long a period for *recaka* following *kumbhaka* may aggravate the problem of anoxia of the cerebral cells.

Alternate breathing (left→right→right→left) has much scientific significance. It may briefly be mentioned here. *Prāṇa* flows in *iḍā, piṅgalā* and *suṣumṇā*. If the spine is taken as a reference point, *suṣumṇā* traverses a centrally vertical path, *iḍā* to the left of *suṣumṇā* and *piṅgalā* to the right of *suṣumṇā*. It may be noted that the spine or the vertebral column and the spinal cord inside it are structures of the gross body whereas these *nāḍī*s are structures of the subtle body.

All *nāḍī*s originate from the bulb (*kanda*) of the *mūlādhāra-cakra* and go to different parts of the body. The *suṣumṇā* travels a straight path from the *mūlādhāra* to the *ājñā*. The *iḍā* and the *piṅgalā* travel on the left and the right side, respectively, in a bow-shaped manner except forming three knots. The first knot (*brahmagranthi*) is at the *mūlādhāra*. The third knot (*rudragranthi*) is at the *ājñā*. The two bows are constricted at the *anāhata-cakra* (the heart centre) to form a knot (*viṣṇugranthi*). The *suṣumṇā* proceeds in a straight path from the *ājñā* to the *sahasrāra* where it branches into two flexures. The right flexure comes down from the *brahmarandhra* area to the left nostril. The left flexure comes down from that summit to the right nostril. Thus the sides are reversed.

Now we discuss the gross anatomy of the brain and the reversal of the nerve pathways. There are two cerebral hemispheres — the left and the right. The left cerebral hemisphere is the logical, rational and scientific brain. The right cerebral hemisphere is the artistic, emotional and sentimental brain. Nerves from the left side of the brain change their course and innervate the right side of the body. Nerves from the right side of the brain change their course and innervate the left side of the body. For this reason, any lesion in the left brain produces symptoms (like paralysis) in the right side of the body and vice versa.

We discussed the subtle anatomy of the *nāḍīs* and the gross anatomy of the central nervous system to focus on some important aspects of the *nāḍī-śodhana prāṇāyāma.* The alternate breathing has direct bearing on the anatomy, both subtle and gross. Secondly, although we do deal with breathing air and the mechanics of the respiratory system, at the subtle level, we deal with the flow of *Prāṇa* in the *nāḍīs.* Thirdly, in the *pūraka* and the *recaka* processes of the *prāṇāyāma,* we consciously shift our awareness on the flow of *Prāṇa* either in *iḍā* or *piṇgalā. Prāṇa* also flows in *suṣumṇā. Nāḍī-śodhana prāṇāyāma* purifies and cleanses the *suṣumṇā nāḍī,* in addition to the other *nāḍīs.*

Now we come back to the *prāṇāyāma* proper. In *nāḍī-śodhana prāṇāyāma* with *kumbhaka,* supplement the following two steps for *kumbhaka* and *recaka*:

1. Remain in *jālandhara-bandha* and *mūla-bandha* throughout the period of *kumbhaka.* Release the *jālandhara-bandha* at the termination of *kumbhaka* and beginning of *recaka.*
2. Impose the *uḍḍīyāna-bandha* in addition to the *mūla-bandha* during the whole period of *recaka.* Release the *uḍḍīyāna bandha* at the termination of *recaka* and just before the onset of the subsequent *pūraka.* Never remain in *uḍḍīyāna-bandha* during *kumbhaka.*

These two supplementary steps are not optional. They cannot be dispensed with. They are integral parts of the *nāḍī-śodhana prāṇāyāma* with *kumbhaka.* It may be emphasised that *kumbhaka* without the *jālandhara-bandha* and the *mūla-bandha* is contraindicated.

### C. *Nāḍī-śodhana prāṇāyāma with antara and bāhya kumbhaka*

After sufficient practice of stage A and B of the *nāḍī-śodhana prāṇāyāma,* one may go for stage C. It is the same as B except the following addition.

Allow a *bāhya kumbhaka* after each *recaka* and before the subsequent *pūraka.* In this process, the breath is retained outside. The word *antara* means 'inside' and *bāhya* 'outside'. The recommended proportion of duration of *pūraka, antara kumbhaka, recaka* and *bāhya kumbhaka* is 1:4:2:2. This may again be noted that our recommendation is a proportion of approximation established through practice and experience rather than counting of numbers or mental repetition of *mantra*s and taking account thereof.

*Nāḍī-śodhana prāṇāyāma* without *kumbhaka* is a safe one for all except for persons with serious pulmonary and bronchial ailments, serious cardiac problems and *uncontrollably serious* hypertension. This *prāṇāyāma* is highly recommended for meditation to be preceded.

The effects of *nāḍī-śodhana prāṇāyāma* with *kumbhaka* are much better than those of this *prāṇāyāma* without *kumbhaka.* If *kumbhaka* and the associated *bandha*s are learnt and well practised under the guidance of a competent *guru,* it is advisable to practise *nāḍī-śodhana* with *kumbhaka* before meditation. If this condition is met with, one may adopt Variety III of ths *prāṇāyāma* to be followed by meditation.

# 1.5

## Pratyāhāra Preparatory to Meditation

PRATYĀHĀRA means 'withdrawal'. In yogic context, it means 'withdrawal of senses'. We have five gross organs of perception, namely, two eyes (the organ of vision), two ears (the organ of audition), the nose (the organ of olfaction), the taste buds in the oral mucous membrane and on the tongue (the organ of gustation) and the skin (the tactile organ). These gross organs of perceptions cannot be withdrawn. They receive stimuli from the external world. The input data are subjected to a preliminary processing in the gross organ of perception. Information is transmitted from the gross organ of perception to the corresponding cerebral centre in the uppermost part of the brain. This is electromagnetic transmission on the nerve-pathway. We do not know what exactly happens thereafter. The corresponding cerebral centre makes a connection with the *manas, ahaṅkāra* and *buddhi* — the *antaḥkaraṇa*, which is lighted by the *jīvātmā* sitted at the *bindu* in the blissful sheath. It is the *antaḥkaraṇa* that perceives and conceives. It orders the subtle organs (*indriyas*) to contact the source of stimulus. The olfactory subtle organ (*ghrāṇendriya,*) gustatory subtle organ (*rasanendriya*), visual subtle organ (*darśanendriya*) tactile subtle organ (*sparśanendriya*) and auditory subtle organ (*śravaṇendriya*) are located in the *mūlādhāra, svādhiṣṭhāna, maṇipūra, anāhata* and *viśuddhi cakra,* respectively. Each of these subtle organs goes out to reach the source of the stimulus. Thus there is a two-way communion between the source of stimuli and the *antaḥkaraṇa-indriya*-complex.

In the process of *pratyāhāra,* the subtle sense-organs (*jñānendriyas*) are withdrawn into Egoity (*ahaṅkāra*) which is an evolute of the evolvent *buddhi* (intellect). In the course of evolution, *ahaṅkāra* is the evolvent and the five sense-organs are the evolutes. It is the general rule that evolutes are withdrawn into the evolvent. As a result of this withdrawal, the subtle sense-organs cannot reach the sources of stimuli and sense-perceptions are blocked.

The theory of *pratyāhāra,* as outlined here, has not been well spelt out in most modern books on *yoga.* The practice of *pratyāhāra* is still more hazy. Here we propose to present the concrete steps that may be adopted and practised for getting success in *pratyāhāra.*

We recommend *prāṇāyāma* to precede each session of meditation, although we do not propose to make it compulsory. *Pratyāhāra* stands on a different footing, however. It should be a regular practice of the *yogī,* but is not necessary to precede every session of meditation. It improves the power of concentration. A meditator, without the previous practice of *pratyāhāra,* can hardly get full success in meditation.

## Techniques of pratyāhāra

Intense concentration on the activity of one sense keeps the other senses withdrawn. This principle is made use of by using one of the three sense-organs, namely, eyes, ears and nose.

## Use of olfactory concentration for pratyāhāra

Any aromatic substance may be used for this purpose. The aroma should be soothing and pleasant; not obnoxious, unpleasant and repellent. The *yogī* should be fully absorbed in sensing the aroma with pin-pointed focus on it. If this is done, the other senses remain withdrawn. However, the sense of smell is less commonly used for *pratyāhāra* in comparison with the visual or the auditory sense.

## Use of visual concentration for pratyāhāra

### TRĀṬAKA

Do *trāṭaka* on a black spot drawn on a white paper, on a crystal, on the tip of the flame of a candle or lamp, on the vermilion spot of a deity, on the sandalwood spot of a deity, on the letter *AUṀ*, on the picture or statue of a deity, or on any such other thing already indicated in the section under *trāṭaka*. If you have made some progress in *yoga* and you are well acquainted with the subtle anatomy of the *cakra*s of the subtle body, you may do *trāṭaka* on the inner *maṇḍala* of a *cakra* or on the *jyotirliṅga* in *sahasrāra*.

### MUDRĀ

Sit with *śāmbhavī-mudrā, agocarī-mudrā* (*nāsikāgra dṛṣṭi*), or *yoni-mudrā*. The techniques of these *mudrā*s have already been described. The vision may be inner (*antardṛṣṭi*) or outer (*bahirdṛṣṭi*). In the former, the eyes are closed. Concentrated vision brings to a state of *pratyāhāra*.

## Use of auditory concentration for pratyāhāra

### LOW-PITCHED SOUND IN HARMONY AND SYNCHRONY

Such sound may be orally produced by the *yogī*. It may also be an instrumentally recorded sound. Traditionally it is a *mantra* repeated for a period. The best *mantra* is *AUṀ*.

### KĪRTANA

For the present context, *kīrtana* is the loud repetition of a *mantra* in a devotional ecstasy. It has characteristics apparently opposed to *yoga*. Nevertheless, here it is recommended for *yoga*. It may or may not be accompanied with instrumental music. *Kīrtana* brings to a state of *pratyāhāra*.

### Concentration on the anāhata dhvani for pratyāhāra

*Dhvani* means 'sound'. The literal meaning of the word *anāhata* is 'unbeaten'. That sound which is produced otherwise than by beating is *anāhata dhvani*. It is the sound *AUṀ*, which is otherwise known as *praṇava*.

Ordinarily vibrations are produced by beating and sound is produced by vibrations. The *anāhata dhvani* is an exception, however. Nature and everything of Nature constantly and continuously produce the sound *AUṀ*. And this sound is produced without beating and vibrations. The whole of Nature and all parts of Nature do *mantra-japa* by continuously repeating the one-syllabled *praṇava* (*AUṀ*) which verbally stands for *Brahman*.

By listening to the *anāhata dhvani* and concentrating on it for about ten minutes a day, one may attain to the *pratyāhāra* state. Here is a problem, of course. Persons, without practice of meditation, can hardly listen to the *anāhata dhvani*. And concentration on the *anāhata dhvani* takes to the ṣtate of *pratyāhāra* which prepares the seedbed of meditation. Hence this technique cannot be suitable for beginners in meditation. This is, however, a very potent and useful technique for persons who have already made some practice of meditation.

### Use of mantra-japa for pratyāhāra

The repetition of a *mantra* is known as *japa*. Every *mantra* has a deity (*devatā*) and contains the name of that deity. *Mantra-japa* is done in one out of three-ways, namely, *vaikharī, upāṁśu* and *mānasika*. Verbal repetition of the *japa* is done in the *vaikharī* variety. Repetition in a whisper or humming, with the movements of the lips, without the *japa* being made audible to others, is known as *upāṁśu*. The mental repetition of the *japa* is known as *mānasika*. Maharṣi Patañjali recommends meditation on the meaning of the *mantra* while doing the *japa.*[5]

For non-adepts in *yoga, vaikharī japa* is recommended for the initial stage. The loudness of the *japa* shuts out all extraneous thoughts and stops them from entering into the mind. One may proceed from *vaikharī* to *upāṁśu* and finally to *mānasika* in the course of the practice of *japa. Upāṁśu japa* is better than *vaikharī* and *mānasika japa* is better than *upāṁśu*. However, *mānasika japa* is not very suitable for the beginner due to the fact that all sorts of extraneous thoughts and external sounds enter into the mind during the *japa* in silence.

*Japa* should be done with unwavering faith (*śraddhā*), devotion (*bhakti*) and intense love (*prema*). When this is done, the mind stays in an emotional state with pin-pointed attention to God. In this mental state, all the subtle senses (*indriyas*) are withdrawn into *ahaṅkāra* (Egoity) and hence are rendered non-receptive.

In all the three varieties of *japa,* the state of *pratyāhāra* is attained partially or wholly. But the *mānasika* (silent and mental) *japa* is the most effective one in producing the state of *pratyāhāra. Japa* has other benefits too. One gets all those benefits in addition to getting the *pratyāhāra* state preparatory to meditation.

5. *PYD*, I.28 (*tajjapastadarthabhāvanam*).

# 1.6

# The Practice of Meditation

DHĀRAṆĀ, *dhyāna* and *samādhi* are the last three limbs of *Pātañjala Yoga*. These three, done together, are combinedly known as *saṁyama*. Here we are using the English word 'meditation' for *saṁyama*.

## Practice of dhāraṇā

In *dhāraṇā*, concentration is focussed on a spot. It is not necessarily gazing with eyes open. To use the yogic language, it may also be focussing the vision with eyes closed. Generally, in meditation, the eyes are closed and *dhāraṇā* is done with inner vision.

### FIRST STAGE

The spot on which *dhāraṇā* is practised may be external or internal. A beginner may practise *trāṭaka* on a black spot drawn on a white paper, on a crystal, on the tip of a flame of a candle or a lamp, or on the vermilion spot or sandalwood spot at the eyebrow centre of a deity. It is the first stage in the practice of *dhāraṇā*.

### SECOND STAGE

In this stage, the spot on which *dhāraṇā* is practised is some locality on the external body of the meditator. Nose-tip-gazing is one such *dhāraṇā*. *Śāmbhavī-mudrā* is also another *dhāraṇā*, belonging to this second stage.

THIRD STAGE

In this stage, *dhāraṇā* is done with closed eyes and the spot on which the inner vision is focussed is some locality which is internal to the body. *Dhāraṇā* may be done on any gross organ of the body. It may be done on any *cakra* of the subtle body. In usual meditation, the meditator does *dhāraṇā* on his eyebrow centre (*ājñā-cakra*) with closed eyes.

If you are a beginner in meditation, sit in *dhāraṇā* sessions twice or thrice a day, each session being for a period of five to ten minutes. Begin with stage I, and passing through stage II, come to stage III where you stabilise your *dhāraṇā.*

**Practice of dhyāna**

In *dhyāna,* the meditator focusses his attention on a single idea which flows in the mind uninterruptedly like the flow of oil in a continuous stream, when poured from one vessel to another. Here it may be emphasised that the idea should be one only and not more than one.

For practising *dhyāna,* the following preliminary steps may be taken. These are common to all forms of *dhāraṇā, dhyāna* and *samādhi.*

1. Sit in *siddhāsana, padmāsana, svastikāsana* or *sukhāsana,* in order of preference. Sit on a four-folded blanket or a small carpet specially made for such a purpose. Foam bed or any such soft material is not good for this purpose. If a bed is used instead of a floor, it should be a hard bed rather than a soft one.
2. Sit in a vertically erect position so that the head, neck and torso remain perpendicular to the ground level and the spine does not sag or bend.
3. Close the eyes.
4. Relax the body and the mind. The limbs and muscles

should be free from tenseness and all organs and tissues shall be free from straining.

5. Remain in *cin-mudrā* or *jñāna-mudrā.* If you sit in *sukhāsana,* keep your hands on your lap, placing the dorsal right hand on the left palm (*bhairava-mudrā*), or the dorsal left hand on the right palm (*bhairavī-mudrā*), both the palms facing upward in both the *mudrā*s (*fig.* 1.18 and 1.19).
6. It would be preferable to meditate in the same place at the same time daily. This would condition your mind favourably.
7. If you are a theist, sit before your favourite deity in the meditation room. If you are an atheist, you may still reserve a room for meditation, and this room may be calm, quiet and aesthetically pleasing to the mind.

*fig.* **1.18** ***Bhairava mudrā***

*fig.* **1.19** ***Bhairavī mudrā***

TECHNIQUE I

Meditate on the idea of earthen solid, aquatic fluid, fire, airy gases and *ākāśa* (Space) in succession, the duration of each one being about two minutes.

When you think of water, mentally visualise a vast mass of water like the sea or a lake and think of water only. Do the same thing with earth, fire, air or *ākāśa*.

TECHNIQUE II

Meditate on the colours of the spectrum, namely, violet, indigo, blue, green, yellow, orange and red, individually in succession. If time is a limiting factor, take one colour like red, yellow or blue. The idea of the chosen colour should be continuously flowing in the mind's stream.

TECHNIQUE III

Meditate on a form. It may be the form of a deity — Kālī, Durgā, Lakṣmī, Sarasvatī, Brahmā, Viṣṇu, Śiva, Kṛṣṇa, Buddha, Mahāvīra, Guru Nānak, Jesus Christ, or any other. It may be the form of a symbol like *AUṀ, SVASTIKA, LIṄGA, CROSS,* or any other.

TECHNIQUE IV

Advanced practitioners of *yoga* may meditate on a *cakra — mūlādhāra, svādhiṣṭhāna, maṇipūra, anāhata, viśuddhi, ājñā, bindu,* or *sahasrāra.* Knowledge on the anatomy of the *cakras* is a prerequisite for this meditation.

TECHNIQUE V

Mentally and silently repeat the *mantra* of your *iṣṭa-devatā* (chosen tutelary deity) with your concentrated thought on the meaning of the *mantra.*

TECHNIQUE VI

In this technique, there is a target object (person, thing, organ, tissue, chemical, etc.) and a suggestion or a command (*saṅkalpa*). This is really a fusion of *dhāraṇā* and *dhyāna.* The meditator takes a deep breath through both nostrils while remaining in *mūla-bandha.* In the state of *antara kumbhaka* (internal retention), he orders the target object to obey the command or the suggestion. He meditates on the target object and the *saṅkalpa* simultaneously. He goes on repeating the *saṅkalpa* while in the *kumbhaka* and then exhales when he can no longer retain the breath. He again takes a deep breath and mentally repeats his *saṅkalpa* while focussing his attention on the target object. This process is repeated for five to ten minutes per session.

## Practice of samādhi

In *dhyāna,* the meditator fixes his attention on one idea only and the idea flows continuously without interruption. In *samādhi*, the meditator remains in a thoughtless state. This state is devoid of material existence, devoid of forms, attributes and actions, and devoid of thoughts.

For the beginner whose meditation has not attained the stage of maturity, the state of thoughtlessness becomes transient with frequent interruptions of extraneous thoughts coming from all sides. As a whirlwind is created around the nucleus of a vacuum, so does occur the intrusion of sundry ideas into the thoughtless mind. To get rid of this difficulty, the meditator has to take the help of an *ālamba* (support). He uses the *ālamba* only when thought-intrusion takes place. Again he gives up the *ālamba* and remains in thoughtless state.

As a molecule of sodium chloride (salt: NaCl) dissolves in the sea-water and *apparently* loses its separate identity, so does a *yogī* become completely absorbed in *Brahman* in the *samādhi* state. *Samādhi* is perfect in the fourth state of existence (*turīya*).

TECHNIQUE

1. Take a symbol and name it by a word which must be a monosyllable. The Vedic ॐ (*OṀ=AUṀ*) is such a symbol which stands for *Brahman*[6]. Any other symbol like the *svastika* (卐), the *triśūla* (trident), the *cakra* (discus), the *liṅga* (the Divine Father) with the *Śakti* (the Divine Mother), the Christian cross (✝), or any one else may be adopted, provided a monosyllable may be accepted to represent the particular symbol. The symbol should have preferably been an archetype, classically meaningful for the Unconscious. The symbol with its *vācaka* is the *ālamba*.
2. Sit in a meditative posture with closed eyes. Visualise the symbol at the eyebrow centre which is the seat of *buddhi, ahaṅkāra* and *manas*. Do *dhyāna* on the symbol

6. *PYD*, I.27 (*tasya vācakaḥ praṇavaḥ*).

and mentally repeat the *vācaka* (the designator of the symbol). Abruptly erase the picture of the symbol from your mind's screen and erase the idea of the symbol from your mind's memory. Remain in a thoughtless state. Continue to remain in that state as long as you can.

3. Whenever any thought intrudes into your mind from inside or outside, take the help of the *ālamba* on which *dhyāna* is to be done. After doing *dhyāna* for a few seconds, come back to the *samādhi* state again. Repeat *ālamba-dhyāna* if and when necessity arises in the midst of *samādhi*.

4. Remain in *samādhi* for five to twenty minutes or more.

MEDITATION

*Pātañjala Yoga* has eight limbs. Out of these, the last three limbs, namely, *dhāraṇā, dhyāna* and *samādhi*, practised together, constitute the yogic process known as *saṁyama*.[7] What is known as meditation in general will be described under the heading *saṁyama*.

### *Āstika saṁyama*

Follow the following steps for doing theistic meditation:

1. Follow the seven pre-meditational steps outlined for *dhyāna*.

2. With eyes closed, visualise the form of your *iṣṭa-devatā* at the eyebrow centre.

3. Do *mānasika* (mental) *japa* of the *mantra* of your *iṣṭa-devatā*. The total number of syllables (*akṣaras*) in the *mantra* should not preferably exceed sixteen. If you are initiated by a *guru*, do *japa* on the *mantra* given by

7. *PYD*, III.4 (*trayamekatra saṁyamaḥ*).

the *guru*. The visualisation of the form and the *mantra-japa* may be done for a couple of minutes.

4. Discontinue the visualisation and the *mantra-japa*. But continue the *japa* of the monosyllabic *ālamba*.

   Some Western scientists who have done research on this aspect equate the *praṇava* (*AUṀ*) with any other monosyllable sound such as 'ONE'. We do not agree with them. Their experimental subjects did not meditate on the meaning of *AUṀ*. The concept of *Brahman* is alien to them. They mechanically uttered *AUṀ* and other monosyllables mentally. Hence *AUṀ* was not better than other monosyllables for them. We highly recommend the meditation on *AUṀ* which is the quintessence of all the Vedas.

5. Suspend the mental repetition of the *ālamba* and meditation thereon.

   So far you were doing *dhāraṇā* and *dhyāna*. Hereafter you plunge into *samādhi*.

6. Remain in thoughtless condition.

7. If and when thoughts trespass upon your mind, immediately do mental *japa* of your *ālamba*. But this is a temporary phase for a few moments. Jump into the thoughtless state again and remain in that state for a period as long as possible.

After the meditation, sit for a while, relax and then get up.

## SECULAR MEDITATION

This meditation is the same as the foregoing one except a few changes to suit the temperament of the ones who do not believe in God or who are agnostics.

Follow the following steps for doing secular meditation:

1. You may sit on the floor in any one of the meditational *āsana*s. Alternatively, you may also sit on a *hard* bed in any of the meditational *āsana*s. If *āsana*s are not convenient for you, you may sit on a hard chair. Except this deviation, follow the seven pre-meditational steps outlined for *dhyāna.*
2. With eyes closed, visualise a lighted point at the eyebrow centre.
3. Select a monosyllable for you or get it from your instructor. This would be your *ālamba.* Silently repeat this monosyllable.
4. Discontinue the visualisation of the light-point; but continue the mental repetition of the monosyllable (*ekākṣara*).
5. Suspend the mental repetition of the monosyllable.
6. Remain in thoughtless condition.
7. If and when thoughts trespass on your mind, immediately repeat your *ālamba* silently. After a while, again plunge into the thoughtless state.

**Total absorption and unification**

In both types of meditation, theistic and secular, *anāhata dhvani* (unbeaten sound) is listened to after some practice of *samādhi.* It is a harmonious, synchronous humming sound, very low in pitch, but orderly and melodious. Hearing of this sound is an index of the maturation of the yogic practice.

Many Indian *yogī*s believe that every created entity in Nature continuously repeat the *praṇava, AUṀ* which designates *Brahman.* In the full state of *pratyāhāra* and in the state of the full absorption of one's self into *Brahman,* the unbeaten sound becomes clearly audible.

Both the Great Self (*Paramātmā*) and the individual self

(*jīvātmā*) reside in the body of each person.[8] The Great Self or God, although One and One only is functionally named as three — Brahmā, Viṣṇu and Rudra. 'Brahmā' the creator, resides in the *mūlādhāra-cakra*. Viṣṇu the sustainer and nourisher, resides in the *anāhata-cakra*. Rudra the destroyer, resides in the *ājñā*, the *bindu* and the *sahasrāra*. The *anāhata dhvani* emanates from the *anāhata-cakra* (heart centre) of every person.

The *samādhi* state is the *turīya* state. It is the culmination of *yoga*.

8. *AV*, IX.9.20: *ṚV*, I.164.20.

# PART 2
# THEORY OF MEDITATION

# 2.1

# What is Meditation?

THE English word 'meditation' has no exact equivalent in Indian *Yoga*. It means the act of exercising the mind in contemplation, and especially in religious contemplation. One meditates on a subject, when one focusses one's attention on it in this manner.

## Mind in a whirl

Calmness and stillness are not the natural properties of mind which is always in motion and whirling motion. The natural motion of mind is vortical. It is usually in whirls. Sometimes the whirls are slow and smooth in movement. Some other times, they are turbulent and tumultuous. When a thinker, a philosopher, a mathematician thinks, the wagons of thought may move linearly and sequentially; but such linear movements of thoughts occur over an underlying whirling movement of the mind.

We have observed whirlwinds and whirlpools. In both cases, the medium is a fluid. The former takes place in gases or mixtures of gases such as air; the latter in liquids such as moving water in streams and rivers in spate. In a similar manner, mind has whirlwinds and whirlpools. The whirling movement is intrinsic to all minds. Ripples and waves appear in mind as superimpositions on the underlying whirls. But whirls are invariably present and active.

The *Bhagavad Gītā* has emphasised the fact that mind is always in motion,[1] and that the moving nature of mind is to

1. *BG*, VI.26; VI.34.

be controlled.[2] The *Gītā* admits that it is difficult to control the mind; still it prescribes yogic methods to restrain and calm the mind. The *Gītā* asserts that it is possible to yoke and still the mind if one sincerely and meticulously practises the prescribed yogic methods.

*Ṛṣi* Patañjali has defined *Yoga*. *Yoga* is restraint of the whirls of the mindstuff.[3] When *Yoga* is perfected, the mind stays at absolutely complete rest. It is a state of a motionless point, without whirls, ripples and waves. In the mental world, it is a state of zero or at least minimum entropy. A state of zero entropy is reserved for *Brahman*, which is *Cit* or the Fundamental Consciousness. The yogic mind, in the state of zero whirls, ripples and waves, attains to the stage of *Saccidānanda* (*Brahman* = Existence, Consciousness and Bliss), or at least, it tends to that stage. Entropy is a measure of disorder. A yogic mind, in the state of zero *vṛtti* (whirls), has minimum entropy or no entropy at all.

According to the Indian concept of Sāṅkhya-Yoga and Vedānta, mind and brain are different. The brain is a gross organ of the body. It is a highly specialised nervous organ; but it belongs to the body rather than the mind. In contrast, mind is too subtle to be perceived by the senses. The brain is the apparatus of the mind. Mental phenomena are exhibited through the brain which functions as an instrument of the mind.

Most scientists and modern psychologists identify the brain and the mind. The doctrine of brain-mind-identity has been rejected by Indian psychology, however. The whirls of mind have not been detected in science. But brain-waves have been identified. We can infer the existence of the whirls of mind

---

2. *BG*, VI.26; VI.34-35.

3. *PYD*, I.2 (*yogaścittavṛttinirodhaḥ*).

(*cittavṛtti*) from that of the brain-waves. The brain-waves are the spontaneous discharges of the brain, as recorded by an electroencephalogram (EEG).

Hansberger, a German scientist, discovered brain-waves (alpha and beta) shortly after the First World War. The beta waves have a frequency of 14 to 28 cycles per second. Their pattern predominates during our daily wakeful state. When we are in our busy frame of mind, in tension, worries and anxiety, or when we engage our brain in serious logical thinking, mathematical exercises, or any other problem-solving activity, the beta waves predominate in our brain. These waves are small, coming faster than 13 cycles per second. The alpha waves have a frequency of 8 to 13 cycles per second. They are slightly larger than the beta waves. They are emitted from the brain during milder states of meditation. They are also dominant during states of relaxation and passivity, ecstatic state of creativity and states free from anxiety and tension. In the state of alpha waves, the mind is neither active nor drowsy, but is in a neutral condition. It is an alert state, devoid of concrete visual imagery, with a lack of tension and anxiety, and with a feeling of tranquillity. The theta waves have a frequency of 4 to 7 cycles per second. They are prominent in children and young adolescents in their waking state. They appear just before the onset of sleep. They are rare in waking adults.They are emitted during dreaming and are associated with the unconscious mind. They are also dominant in the deeper states of meditation, intense creativity, ecstasy and receptivity to ESP (extrasensory perception). The frequency of the delta waves is 2 to 3 cycles per second (below 4). They are large and slow waves. They predominate in dreamless sleep or in the unconscious state. They have also been recorded in deep states of meditation.

Many people generally think that the mind is non-functional during sleep and in unconscious states. It is, however, a misconception. The mind is always busy, sometimes more, sometimes less. When we sleep, the mind becomes busy in dreaming. We remember a few dreams, while most dreams are forgotten. The mind still functions as a whirlpool or whirlwind when we are asleep or unconscious.

## The form of the whirling mind

Mind is too subtle and has no form of its own. The grosser a substance, the more definite and firm its structural form. An earthen statue has a form. We can think of a watery or an airy statue; but, practically it has no structural form. Mind, being too subtle, has no definite form of its own. But it acquires forms which are varied and diverse. Water takes the geometrical form of its container. Mind takes the form of its own whirls (*vṛtti*).

*Ṛṣi* Patañjali has an aphorism on the form of the mind.[4] In the analogy of water and its container, mind takes the form of its whirls. The analogy is not 100 per cent identical, however. In the case of the mind, the whirls are produced by the mind itself, and they are not its container. Nevertheless, it is correct to say that the mind assumes the forms of its whirls. Since whirls are not constant in kinds and shapes, the forms which mind takes are diverse in kinds and variable in shape.

## The formless in its own form

Patañjali's definition of *Yoga* has already been stated. *Yoga* is the restraint of the whirls of the mind-stuff. In that state of the mind, whirls cease to be generated; the mind becomes calm and motionless, the stilled mind becomes inactive; due to the absence of whirls, and impliedly the absence of their

---

4. *PYD*, I.4 (*vṛttisārūpyamitaratra*).

forms, mind does not and cannot acquire any form in that quiescent state.

*Ṛṣi* Patañjali's aphorism says:

> At that time, the individual self (*jīvātmā*) stays in the own state of the Universal Self (*Paramātmā* or *Brahman*) who is the Omniscient Seer (*draṣṭā*).[5]

The word *draṣṭuḥ* means 'of the One who sees', and the word *svarūpe* means 'in the own form'. Since *Brahman* or the Fundamental Consciousness (*Cit*) is formless, *svarūpe,* in this context, means 'in its own state'.

The word *Yoga* (*yuj* + *ghañ*) etymologically means 'addition' or 'union', the Sanskrit verb root *yuj* meaning 'to unite'. The mathematics of addition or of subtraction is a special one for *Brahman.* It is unlike 5+3=8 or 5-3=2. *Brahman* is immeasurable (*aprameya*) and illimitable (*asīma*) and thus is infinite. The Vedānta uses the word *Pūrṇa* for *Brahman* in a special sense. The sum of *Pūrṇa* plus *Pūrṇa* is equal to *Pūrṇa.* When *Pūrṇa* is subtracted from *Pūrṇa,* the remainder still remains *Pūrṇa.* (*Pūrṇamadaḥ pūrṇamidaṁ pūrṇāt pūrṇamudacyate. pūrṇasya pūrṇamādāya pūrṇamevāvaśiṣyate.*) Thus, philosophically speaking, the yogic state of the individual self staying in the Universal Self is not a ***usual*** case of addition; neither is it a ***usual*** case of union. In the Vedāntic sense, the individual self and the Universal Self are one and the same, with the exception that the individual self is encased by *upādhi*s (limiting adjuncts). The gross body, the subtle body and the causal body serve as the *upādhi*s. The external world serves as the *upādhi.* The mental

---

5. *PYD, I.3* (*tadā draṣṭuḥ svarūpevasthānam*). We have made the English rendering of this aphorism in conformity with the Vedāntic metaphysics. Patañjali, however, takes *draṣṭā* (seer) as the *puruṣa* or the sentient individual self and not as *Īśvara* or *Brahman.*

impressions (*saṁskāras* and *vāsanās*) serve as the *upādhis*.The whirls of the mind (*cittavṛttis*) are also the *upādhis*. Divested of all these *upādhis*, the individual self re-establishes its identity with the Universal Self.

But this re-establishment of identity is temporary rather than permanent. It lasts as long as the *yogī* remains in the state of zero emergence of the whirls of the mind. Notwithstanding the temporariness of the yogic trance, the effects of *Yoga* on the body and the mind are not transient, however. This will be explained in some subsequent chapter of this book.

# 2.2

## The Four-fold Existence of the Self

IN the previous chapter, we have mentioned that the individual self merges with the Universal Self in the state of the complete cessation of the generation of the whirls of the mind. In this chapter, we will give the description of the four-fold existence of the Self.

The *Māṇḍūkya Upaniṣad*[6] says that the Self is *Brahman* (*ayamātmā brahma*) and that it has four quarters (*catuṣpāt*). These four are: the *Vaiśvānara,* the *Taijasa,* the *Prājña* and the *Turīya.*

### The waking state

The sphere of activity of the *Vaiśvānara* is the waking state (*jāgarita*).[7] This is the state in which the Self cognises the external world and experiences the gross material objects (*sthūlabhuk*). The gross world which every human being experiences in the waking state is perceived and conceived through the activity of the Self (*Vaiśvānara*). For the cognition of the external as well as the internal world in the waking state, the five organs of perceptions are utilised. Stimuli for both pleasure and pain are received in this state. The five motor organs of actions are also utilised in the gross experience. The mind is involved in the stimulus-response reactions, in mental experiences of pleasure and pain, and in emotional activity.

---

6. *MAU*, 2.

7. *MAU*, 3.

## The dream state

The Self is known as *Taijasa* in the dream (*svapna*) state.[8] It cognises the internal mental impressions (*antaḥprajña*) and experiences objects isolated and stored in the mind (*praviviktabhuk*).

In the waking state, stimuli come to the five organs of perceptions from the gross objects of the world. In contrast, no such external stimuli are received in the dream state. The Self (*Taijasa*) makes use of the impressions stored in the mind and fashions a dream-world. Out of such fashioning, it experiences pleasure and pain, and builds up its own emotional edifice. Although the origin of the data stored in the mind is the gross world of the *Vaiśvānara*, the dream-world, created by the *Taijasa*, is not exactly the experienced world of the waking state. The data-source of the dream-world is the *karmāśaya* (the store of the *kārmik* impressions) and the *saṁskāra-piṇḍa* (all the stored mental impressions). The *Taijasa* makes use of these mental data and synthesises dream-stories through permutations and combinations of the mental data. The dream-story is not necessarily a replica of any incident experienced in the waking state.

## The state of deep sleep

When an individual is fast asleep, his sleep is very deep, he does not desire anything in that state, and he does not experience any dream, he is said to be in a state of deep sleep (*suṣupti*). The Self in this state is known as *Prājña*.[9] In this state, the previous impressions, acquired from the external world and generated in the mind, are unified and condensed into a mass of consciousness (*ekībhūtaḥ prajñānaghanaḥ*). *Prājña* is full of bliss and experiences bliss (*ānanda-bhuk*). It is *cetomukhaḥ*

8. *MAU*, 4.

9. *MAU*, 5.

(one who heads towards the pure, Fundamental Consciousness of *Cetas* or *Brahman;* one who is at the doorway to *Turīya*).

In the state of deep sleep, the external world of sense-perception and the internal world of mental impressions are kept in abeyance. All impressions stored from perceptions of the external world and from conceptions of the mental dispositions become condensed and unified into a potential, non-functional mass in this state of deep sleep.

The Self as *Prājña* is *Īśvara* (God).[10] He controls all. He is the knower of all. He is the inner controller (*antaryāmī*). He is the source of all. He is the starting source and the final, receiving receptacle of all created entities.

## The fourth state

The fourth state is known as *Turīya.*[11] It is a Sanskrit word whose literal meaning is 'fourth'. This is the state of Absolute *Brahman,* Pure and Fundamental Consciousness. It does not cognise the objects of the external world. It does not cognise the internal world of mental impressions and mental conceptions. It does not cognise both. It is not a unified, supercondensed mass of cognitions. It is neither cognitive nor non-cognitive. It is unseen, unusable, ungraspable, devoid of distinguishing marks, unthinkable, and unnameable. It is the essence of the knowledge of one self. It is the one into which the universe is resolved. It is the peaceful, the benign, the non-dual. The *Turīya* is the Self. He is to be known.

The *Māṇḍūkyopaniṣad*[12] says that the monosyllable *AUṀ* (*OṀ*) is the symbol for *Brahman.* It stands for the manifested universe of the past, the present and the future; it also stands

---

10. *MAU,* 6.

11. *MAU,* 7

12. *MAU,* 1.

for the unmanifested Absolute that is beyond the three-fold time and that is unchangeable, unmodifiable and ever constant. *Turīya* is symbolised by the monosyllable *AUṀ*,[13] which is otherwise known as *Praṇava*. The first element (*A*) of the syllable stands for *Vaiśvānara*, [14] the second element (*U*) for *Taijasa*;[15] and the third element (*Ṁ*) for *Prājña*.[16] The fourth (*Turīya*) has no element (*amātra*). The fourth is the Self (*Ātmā*). *Brahman*, the non-dual, is the *Turīya* for which the universe ceases to be (*prapañcopaśama*). He who knows it thus enters the Self with his self.[17]

This *Turīya* state is the goal of every *yogī*. It is not enough for him to withdraw his mind from the objects of perception and from dream experiences. Simultaneously with the withdrawal, he has to become one with *Brahman*. This is the ideal state of *Yoga*.

## The seed-bed of the whirls of mind

A discussion on the *Māṇḍūkya Upaniṣad* reveals that whirls of the mind sprout not only in the waking state, but also in the dream state. What are the causal factors for the germination of the *cittavr̥ttis* ? A brief discussion on the seed-bed of *cittavr̥ttis* will be made here.

*R̥ṣi* Patañjali enumerates five types of *vr̥ttis* (whirls), namely, *pramāṇa-vr̥tti, viparyaya-vr̥tti, vikalpa-vr̥tti, nidrā-vr̥tti* and *smr̥ti-vr̥tti*.[18]

---

13. *MAU*, 8.
14. *MAU*, 9.
15. *MAU*, 10.
16. *MAU*, 11
17. *MAU*, 12.
18. *PYD*, I.5-6.

The sources of *pramāṇa-vṛtti* are three in kinds. They are *pratyakṣa, anumāna* and *āgama.*[19] *Pratyakṣa* is direct sense-perception. This knowledge we acquire through the mediation of the eyes, the ears, the nose, the taste-buds and the cutaneous receptors. The *anumāna-vṛtti* springs from our knowledge on inference (*anumāna*). We observe smoke in fire, and, in this direct observation, we see both smoke and fire. Sometimes, we see smoke only, and from our observation of smoke, we infer the existence of fire. This is *anumāna* or inference. Both *pratyakṣa* and *anumāna* involve mediate knowledge. We get immediate knowledge too and that is *āgama.* When one gets knowledge from one's intuition, that knowledge is *āgama.* When one gets knowledge from the revealed or intuitional knowledge of seers, that is *āgama.*

The *viparyaya-vṛtti*[20] comes from false knowledge. An object *B* is mistakenly known as *C* or *D*, but not as *B*. This type of knowledge is false, and the *vṛtti* generated out of it is *viparyaya-vṛtti.*

The *vikalpa-vṛtti*[21] is produced by verbal knowledge only, without the existence of a corresponding material or spiritual entity. The word 'unicorn' leaves some impression on our mind whereas, in reality, there is nothing like a unicorn. A winged fairy or a ferocious demon, through hearing or reading, imprints some image on our mind. This type of knowledge, without corresponding reality, produces *vṛtti*s which are known as *vikalpa*. We are not raising the question here whether ghosts exist or not. But our experiences say that some of the persons allegedly affected by ghosts were really troubled by *vikalpa* ghosts. On examination, it was found that these persons

19. *PYD*, I.7.

20. *PYD*, I.8.

21. *PYD*, I.9.

were not affected by real ghosts. They have been listening to or reading ghost stories. Ghosts have been printed in their minds' tapes. They suffer from ghost-attacks by their *vikalpa-vṛtti. Vikalpa* includes all hallucinatory phenomena.

*Nidrā-vṛtti*[22] is a type of mind's whirls. *Nidrā* literally means 'sleep'. During sleep, the five organs of perceptions cease to function. Hence there is lack of knowledge about the external world in sleep. However, persons dream in sleep. They remember a few dreams after waking and they forget most of the dreams. The *antaḥkaraṇa* (internal instrument of the mind) synthesises dream-stories by imagination, but by drawing the elements out of the printed impressions on the mind. Dreams are generally not verbiose. They use less of language and more of symbols. Dreaming is a usual phenomenon with everybody during sleeping. The *nidrā-vṛtti* is really the *svapna-vṛtti* (*svapna* means 'dream').

*Smṛti-vṛtti*[23] is the fifth type of mind's whirls. The Sanskrit word *smṛti* means 'memory'. When something already experienced and impressioned in the mind is brought to the surface of consciousness, it is called memory. *Smṛti-vṛtti* pertains to not only the past experiences of the present life, but also the experiences of the past lives. Some memories generate mild *vṛtti*s while some others produce strongly turbulent whirls.

Two words, namely, *saṁskāra* and *vāsanā,* are important in the karmic theory. There is a *karmāśaya* in the subtle body (*sūkṣma* or *liṅga śarīra*) of every individual. The karmic impressions are stored there. *Saṁskāra* is the Sanskrit word for the karmic impressions. The sum total of the *saṁskāra*s is collectively known as *saṁskāra-piṇḍa.* The potent urges and

---

22. *PYD,* I.10.

23. *PYD,* I.11.

desires of life, otherwise known as *pravṛtti*, are stored in the *karmāśaya* as *vāsanā* traces. All *vāsanā*s are *saṁskāras*, but the reverse is not true. Thus, in the *karmāśaya*, there is a sub-compartment known as *vāsanāśaya*. Some karmic impressions are deeply buried in the *karmāśaya*. This deep layer may be compared with the basement of a building. Mental impressions, undesirable and unwanted, are thrown in the basement. *Karma*s of different lives are stored in the *karmāśaya*. They are erased only when they are fructified (*karma-vipāka*).

Freudian psychology has a provision of the Unconscious and repression. But Sigmund Freud was an atheist who did not believe in reincarnation. According to him, the mind begins with the conception and ends in death. Secondly, his psychological terms such as Id, Ego, Superego and the Unconscious have no locational relevance in the brain and spinal cord. The brain-mind identity theory cannot satisfactorily explain these functional terms on anatomical basis. In contrast, Indian psychology adequately explains the location of the Unconscious and its functioning through different births. The depth psychology of India has so far not received that attention which it deserves.

Whirls of the mind, arising out of memory, may be of recent origin, may be of distant past of the present life, or may be of past lives. *Saṁskāra*s may be brewing in the form of memory. *Vāsanā*s may be boiling in the form of memory. All these mental imprints produce whirls in the mind.

## Hindrances to Yoga

The five types of *vṛtti*s that have been described here may or may not be producers of hindrances. They are *kliṣṭā* when they produce hindrances to *Yoga*. They are *akliṣṭā* when they do not produce hindrances to *Yoga*.

There are five types of *kleśa*s or hindrances to *Yoga*. They are: ignorance (*avidyā*), egocentricity (*asmitā*), passion (*rāga*), aversion (*dveṣa*) and the clinging urge to live (*abhiniveśa*).[24] Out of these, *avidyā* is the most important hindrance. It leads to *asmitā*. A person develops passion for a thing or an activity when he gets pleasure out of it.[25] Passion is a very potent impediment to *Yoga*. Contrary to passion is the case with aversion. The repulsion, wrath or anger generated in one's mind for an unfavourable thing, person or activity that imparts pain is aversion.[26] The will-to-live is *abhiniveśa*.[27] Any living organism, from microbes to human beings, cling to life. They want to live and live for eternity with the present body. They are terribly afraid of death (*maraṇatrāsa, mr̥tyubhaya*). This clinging to life is a great impediment to *Yoga*.

It has already been said that *vr̥tti*s may or may not produce hindrances to *Yoga*. The former type is *kliṣṭā* and the latter *akliṣṭā*. The *yogī* first tries to restrain the *kliṣṭā vr̥tti*s, and then the *akliṣṭā vr̥tti*s.

## Practice and dispassionateness

For a novice, the restraint of the *vr̥tti*s seems to be impossible. But it is not really so, although not too easy. *R̥ṣi* Patañjali says that *vr̥tti*s can be restrained by practice (*abhyāsa*) and dispassionateness (*vairāgya*).[28] Emphasis on *abhyāsa* and *vairāgya* has also been laid by the *Bhagavad Gītā*.[29] The *Gītā* recognises the fact that mind is always movable and that a wavering

---

24. *PYD*, II.3.
25. *PYD*, II.7 (*sukhānuśayī rāgaḥ*).
26. *PYD*, II.8 (*duḥkhānuśayī dveṣaḥ*).
27. *PYD*, II.9.
28. *PYD*, I.12 (*abhyāsavairāgyābhyāṁ tannirodhaḥ*).
29. *BG*, VI.35.

mind disturbs the gross body and scatters the sensory as well as the motor subtle organs (*indriyas*).[30]

Repetition of a physical or a mental activity is known as *abhyāsa* (practice). Whether physical or mental, if an action is repeated, a programme is imprinted on the mind. Once the programme is imprinted, the action becomes automatic subsequently.

*Rāga* (derived from the Sanskrit verb root *rañj*) or passion as a *kleśa* (hindrance or impediment to *Yoga*) has already been mentioned. Desire for pleasure and worldly passion are designated by the word *rāga.* The absence or lack of *rāga* is *vairāgya.* It may not be mistaken that *vairāgya,* for this purpose, stands for renunciation of the world or utter disgust with the worldly affairs. Neither is it pleaded here that a *vairāgī* (one who shuns passion) should seek for pain rather than pleasure. A *yogī* forsakes *indulgence* in worldly desires, *indulgence* in seeking for pleasure and *indulgence* in becoming passionate.

---

30. *BG,* VI.34.

# 2.3

## Tanhā: Unquenched Thirst

THE Sanskrit word *tṛṣṇā* means 'thirst'. The Pāli equivalent of *tṛṣṇā* is *tanhā*. Lord Gautama Buddha has used the word *tanhā* in his teachings. He says that *kāmanā* (desire) is the cause of suffering (*duḥkha*). To get rid of suffering, one has to annihilate one's desires.

Any individual, society, state or country cannot prosper and progress without desire. Satisfaction with what little one has is the enemy of one's progress. Dissatisfaction with the existing conditions with simultaneous desire for more and more is the key to progress. This principle has been accepted in economics and political science. It is a general observation that individuals acquire more and more wealth, more and more power and position, more and more fame and more and more all-round prosperity through incessant desire and continuous striving. No material prosperity is feasible without desire and struggle for achieving more and more. Materialistically speaking, sky is the limit to progress. Some very successful materialists stride one step farther; they pierce the sky and go beyond it in their limitless search for further acquisition and achievement.

The materialists' viewpoints have been tested and retested in all countries and all ages. How do we reconcile with Buddha's teachings then?

### Darwinian motto

Darwinism is atheistic, materialistic and anti-spiritual.

'Struggle for existence and survival of the fittest' is a key principle in Darwinism. This principle is applicable not only for human beings but also for all plants and animals, starting from viruses, bacteria, protozoa, algae and fungi. That it is a well-tested, sound principle at the materialistic level cannot be denied. Inaction is anathema to struggle. Complete or partial inaction is involved in lack of desire. Hence, analytically speaking, Buddha's teaching on the annihilation of desire (*kāmanā-vināśa*) and Darwinism cannot go together.

**Rat race in modern life**

The annihilation of desires is anathema to material prosperity and to Darwinian struggle. Notwithstanding this statement of fact, it is also to be admitted that rat race is a major malady in modern life. The modern man is busy with a fiercely competitive struggle for money, comfort, luxury, position and power. Poverty is rampant in the modern world. But affluence is not rare too. The pity is that affluence and rat race run parallelly. The more affluent a person, the more hungry or thirsty he is for wealth, luxury, position and power. He has such a ravenous appetite that he voraciously devours anything he gets. He is a raver, an uninhibited pleasure-loving person. He wants to amass more and more wealth and that too all of a sudden. He wants to ascend the steps to power and reach the peak without delay. He gets more and more comfort — better and better houses, better and better cars and better and better amenities. His or her thirst for sex is never quenched; the flame of lust goes higher and higher. For him or her, there is always a chance of getting a more beautiful and a sexier partner. The modern man, with some creative talent, becomes a poet, a painter, a musician, a dancer, a player, an actor, a discoverer, or an inventor. He earns recognition and fame. Recognitions pour on him. But he wants more and more, and that too in quick succession. He is ever insatiate.

The insatiable, modern man, albeit affluent, is stricken with perpetual poverty. He is in plenty except the fact that peace is a rare commodity for him. In the vacuum of peace, his mind swirls in whirlwind and churns in whirlpools. Life becomes unbearable for him. He manages to live it. When he fails to manage, he commits suicide.

## Three types of desire

There is no life without actions. Actions germinate in desires. Hence a desireless, actionless life is not pleaded for. Only *saṁnyāsīs* (ones who have renunciated the world) cease to act. And they too do not stop their daily actions, inevitable for living. Inaction is to be condemned for householders, businessmen, farmers, fighters, administrators, statesmen and all others who have to perform their duties. The *Gītā* proscribes inaction.[31]

The Vedas and the Upaniṣads declare that, prior to the creation, God desired the creation of the universe. Although He has no unfulfilled desire and no want at all, He, for His sportive play (*līlā*), desired to create a universe.[32] He had designed[33] a blueprint of the universe before He really created it. He engineered the design and continues to do so. His artistic hand creates the art on the canvas of the Cosmos. Whatever God does is executed through the agency of the Divine Mother, the Consort and the Power of God.[34] He becomes the

31. *BG*, III.8.

32. *AV*, 52.1-5; *Ṛ̥V*, X.129.4; *BS*, I.1.5; I.1.18; I.4.24; II.3.12-13; *AU*, I.1.1; *BU*, I.2.1; III.7.3; III.7.23; *CU*,VI.2.3-4; *PU*, VI.3; *TU*, II.6.1.

33. *BS*, II.2.1.

34. *BS*, I.4.3; II.2.2; *BSŚB*, I.4.2-3; II.1.14; II.1.24-25; II.2.2; *BG*, III.27; VIII.18-19; XIV.3-4; *BGŚB*, VII.6; VIII.18-19; IX.7-8; IX.10; XIII.19; XIII.29; XIV.3; XV.16; *ŚU*, I.3; IV.10; *ŚUŚB*. I.3; I.4; AL.I.1; *DBhā*, I.2.5; *SPS*. I.96; I.164; II.35.

Chairperson (*adhyakṣa*)[35] of the creation, evolution, involution, and dissolution of the universe. If this is the case with God Himself, there is no question of the abandonment of desire and activity for man.

There are three types of desires, namely, *sāttvika, rājasika* and *tāmasika.* Mahatma Gandhi desired the freedom of India. One benevolent person has a desire to open a school and a hospital for the poor people. A *yogī* has a strong desire to liberate his self. These are cases of *sāttvika* desire. A politician desires to be a Prime Minister. A reputed writer desires the Nobel Prize. A businessman desires to be a multimillionaire. These are cases of *rājasika* desires. A perverted person desires sex-indulgence with many beautiful women. A notorious criminal has a desire to murder the Prime Minister of a country. A terrorist desires genocide in a village of a certain community. These are examples of *tāmasika* desires.

If desire is proscribed, it becomes difficult or impossible for an individual or a society to live meaningfully. A life without a purpose is no life. A life without desires is impossible to think of. Hence desires, as such, are not to be condemned, without an in-depth analysis of their merits and demerits. *Tāmasika* desires are to be condemned, of course. *Sāttvika* desires are to be recommended. *Rājasika* desires are to be critically examined for their adoption or rejection.

## A lotus leaf in water

A lotus leaf floats on water. It is on water and in water. But water does not moisten it. Even in close contact, it is detached from water. This exactly what a *yogī* does.

The *Bhagavad Gītā* has a famous verse which prescribes

---

35. *ṚV*, X.129.7; *BG*, IX.10; *BU*.I.4.7; *CU*. VI.3.2; *ŚU*,VI.11.

detached actions.[36] 'You have a right on your work, never on the fruits thereof. Let not actions be for fruits. Let not your attachment be with inaction.' There is a word *saṅgaḥ* in this verse. It has been derived from the Sanskrit verb root *sañj* which means 'to attach'. *Saṅgaḥ* is attachment and *asaṅgah* is detachment. The *Gītā* prescribes unattached actions.

Some economists and psychologists are very much critical of this verse of the *Gītā*. They plead for incentives and they state that the fruits of actions serve as incentives for exerting maximum efforts in doing a work. They allege that work without attachment to fruits thereof does not provide incentive to a person for hard work. Of course, such an allegation is not unfounded. But this plea has truth in it at the materialistic plane and at a level where man's spiritual evolution has not crossed the threshold level.

Most persons live a sad life for this attachment. The first chapter of the *Gītā* is the *viṣāda-yoga* of Arjuna who is an algebraic × for all humanity. His agony (*viṣāda*) springs from his attachment. The major root of man's agony is his attachment (*āsakti*). If somebody can forsake attachment, he can be happy.

The verse of the *Gītā*, referred to here, is sometimes misinterpreted as pleading for renunciation of fruits of actions. If I work for an Institute or an Organisation or an individual person, I have the right to get my wage or salary. The advice of the *Gītā* is something else. In any enterprise, the result may be a success or a failure, or a partial success or a partial failure. We rejoice a success. We suffer due to failure. A student labours hard for getting success in a competition. The outcome may be plus or minus. If he maintains equanimity of mind in either of the situations, he becomes happy. It is his duty to do hard labour. In spite of sincere and hard labour, the result

---

36. *BG*, II.47.

may be unfavourable. If he is not perturbed even if his result is unfavourable, he has achieved detachment. The *Gītā* prescribes detached actions, actions without attachment to fruits, but not renunciation of fruits.

*Tanhā* or *tṛṣṇā* (ever unquenched thirst) is a concomitant feature or modern life. Man is thirsty even if he gets plenty of water to drink. This thirst is not the natural physiological phenomenon. It is a psychological morbidity. It generates frustration. It is the major cause of anxiety or tension. A person may be physically or mentally busy. Still such a person is not subject to stress and strain, except periodical exhaustion, if his actions are detached (*anāsakta karma*). If he is attached to the duality of success or failure, he succumbs to stress and strain.

A *yogī* aspirant should train himself to give up *tanhā*. He should not renunciate actions. But his actions should be detached.

## 2.4

# The Six-fold Enemy

AN individual himself is his own friend and own enemy.[37] The *Bhagavad Gītā* has used the word *ripu* for 'enemy' in this context. Even if others become inimical, their enmity may be traced to the root which is the activity of the individual.

A person has six *ripu*s that are engendered by himself. These are: lustful desire (*kāma*), anger (*krodha*), greed or covetousness (*lobha*), delusion (*moha*), pride mixed with arrogance (*mada*) and jealousy, malice or envy (*mātsarya*).

The *Gītā* used the word *ātmā* for the self that is said to generate the six *ripus*. If we examine this issue more closely, we find that it is really the Primordial Nature (*Mūla-Prakṛti*, constituted by three strands or *guṇa*s, namely, *sattva, raja*s and *tama*s) that acts as the agent at the cosmic level. Through the reflection of the light of the Consciousness (*Puruṣa* or the Cosmic Person), *Prakṛti* is induced to act. Thus, in a true sense, *Puruṣa* does not act, and it is *Prakṛti* that is the doer of all actions.[38] What is said holds true for the totality of the universe (*samaṣṭi*). But, in consideration of an individual (*vyaṣṭi*), it is the *antaḥkaraṇa* (internal instrument) that assumes the doership of actions.[39] *Prakṛti* is the non-evolute evolvent, from which *Mahat* (the Great, the Cosmic Intellect or the Cosmic Mind, the *Virāḍ* of the Vedas) evolves. What is *Mahat* for the entire

37. *BG*, VI.5.

38. *BG*, XIII.29.

39. *SPS*, I.99.

Cosmos is *buddhi* (intellect) for an individual. *Ahaṅkāra* (Ego) evolves from *buddhi. Manas* (mind), the five subtle sensory organs, the five subtle motor organs and the five subtle fields (*tanmātras*) are produced from *ahaṅkāra. Buddhi, ahaṅkāra, manas,* the five subtle sensory organs, the five subtle motor organs and the five subtle fields (*tanmātras*) constitute the *liṅga* or the *sūkṣma śarīra*[40] (the subtle body). The subtle body survives death. But the gross body (*sthūla śarīra*),[41] inherited from the parents and further grown by assimilation of nutrients, disintegrates in death. *Buddhi, ahaṅkāra* and *manas* are the three major components of the internal instrument (*antaḥkaraṇa*), which works due to its proximity with the individual self (*jīvātmā*). The self is Consciousness (*Cit*), whereas the *antaḥkaraṇa* is insentient. In spite of the insentience of the *antaḥkaraṇa,* due to its induction by the self, it is rendered conscious, and the *antaḥkaraṇa,* thus made conscious, functions in the body.

Unquenched thirst in general and sex-perversion in particular are expressed by the term *kāma.* It is a potent enemy of man. It degrades and devalues him. The harm done by unquenched thirst has already been discussed in the previous chapter. Here is stressed the malignancy of unbriddled sexual lust. Infidelity of a male or a female spouse is a major cause of family discord and strife. The children of broken homes are the worst affected. Sex-perversion is pernicious to the family as well as the society and psychologically lethal to the perverted person. Sex-morality is conducive to healthy families and healthy societies. Further, a sexually insatiable person creates whirlwinds in his/her mind. It is detrimental to yogic attainments.

---

40. *SPS,* III.7.

41. *Ibid.,* III.9.

Anger is another enemy that deteriorates the quality of a person. It hurts the other person with whom one is angry. Thus, it creates enemies and very often enemies without any valid and unavoidable reasons. It disturbs the mind of the one who gets angry. The mental balance of an angry person is very much upset by anger. A disturbed mind brings about psychosomatic disorders, and thus serious physical ailments ensue from the anger of a person. An angry person does not stay in his own control at the angry moment. He may otherwise be a very nice person. But he can be a devil at the angry moment and can do anything that is unexpected from him. The harm done during the duration of anger can hardly be repaired later. Some persons suffer from peptic ulcer due to habitual anger. Some die of cardiac attack as a result of intense anger. Some get cerebral stroke, coma and paralysis due to anger and the consequent sudden spurt of hypertension. Some permanently lose bosom friends due to a momentary short-temperedness. Anger is the cause of quite a number of divorces. The *Bhagavad-Gītā* has proscribed anger in unequivocal language.[42]

Greed (covetousness) is another potent enemy of man. He wants to possess more and more. He wants to acquire other people's property. Exploitation is rooted in greed. A greedy man swallows everything, devours everything; by this he swells up until he bursts. Any amount of possession is not enough for him. He craves for more and more. He is an ever dissatisfied man. His physical greed becomes a mental malady. Anybody with such mental malady cannot progress in *yoga*. The *Yajurveda* and the *Īśopaniṣad* proscribe covetousness.[43] The

---

42. *BG*, II.62-63; III.37; XVI.18 & 21; XVIII.53.

43. *YV*, *XL*.1; *IU*.1.

*Bhagavad-Gītā* advises to abandon the bad quality of covetousness.[44]

The *Bhagavad-Gītā* states that lustful desire, anger and covetousness are the three *ripus* that open the door to the hell.[45] Anyone, desirous of being a *yogī,* should give up these three base qualities.

Delusion (*moha*) is a potent impediment to *Yoga*. The Sanskrit word *moha* has been formed from the verb root *muh,* meaning 'to become stupefied or unconscious', 'to be bewildered or perplexed', or 'to err, to be mistaken, to go astray'. Thus *moha* means 'loss of consciousness, bewilderment, perplexity, distraction, infatuation, delusion, error or folly'. For our purpose of yogic discussion here, the meaning 'delusion' or 'infatuation' may be accepted. Delusion is a false belief or impression. Infatuation is an intense fondness or admiration with extreme folly. In exhibiting the property of *moha,* one is intrinsically affected with ignorance. He has some erroneous belief due to lack of right knowledge. Secondly, he is exaggeratingly fond of or admirer of the thing, the person or the idea which he loves so passionately. And such a passionate love coupled with error or folly stupefies the person. Under the influence of *moha,* a person loses his discriminating power. He cannot distinguish good from bad and right from wrong. The *Bhagavad-Gītā* has referred to *moha* in a number of places.[46]

*Mada* is the fifth *ripu* that acts as the enemy of the self. It is a Sanskrit word, derived from the verb root *mad,* meaning 'to gladden, exhilarate, intoxicate, animate, or inspire'. The word *mada* means 'hilarity, rapture, excitement, intoxication, pride,

---

44. *BG, XIV*.12 & 17; XVI.21.

45. *BG, XVI*.21.

46. *BG*, XI.1; XIV.13; XVI.10; XVIII.7, 25, 60 & 73.

arrogance, conceit, or an intoxicating drink'. For the purpose of this yogic discussion, we may take *mada* to mean force, pride, arrogance, conceit and excitement together.[47] The *Bhagavad-Gītā* has a reference to *mada*.[48] Persons in whom *mada* is predominant exhibit their malignancy through self-conceit, force, pride, lust and anger.[49] They think themselves as the Lord of the universe.[50] They make all attempts to achieve power, to exercise sovereignty, and to dominate and to enslave others. *Mada* is a pernicious foe of man. It is a bad trait which is repellent to *Yoga*. It must be given up in order to ascend the ladder of *Yoga*.

*Mātsarya* is the sixth *ripu* which debases the self. The Sanskrit word *mātsara* means 'one who is envious, jealous, malicious'. *Mātsarya* is envy or jealousy. The opposite of *mātsarya* is *muditā,* to be happy with others' success and delight. Envy or jealousy is a base quality with human beings who have not refined themselves. It is a type of flame that is meant against others, but that burns and agonises the Ego of the envious person. *Saṁskāra*s (imprints on the *antaḥkaraṇa*) of a person afflicted with envy become poisonous seeds. They sprout in this life or subsequent lives to become poisonous trees and yield poisonous fruits. Envy is very harmful to yogic attainments.

It may not be misunderstood that *yoga* cannot be initiated before all the six *ripu*s are completely subdued and annihilated. It is not so easy to achieve full success in completely subduing all the *ripu*s within a short period. It may not be possible to fully subdue the *ripu*s unless and until one becomes a perfected

47. *BG,* XVI.10

48. *BG,* XVIII.35

49. *BG,* XVI.18

50. *BG,* XVI.14.

*yogī*. Hence the idea of subduing the *ripus* first and starting the practice of *yoga* next is to be given up. One should start practising *yoga* and start making conscious effort for subduing the *ripus*. Both may be done simultaneously in a parallel manner. It is a fact that *yoga* facilitates and accelerates controlling and subduing the *ripus*.

Perfectionism is a utopian idea. It should be the goal which may never be attained in one's life. It should be the final point on the arduous path of the long journey. But it should not be a prerequisite for the initiation of the journey.

We may take the simile of an examination. To secure one hundred marks out of a total of one hundred should be the goal. But the reality of life may be different. One may secure 80, 70 or 60 per cent. Still it is worth appearing an examination and get a good pass mark.

*Ripus* are the mud of life. One must get out of the mud and wash the feet in order to be clean. Very little success in *yoga* is achieved if one persists to stand in the mud and to be clean at the same time.

# 2.5

## Yama: The Five Great Vows

Jainism prescribes good conduct (*samyak caritra*). Five conducts are prescribed for this purpose. They are: non-violence (*ahiṁsā*), truthfulness (*satya*), non-stealing (*asteya*), abstinence from sexual indulgence (*brahmacarya*) and non-accumulation of property (*aparigraha*). These are the five great vows (*pañca mahāvrata*).

The five great vows of Jainisim are the same as the five *yamas* of *Yoga. Maharṣi* Patañjali has given an aphorism (*sūtram*) in this context.[51] Five conducts, namely, non-violence, truthfulness, non-stealing, sex-abstinence, non-accumulation of property, have been prescribed for a *yogī*. All these five have been grouped under the name *YAMA*. It has been derived from the Sanskrit verb root *yam*. It means 'restraint', 'self-control', 'the act of reining, curbing, bridling or controlling'. *Maharṣi* Patañjali has also used the word *mahāvratam*.[52]

### Non-violence

Non-violence is the *yama* of priority. It proscribes violence against human beings, animals, birds, microbes, plants and the non-living world. Any injury to others, living or non-living, should be avoided. Violence may be physical, mental or verbal. Violence of any of these types should be given up. Once the *yogī* gets full success in shunning violence, persons and animals

---

51. *PYD*, II.30 (*ahiṁsāsatyāsteyabrahmacaryāparigrahā yamāḥ*).

52. *PYD*, II.31.

in his vicinity are induced to become non-violent.[53]

## Truthfulness

The second restraining conduct of a *yogī* should be truthfulness. He should speak the truth to the best of his knowledge. Of course, if truth is unpleasant, hurting and harmful, discretion must be exercised by observing silence or by a pleasant mode of expression. Principles of psychology should be made use of to avoid hurting others, since hurting is a type of violence.

In some uncommon situations, however, truth may be spoken boldly and openly even if the other man or party is *apparently* hurt, if the expected benefits to be resulted from this truth are to be corrective in nature and the expected consequences are nobler at a greater level and in a greater context.

If one is certain of avoiding a devastating calamity and an impending disaster of great magnitude, if one's selfish interest is not involved in the action, and if the good of the society, the earth or the universe is the sole concern, speaking an untruth may be necessary. And such untruth is a benign untruth which is a non-violent truth. There was such an occasion in the Mahābhārata War when Śrī Kr̥ṣṇa induced Yudhiṣṭhira to announce that human or elephant Aśvatthāmā has been killed.

Some may mistakenly consider the idea of a benign untruth of being a non-violent truth as sacrilegious. It is really not so if they appreciate the action in the following situation:

A monk sits in meditation under a banyan tree on the outskirt of a forest. A beautiful young woman runs in a distressing mood and hides herself inside the hermitage. A robust man of bad character who chases the woman for rape

53. *PYD*, II.35.

reaches the hermitage five minutes later and asks the monk her whereabouts. The monk tells a lie by saying that the woman ran to the north and entered the dense forest. An analysis of this situation would clearly indicate that the so-called lie of the monk is a benign lie and a non-violent truth.

The exceptional situation mentioned here should not be made common. Barring exceptions which are rare, a *yogī* should practise truthfulness and he should speak pleasant truth.

## Non-stealing

A person may become a theif due to impelling environmental causes. Someone is too poor and deprived of the basic necessities of life. He does not get food to eat; he does not get a loin-cloth to wear; he does not get money to buy medicine for saving the life of his sick child. Under such compelling circumstances, he finally takes to stealing. A second type of persons do not want to work. They, under the strong influence of *tamas,* are indolent in nature. They idle away their time. They are reluctant to put up hard labour. Although slothful, they wish easy money. They commit theft, burglary and robbery. There are others of a third type who are indifferent to ethical values. They are die-hard materialists. They steal private and public money to be richer and to enjoy more of luxury and comforts. There is a fourth category of persons who have accumulated bad *vāsanā*s in their Unconscious through different births. The *vāsanā* greed stimulates them from within to steal both private and public properties. Their *lobha* (greed) impels them to adopt *parigraha* (accumulation) which gives them pleasure.

An aspirant for *yoga* may not belong to the first category, the unfornate poor and needy. He may belong to the second category of inertial nature, the third category of unethical materialism with addiction to luxury, or to the fourth category of covetous *vāsanā*. An unscrupulous person who steals may get benefits from yogic practices of *āsana*s (yogic postures) and *prāṇāyāma* (yogic breath control); but he can hardly purify his mind through yogic meditation. Stealing is counteractive to mental calmness and peace.

## Brahmacarya

The word *brahmacarya* has been coined by the union of two words, namely, *brahma* and *carya*. The word *carya* has been derived from the Sanskrit verb root *car* which means 'to go, to move'. A *brahmacārī* is one who walks the path of *Brahman*. This is the etymological meaning, used in a wider context. The word has a special meaning with reference to spiritual, yogic life and Hindu monastic life. *Brahmacarya* is the state of an unmarried student of the Vedas; it is a state of continence and chastity. The first quarter of the one hundred years of a life is usually the period of *brahmacarya* for a man of society. He enters into *gārhasthya* (life of a householder) in the second quarter of his life.

In the context of religious and yogic life, *brahmacarya* carries a usual connotation of sex-abstinence, a completely sex-free life. The Vedic *ṛṣis* were mostly married. In the second quarter of their life, they lived a life of regulated sex. The spouses were faithful to each other. They were avoiding sexual excess and sexual indulgence. Ethical and regulated sex can be pure, divine and holy. Such a sex-life for a householder does conform to the standard of *bhrahmacarya*. It is far better to marry and live a *brahmacārī* life with regulated sex than to live a life of a pseudo-bachelor and a pseudo-*brahmacārī* through immoral sex-indulgence. Man lives in society. For the good of the society, sex should be confined to both the members of a spouse. Extra-marital sex-relation is harmful to the individuals and to the society. Sex-indulgence and any type of indulgence is unwholesome to *yoga.* Sexual excess tells upon the health of an individual. Sex-abuse is a pernicious practice. Abnormal sex-behaviour is harmful to the individual as well as the society. There is also violence in some types of sex-conduct. If these malpractices of sex are avoided, there is no reason why sex would be a taboo for *yoga.* Sex can be sanctified in spiritual life. It is a biological necessity and has emotional value. Sex-repression and forced sex-restraint bring about serious psychological disorders. A regulated, moral sex-life may be termed *brahmacarya* for our purpose of meditation for all. Full-time perfected *yogī*s are exceptional, however.

Absolute sex-abstinence may be necessary for a whole-time spiritual person at a higher level of spiritual life. But such cases are not common in the society. For such a person, a family may be a physical hindrance to full-time spiritual practices. Where renunciation of the society and of worldly life becomes a necessity, where full attention, without a trace of distraction, is to be devoted to spiritual pursuit, where all energies are to be channellised for a higher cause — spiritual, social or otherwise, there may arise the necessity of a life of celibacy, a commitment to abstention from sexual relations and from marriage.

## Aparigraha

The Sanskrit letter *'a'* means 'not' and the word *parigraha* means 'to accept from others'. We accept kind and cash from others. Every acceptance is not *parigraha.* If one works and accepts one's wages, salary or emoluments for the work done, the acceptance is not *parigraha.* One must earn what one accepts. Some say that *parigraha* is acceptance of gifts. This is also not correct in all cases. A father or a mother gives gifts to the children as tokens of love. So also do children give gifts to parents. A husband's gifts to a wife, a wife's gifts to a husband, a friend's gifts to a friend and a relative's gifts to a relative as a token of love or in conformity with a social custom cannot be considered as *parigraha.* To accept a bribe is a *parigraha.*To accept cash or kind for an illegal favour on the part of a person in power is a *parigraha.* Acceptance of gifts or cash for immoral sex relation is a *parigraha.* Acceptance of anything for any exchange in the form of cash, kind or service, which is illegal or immoral, is a *parigraha. Aparigraha* or non-acceptance of cash, kind or services, not legally or morally due, is strictly prescribed for a *yogī.*

One meaning of *aparigraha* is non-accumulation of property. There is a verse in the *Bhāgavatam:* 'One has right over that much of property which one needs for one's subsistence. One is a theif if one acquires more. Such a one is to be punished.'[54] *Maharṣi* Patañjali prescribes non-accumulation of property for a *yogī.*

---

54. *yāvad bhriyeta jaṭharaṁ tāvat svatvaṁ hi dehīnām. adhikaṁ yo'bhimanyeta sa steno daṇḍamarhati.*

# 2.6

# Niyama: The Performance of Five Prescriptive Duties

OUT of the eight limbs of *yoga, niyama* is the second one. The five controls or restraints of *yama* are proscriptive: (1) Don't do violence, (2) Don't tell lies, (3) Don't steal, (4) Don't do adultery and don't indulge in sexual excess, (5) Don't accept bribes and don't accumulate property. In contrast, the five duties enumerated under *niyama* are prescriptive. They are: cleanliness, contentment, austerity, studies on Self, complete surrender to God.[55]

## Cleanliness (śauca)

The *yogī* should maintain cleanliness of body, mind and speech. Physical cleanliness includes cleanliness of the body, the clothes and the surrounding. If the body outside is clean and the mind inside is dirty, a dirty mind is not conducive to *yoga.* Hence the *yogī* should abandon dirty ideas. His mind should always be replete with good and noble thoughts. Thirdly, his speech should be free from dirt. It should not contain foul words and words that hurt and offend others. Clean speech is the index of a clean mind. Any progress in *yoga* is not possible if the mind is dirty.

## Contentment (santoṣa)

Contentment is a necessary condition of the mind to progress in *yoga.* A dissatisfied person cannot make much progress in

55. *PYD,* II.32 (*śaucasantoṣatapaḥsvādhyāyeśvarapraṇidhānāni niyamāḥ*).

*yoga*. Dissatisfaction is a mental state of unhappiness.The mind of a dissatisfied person is agitated like simmering or bubbling water in a kettle, hissing steam in a pressure-cooker and churning water in a whirlpool. A low pressure is created around the core of the mind of a dissatisfied person. It generates a whirlwind and, in aggravated situations, a tornado, a cyclone or a hurricane. Stillness of mind is a prerequisite for *yoga*. Agitation and violent motion, linear, circular or chaotic, is lethal to *yoga*. Hence the *yogī* should always have a contented mind.

Some critics of the yogic idea of *santoṣa* express a different view. If we are satisfied with whatever we have and whatever we get, our material progress and prosperity would be stalled. *Santoṣa,* as such, is a treaty with poverty, stalemate, inaction and stand-still condition. Dissatisfaction serves as a stimulus to trigger energetic actions, to make rapid strides and to bring about positive improvement to the existing conditions. This is the idea fostered by economics and political science that keep the sky as a limit to material improvements. This is a *rājasika* idea that eulogises dissatisfaction.

The yogic *santoṣa* is a *sāttvika* idea, however. *Yoga* does not plead for inaction. Opting for inaction was the *viṣāda-yoga* (the *yoga* of languor, lassitude, dejection, depression or despondency) of Arjuna. The next seventeen chapters of the *Bhagavad-Gītā* are devoted to the rejection of inaction and the drooping state of mind. The *Gītā* is narrated in the battlefield of Kurukṣetra where inaction is contextually ruled out. Action for a noble purpose, for the purpose of the betterment of individuals, societies and the universe in general, without attachment to the fruits thereof, and for the sole purpose of performing one's duties, is the motto of *yoga,* at least of *karma-yoga* (the *yoga* of action). Hence the charge that *yoga* teaches inertia, inaction and renunciation of actions is unfounded.

*Yoga* prescribes both actions and contentment. In spite of putting hard and sincere labour for getting some good thing achieved, the result may be disastrous or may not come up to expectation. The result may also be very good or beyond expectation. Whatever is the result, good, partially good, bad or very bad, is to be accepted without dissatisfaction and with satisfaction. This is the yogic *santoṣa*. There is no *yoga* without *santoṣa*. A dissatisfied mind is agitated. An agitated mind is not compatible with *yoga*.

Is *santoṣa* practically feasible amid failure, want, poverty, calamity and disaster ? When life is painful, full of inflictions and defeats, when diseases and death threaten life, when sorrows overpower the charm of life, can contentment be a feasible proposition? This sort of pessimism is antithetical to yogic *santoṣa*. The antithesis has some valid points with relevance to the non-*yogī* common man. It is, however, not much meaningful for a *yogī*. A *yogī* trains his mind to maintain equanimity in opposite situations, both favourable and unfavourable. He is contented in both situations. He gets immense pleasure by the practice of contentment.[56]

### Austerity (tapaḥ)

The word *tapaḥ* has been derived from the Sanskrit verb root *tap*, literally meaning 'to heat'. It otherwise means 'to suffer pain, to torment one's self, to undergo self-mortification, to practise austerity'. Through practising *tapaḥ*, one gets rid of impurities and thus purifies one's gross as well as subtle bodies.[57]

Fasting on special occasions is a common *tapaḥ*. Observances of vows (*vrata*) according to scriptural instructions and social-

---

56. *PYD*, II.42.

57. *PYD*, II.43.

cum-religious traditions are also austerities. Some *yogīs* undergo self-mortification through various techniques to suffer pain. They stand on one leg under the scorching sun with face upwards and eyes open directed towards the sun. They lie on fire with face upwards. They lie on thorn-beds. They walk on fire. They protrude their tongues with nails piercing across. They stand in water in a pond or a river, look up the sun and utter *mantras*. Diverse are the techniques of self-mortification and self-torture.

Fasting and special observances of *vratas* are very often useful. The self-torturing and self-mortifying practices are, however, purposeless feats which are in no way connected with *yoga*. Man is born and reborn and thereby he gets a body. The body is necessary to get nobler things done. Births are necessary; they are multiple chances to spiritually evolve and finally to attain to *Brahman*hood. The body must be kept healthy, strong and sound. It is a vehicle to get the mission fulfilled. It is not something unwanted. It is not anti-spiritual and unholy. A healthy body is conducive to a healthy mind. No *yoga* is possible without a healthy mind. Further, there is no sense in suffering physical and mental pain for the sake of suffering only. Every man should try to get rid of pain or at least to minimise pain in life. It is a sheer folly to make efforts to maximise pain. If one gets *sāttvika* pleasure in life, one should make attempts at its augmentation. Life is already intrinsically painful. It is not wise to make it more painful. If suffering pain is *yoga*, that *yoga* is to be forsaken.

Notwithstanding the recommendation for the avoidance of pain and for giving up undesirable practices of self-torture and self-mortification, austerities and even severe austerities at the cost of life are prescribed in *yoga* on special occasions and for special purposes. If the aims are noble and righteous, if suffering is unavoidable to achieve the aims, one may opt for suffering or even for sacrificing one's life.

Seeking after comforts and luxury which are *rājasika* or *tāmasika* in nature is contradictory to *yoga*. In that sense, indulgence in sensual gratification is condemned in *yoga*. In implication, sacrificing luxury and adopting a life of suffering for any noble cause is a *tapaḥ*. In performing *tapaḥ*, the *yogī* does not really suffer; he remains in spiritual ecstasy while and after performing *tapaḥ*.

## Kriyāyogaḥ

The last three *niyamas*, namely, *tapaḥ*, *svādhyāya* and *īśvarapraṇidhāna*, have been grouped by Patañjali under a collective name, *kriyāyoga*.[58] Confusion has been created by the adoption of this classical term by some recent school of *yoga* for some yogic techniques which do not conform to Pātañjala *Yoga* or any classical school of *Yoga-Tantra* which deals with Kuṇḍalinī *Yoga* and the *Yoga* of the *cakras*. A new term should have been used for a new system, instead of using Patañjali's classical term for some other purpose.

## Studies of scriptures of the self (svādhyāya)

*Svādhyāya* is a compound word formed by the combination of *sva* and *adhyāya*. *Sva* means 'own', referring to *Īśvara* (God) or *Brahman;* it does not refer to any individual person, including the *yogī* himself. *Adhyāya* means 'study'. Hence *svādhyāya* is the study of scriptures on *Īśvara* or *Brahman*. It also means repetition of the *praṇava*, the one-syllabled *mantra OṀ* (*AUṀ*). *Brahman* is verbally designated by the monosyllable *AUṀ*,[59] although no language can be applicable to the Absolute Reality. Thus *mantra-japa* (repetition of a *mantra*) is a type of *svādhyāya*. For this purpose, any *mantra* is good enough. Every *mantra*

58. *PYD*, II.1 (*tapaḥsvādhyāyeśvarapraṇidhānāni kriyāyogaḥ*).

59. *PYD*, I.27.

has a deity and the deity's name. All deities are one Deity, not different from God and His Power (*Śakti* or Consort). God is not an entity second to *Brahman*. Almost all *mantras* start with *OṀ* (*AUṀ*). Hence the *japa* of any *mantra*, suitable to the psychological temperament of the devotee, may be considered as *svādhyāya*. *Maharṣi* Patañjali has written an aphorism on *svādhyāya*.[60] According to it, a *yogī* gets a direct perception of his *iṣṭa-devatā* (the deity of his choice and devotion) by *svādhyāya*.

## Surrender to God (Īśvara-praṇidhānam)

The fifth and the last *niyama* is complete surrender to God. This is the last but not the least. In fact, this is the *niyama* of the first priority and of the utmost importance. *Maharṣi* Patañjali says that, by a complete surrender to God, the *samādhi* (complete union or complete identification) of a *yogī* is well facilitated.[61]

What is termed *īśvarapraṇidhāna* by *Maharṣi* Patañjali is *prapatti* or *śaraṇāgati* in *bhakti-yoga* (the *yoga* of devotion). The Sanskrit word *śaraṇa* means 'shelter or refuge'. The devotee seeks refuge at the feet of God. This is the culminating state of *bhakti-yoga*. And so does Śrī Kṛṣṇa advise Arjuna in the concluding chapter of the *Bhagavad-Gītā* on the complete surrender to God alone.[62]

---

60. *PYD*, II.44.

61. *PYD*.II.45.

62. *BG*, XVIII.66.

# 2.7

## Vitalisation and Withdrawal

THE *yogī* sits in some posture for meditation. Yogic postures (*āsanas*) are many. They are generally meant for keeping the body in healthy conditions. The meditational postures should be such that the *yogī* may stay in a firm and a comfortable condition.[63] Four such postures are recommended for this purpose. They are *siddhāsana, padmāsana, svastikāsana* and *sukhāsana* in order of preference. The *Bhagavad-Gītā* has prescribed some criteria for the meditational postures.[64] The place of meditation should be clean. It should neither be too high nor too low. The posture should be firm enough for the body to be free from movements. The head, the neck and the torso should be on a straight line perpendicular to the earth level. The *yogī* should not look at any direction and should concentrate his attention on the locality of the apex of the nose (the spot between the two eyebrows). The *Śvetāśvatara Upaniṣad* has also given a description of the meditational posture.[65]

While sitting on the meditational posture, the *yogī* should relax the body and the mind.[66] All the skeletal muscles should be free from tensity. The mind also should be free from strain. It should be a state of complete relaxation.

---

63. *PYD*, II.46 (*sthirasukhamāsanam*).

64. *BG*, VI.11-13.

65. *ŚU*, II.8.10.

66. *PYD*, II.47.

## Prāṇāyāma

*Prāṇāyāma* is a compound word formed by the combination of *prāṇa* and *āyāma*. The Sanskrit word *āyāma* means 'restraining' or 'expansion in length, breadth, depth and time'. The Sanskrit word *prāṇa* is popularly considered to mean 'vital air', 'the breath of life', 'breath', 'spirit', 'vitality'. Thus *prāṇāyāma* usually carries the meaning of 'breath control'.

The word *prāṇa* has the prefix *prā* which is the lengthened form of the usual prefix *pra*. The verb root is *an* which means 'to breathe', 'to respire', 'to live', 'to move', 'to go'. Hence the word *ana* means 'breath' or 'respiration'.

In *prāṇāyāma*, the inhalation (*śvāsa*) and the exhalation (*praśvāsa*) are regulated. *Maharṣi* Patañjali has defined *prāṇāyāma* in one of his aphorisms.[67] He has described three types of *prāṇāyāma*, namely, *ābhyantara-vṛtti* (inhalation), *bāhya-vṛtti* (exhalation) and *stambha-vṛtti* (retention).[68] The technical words used for these three types are *pūraka*, *recaka* and *kumbhaka*, respectively. Patañjali has also mentioned a fourth type of *prāṇāyāma*, in which the *yogī* becomes unaware of the incoming, the outgoing and the retaining breaths and of the location, duration and enumeration of the breath.[69] We get references to *prāṇāyāma* in the *Bhagavad-Gītā* in a number of places.[70] With special reference to *prāṇāyāma*, the incoming breath is *prāṇa* and the outgoing one is *apāna*.

*Prāṇāyāma* is not confined to the physical processes of breath-control only. For a better comprehension of this important yogic activity, one has to make an in-depth study

---

67. *PYD*, II.49.

68. *PYD*, II.50.

69. *PYD*, II.51.

70. *BG*, IV.29-30; V.27; XV.14.

of the metaphysics of *Prāṇa* with special reference to the Vedic and the Vedāntic cosmogony and cosmology. Mother Sarasvatī, the Power or Consort of Brahmā, played her violin (*vīṇā*) of three strings (*sattva, rajas, tamas*). As a result of the vibrations of the strings, the equipoised state (*sāmyāvasthā*) of the Primordial Nature (*Mūla-Prakṛti*) was disturbed. This disturbance led to creation which was the manifestation from the Unmanifest (*Avyakta*). The first manifested entity was *Mahat* or *Virāḍ*[71], both words meaning 'the Great'. *Virāḍ* was the Cosmic Mind or Supermind or the Collective Intellect (*Samaṣṭi Buddhi*). From *Virāḍ* evolved Cosmic Plasma (*Āpaḥ* or *Nāra* or *Kaḥ*)[72] which was an undifferentiated cosmic micro-fluid (*apraketaṁ salilam*).[73] This Plasma was super-condensed in the beginning to form a Cosmic Egg.[74] *Prāṇa* evolved from *Āpaḥ*.[75] As a result of the vibration of *Prāṇa* and the generation of excessive quantity of heat (*agni*), the Egg exploded.[76] *Ākāśa* (Space) evolved from *Prāṇa*.[77] The Primordial *Ākāśa* was superheated. From the superheated *Ākāśa* evolved the four fundamental forces, energy-quanta and matter-particles.[78]

---

71. *AV*, XI.8.30; *ṚV*, X.90.5; *SPS*, I.61.
72. *ṚV*, II.35.1-15; VI.50.7; X.2.7; X.82.5-6; X.91.6; *AV*, I.4.1-4; I.33.1-4; *YV*, 27.25-26; *TĀ*, X.22; *ŚBrā*, XI.1.6.1; *MS*, I.8 & 10; *BS*, II.3.11; *Bhā*, II.10.10 ff; *VāPu*, VI.1-11, *BU*, I.2.1-3; V.5.1; *KTU*, II.1.6.
73. *ṚV*, X.129.3.
74. *BGŚB*, Intr.; *MS*, I.9.
75. *ṚV*, X.121.1 ff; *YV*, 13.4; 27.25-26; *AV*, IV.2. 6-8; XI.1; XI.7; XI.10; XI.12; *ŚBrā*, VI.1.1.1; *BS*, II.4.8; II.4.12; *BU*, II.1.20; III.9.9; IV.1.3; *CU*, I.11.5; VII.15.1; *MUU*, II.1.3; *PU*, VI.4; *TU*, II.3.1; III.3.
76. *CU*, III.19.1; *KTU*, II.3. 2-3; *BS*, I.3.39; *YV*, 27. 25-26.
77. *KTU*, II.1.7; *PU*, VI.4.
78. *ṚV*, I.89.10; I.164.33; X.72.4 & 6; *BU*, I.2.5; *CU*, I.9.1; *KTU*, II.1.7.

*Prāṇa* is the Unified Field, the Unified Force and the Unified Vitalising Principle.[79] It is the source of all forms of energy. It pervades all Space. It pervades all matter and energy. It was not exhausted subsequent to the evolution of *Ākāśa* from *Prāṇa*. *Āpaḥ*, *Prāṇa* and *Ākāśa* are reversibly inter-convertible in the sequence of *Āpaḥ*↔*Prāṇa*↔*Ākāśa*.[80] The Unmanifest manifested; the Undifferentiated differentiated; the Homogeneous became heterogeneous. *Virāḍ, Buddhi* or the Cosmic Intellect acquired *upādhi*s (limiting adjuncts) and became individual intellects (*vyaṣṭi buddhi*), although the original *Virāḍ* or the Cosmic Mind still remained as the Collective Mind. It was this individual *buddhi* which served as the evolvent of the evolute *ahaṅkāra* (Ego).

*Prāṇa* or the Cosmic Vitalising Principle is ever pervasive in the whole universe. It is to be collected from *Mahākāśa* (Great Space) and stored in the body. The *cakra*s in the subtle body are the storing batteries and they serve as transducers too. They transform the Prāṇic Energy into its daughter forms of energy in the body. *Prāṇa* is the Mother of all forms of energy.

*Prāṇa* enters the body with or without a medium. It is convenient to collect *Prāṇa* through the inhaling air. Impurities of the body and mind are removed along with the exhaling air. The ingoing *Prāṇa* is *prāṇa* and the outgoing *Prāṇa* is *apāna*. Techniques have been evolved by the seers for the efficient collection of *Prāṇa*.

From the foregoing discussion, it is clear that *Prāṇa* is not vital breath and vital air.[81] It had its origin before air and life evolved. It is not *vāyu*. The word *vāyu* has a number of meanings, one of which is 'air'. The word is derived from the

---

79. *TU*, II.3.1; *TUŚB*, II.3.1.

80. *BU*, I.2.3; *CU*, IV.10.4-5.

81. *BS*, II.4.9; *MUU*, II.1.3.

verb-root *vā,* meaning 'to blow', 'to emit', 'to be diffused'. In the *Puruṣa-Sūkta* of the *Ṛgveda, vāyu* is said to have sprung from the *Prāṇa* of the Primordial Cosmic Person (*Puruṣa*).[82] Hence is the association of *prāṇa-vāyu.* Etymologically, both *vāyu* and *prāṇa* have similar meanings. But, contextually, both of these words do not carry the meaning of 'air' or 'vital breath' with special reference to *prāṇāyāma.* Both *Vāyu* and *Prāṇa* are Vedic gods, not connected with the physical air. *Vāyu* or *Prāṇa* is all-pervasive whereas air is not. Air is absent in major parts of the universe. Air is a mixture of some gases present in the earth's atmosphere.

It has already been stated that *Virāḍ* or *Mahat* evolved from *Māyā* (*Mūla-prakṛti* or the Primordial Nature) who is the Mother Creatrix, and that *Āpaḥ* or the Cosmic Plasma evolved from *Virāḍ.* This Cosmic Plasma which was undifferentiated in the beginning super-condensed itself to form a *bindu* (literally meaning 'dimensionless point'). This *bindu* was the 'Cosmic Egg', the 'singularity' of modern cosmology. From the *Āpaḥ* inside the Cosmic Egg, evolved *Prāṇa,* a vibrating evolute. It is the intrinsic nature of *Prāṇa* to vibrate. This vibrating principle is the *nāda* of the Śaiva or the Tantra philosophy. The vigorous vibration of *Prāṇa* inside the cosmic egg caused the latter to explode. Synchronous with the cosmic explosion, evolved *Ākāśa* (Great Space) which itself expanded. Although *Prāṇa* and *Ākāśa* were the evolvent and the evolute, respectively, they co-exist together. Wherever exists *Ākāśa,* there exists *Prāṇa.* Thus *Prāṇa* pervades the whole universe. Both *Prāṇa* and *Ākāśa* combinedly constitute the Cosmic Field (*Kṣetra*) from which quanta and particles emanate and in which they merge. *Prāṇa* is the precursor of all the four fundamental forces and all the forms of energy. Matter, being packets of energy, also evolves from the Cosmic Field. *Prāṇa* is the Super-

82. *ṚV,* X.90.13.

Unified Cosmic principle. It is that which makes everything move. It is that which makes everything work. No matter-particle and no energy-quanta can exist without motion. No motion and no work can be possible without *Prāṇa*. *Prāṇa* is not life (*jīvana*). Life appeared very late in the course of evolution and is still not ubiquitous. But *Prāṇa* evolved inside the Cosmic Egg before the Big Bang explosion. According to the Vedas and the Vedānta, the initial cosmic explosion was not a Big Bang; it was not chaotic; it was orderly, well-planned and intelligently executed.[83] *Prāṇa* is the fundamental motive force of the whole universe, the majority of which is non-living and an infinitesimal minority of which is living.

It is possible to imbibe and assimilate *Prāṇa* without the mediation of the inhaling air. But it is easier to collect *Prāṇa* through a medium. The medium in the process of *Prāṇāyāma* is air. It is a fact that *prāṇāyāma* grossly deals with the nose, the respiratory passages, the lungs and the inhalation and the exhalation of air. In reality, however, it is concerned with the collection of *Prāṇa* from the universe at large and the storage of *Prāṇa* in the subtle body (not in the gross body). The *nāḍīs* (subtle channels for the flow of *Prāṇa*) are the conduit passages. There are 72,000 channels in the body, out of which three (*suṣumṇā, iḍā* and *piṅgalā*) are principal. The *suṣumṇā nāḍī* is the core *nāḍī* that flows vertically in the spine. The *iḍā* is on the left and the *piṅgalā* is on the right of the *suṣumṇā*. In the process of *prāṇāyāma,* we concentrate on the flow of *Prāṇa* through the left nostril via the *iḍā* and through the right nostril via the *piṅgalā* through the *sahasrāra-ājñā-mūlādhāra* axis. The *prāṇa-apāna* combination also flows through the *suṣumṇā* during *prāṇāyāma.*We do not proceed correctly in *prāṇāyāma* if we concentrate on our nasal passages, bronchi, bronchioles and

83. *ṚV*, X.190.1-3.

lungs. Instead, our real concentration should be on the subtle *nāḍīs* through which *Prāṇa* flows.

*Prāṇa* is stored in five batteries in our body. These batteries are: the *mūlādhāra-cakra,* the *svādhiṣṭhāna-cakra,* the *maṇipūra-cakra,* the *anāhata-cakra* and the *viśuddhi-cakra.* The same *Prāṇa,* stored in these *cakras,* has different names. They are the *apāna,* the *vyāna,* the *samāna,* the *prāṇa* and the *udāna,* respectively.[84] Each of these five *Prāṇas* has specific functions, different from one another. Each *cakra* functions as a storage battery and also as a transducer. It converts the Prāṇic Energy into different forms of conventional energy.

The effects of meditation are better facilitated if *Prāṇāyāma* precedes meditation.[85] However, it is not indispensable.

### Withdrawal of senses (pratyāhāra)

The Sanskrit word *pratyāhāra* has two prefixes, namely, *prati* and *ā;* it is derived from the verb-root *hṛ.* It means 'withdrawal' in general, and 'withdrawal of the senses from external objects' in particular with special reference to *yoga.* Patañjali has defined *pratyāhāra* in one of his aphorisms.[86]

We have five organs of perceptions (*jñānendriya*). They are five subtle organs — for vision, audition, olfaction, gustation and cutaneous sensation of touch, pressure, coldness, hotness and pain. Each subtle organ of perception has a corresponding gross organ — eyes, ears, nose, taste-buds in the mouth and skin.

External stimuli — physical or chemical — are received by the gross sensory organs. They are processed and then an

---

84. *CU,* V.19.1; V.20.1; V.21.1; V.22.1; V.23.1; *MTU,* II.6; VI.5; VI.9.

85. *PYD,* II.53.

86. *PYD,* II.54.

electrical message is transmitted through their respective nerves to the respective centres in the brain. The cerebral centres inform the *antaḥkaraṇa* which, in turn, directs the subtle sensory organs (*indriyas*) that get out to reach the objects of perceptions from which stimuli initially originate. The subtle sensory organs (*indriyas*) connect the objects with the *manas* (mind). Thus objects are perceived.

In *pratyāhāra,* the subtle sensory organs (*indriyas*) are absorbed into the *citta* (the word *citta,* meaning 'thinking substance', of the *Yoga* is a component of *buddhi* of the Sāṅkhya) and take forms like the *citta.* This merger follows an intermediate step in which the *indriyas* merge with *ahaṅkāra.* Since the *indriyas* are withdrawn into the *citta,* they cannot get out to reach the external objects. Hence there is no perception even though the gross sensory organs function and sources of external stimuli exist. Thus, through *pratyāhāra,* the *yogī* exerts a full control on his subtle sensory organs.[87]

How to practise *pratyāhāra* is the crux of the problem. For the purpose of meditation, the visual and auditory sense-organs are the main channels of distraction. Pleasant and unpleasant odours may distract attention; but they are less common than the visual and auditory sensations. One may close the eyes and plug the ears with cotton wool. But this is mechanical blocking rather than *pratyāhāra.* If *pratyāhāra* is successful, sense perceptions cease even though stimuli reach the gross organs of sensations and even though the gross sensory organs receive the stimuli.

The subtle sense-organs are withdrawn into the mind when the latter remains completely preoccupied with some concentrated thought or when the mind remains in completely thoughtless condition. Long practice is necessary to get success in attaining the state of *pratyāhāra.*

---

87. *PYD,* II.55.

# 2.8

# The Tripod of Meditation

OUT of the eight limbs of Pātañjala *Yoga,* the first five limbs, already described, are external (*bahiraṅga*) and the remaining three are internal (*antaraṅga*).The internal ones are: *dhāraṇā, dhyāna* and *samādhi.* These three constitute the tripod of *yoga.*

## Dhāraṇā

To fix the *citta* (mind) to a particular location is called *dhāraṇā.* This word has been derived from the Sanskrit verb root *dhṛ,* which means 'to hold'. The place to which the *citta* is bound may be internal or external. When it is internal, it may be a *cakra* inside the body like the *ājñā-cakra* (spot between the two eyebrows) or some tissue, organ, or limb of the body. When it is external, it may be the image of a deity, a crystal, a coloured or a black or a white spot, or any other external object. *Maharṣi* Patañjali has defined *dhāraṇā* in one of his aphorisms.[88]

## Dhyānam

Having fixed the *citta* to a particular location, the *yogī's* mind remains busy with a *single* thought which continues to be one alone and which becomes continuous and uninterrupted. The single thought may be likened to the continuous flow of oil when poured from one container to another. *Maharṣi* Patañjali has defined *dhyāna,* as has been outlined here.[89]

The word *dhyāna* has been derived from the Sanskrit verb-

---

88. *PYD,* III.1 (*deśabandhaścittasya dhāraṇā*).

89. *PYD,* III.2 (*tatra pratyayaikatānatā dhyānam*).

root *dhyai*, which means 'to think, to contemplate, to meditate on, to call to mind'.

Some *Yoga* Schools use the term *bhāvātīta dhyāna* (transcendental *dhyāna*). Such a use does not conform to the usage in classical *yoga,* however. There is a thought in *dhyāna,* although single and continuously flowing. If *dhyāna* transcends thought, it is not *dhyāna* at all (It is *samādhi*). Of course, 'meditation' is a word which is not equivalent to '*dhyāna*'. Meditation may be transcendental, but not *dhyāna.*

Patañjali has used the word *pratyaya* in his aphorism. It contextually means 'conception, notion or idea'. What flows in *dhyāna* is one idea.

## Samādhi

The word *samādhi* has two prefixes, namely, *sam* and *ā*. It is derived from the Sanskrit verb-root *dhā*. It literally means 'to place, to put, to hold or to fix together'. It may mean 'joining or combining with'.

Here we introduce a word *dhyeya.* What is meditated on is *dhyeya.* It is the idea or notion on which *dhyāna* is done. It is the object on which one meditates.

Patañjali's definition of *samādhi* is stated here: When the contemplation shines forth in consciousness as the intended object and nothing more, and, as it were, emptied of itself, is *samādhi.*[90]

We may discuss the topic of *samādhi* in two stages, the initial and the final. The initial ones are with seed (*sabīja*) or with support (*sālambana*) whereas the final ones are without seed (*nirbīja*) or without support (*nirālambana*). *Samāpatti* is the *samādhi* with seed. The word literally means 'to be like that'. According to Patañjali's definition, the *rajas* and *tamas* whirls

---

90. *PYD,* III.3. (*tadevārthamātranirbhāsaṁ svarūpaśūnyamiva samādhiḥ*).

of mind being dwindled away, and the *citta* being crystal-clear, with reference either to the knower or to the process-of-knowing or to the object-to-be-known, the *citta* attains *samāpatti* by acquiring the form of one of these three, being tinged by one of these three.[91]

The *dhyeya* (the object meditated upon) is gross in the deliberative (*savitarka*) and super-deliberative (*nirvitarka*) *samāpatti*s whereas it is subtle in the reflective (*savicāra*) and super-reflective (*nirvicāra*) *samāpatti*s. The subtle *dhyeya* is one of the five *tanmātras*.

In the *savitarka samāpatti,* distinctions among the word (*śabda*), intended-object (*artha*) and idea (*jñāna*) are maintained and the *citta* becomes one with each of them.[92] In the *nirvitarka samāpatti,* the *yogī*'s *citta* gets rid of the word and the idea and becomes identified with the intended-object (*dhyeya*) only.[93]

In the *savicāra samāpatti,* the place (*deśa*), time (*kāla*) and cause (*nimitta*) of the subtle *dhyeya* are distinguished and the *yogī*'s *citta* becomes one with each of them. In the *nirvicāra samāpatti,* the *yogī*'s *citta* makes no distinctions of the place, time and cause of the subtle *dhyeya* and becomes one with the subtle *dhyeya* only.[94]

All the four types of *samāpatti,* described here, are with seed (*sabīja*). Patañjali names them as *sabīja samādhi.*[95] The *savitarka* and *savicāra* types of *samādhi* are *savikalpa* whereas the *nirvitarka* and *nirvicāra* types of *samādhi* are *nirvikalpa.* The *sabīja samādhi* is otherwise known as *samprajñāta samādhi* and the

---

91. *PYD,* I.41.
92. *PYD,* I.42.
93. *PYD,* I.43.
94. *PYD,* I.44
95. *PYD,* I.46.

*nirbīja samādhi* as *asamprajñāta samādhi*. In the latter, the *citta* rests in the *puruṣa*.

In the *nirvitarka* and *nirvicāra samādhi*s which are devoid of *vikalpa*s (distinctive deliberations and reflections), the *dhyeya* is gross and subtle, respectively. It is the *dhyeya* that serves as the support. In this meditational state, the whirls of mind (*cittavṛtti*) do not *completely* cease to be. And hence this *samādhi* is *sabīja*. There is some sort of *cittavṛtti* since there is awareness of the *yogī* on his identification with the *dhyeya*.The emerging *cittavṛtti* is the seed (*bīja*) that still remains.

By the efficient and prolonged practice of *nirvikalpa samādhi,* the refined intellect (*prajñā*) of the *yogī* realises the Truth. *Maharṣi* Patañjali uses the term *ṛtambharā prajñā* which also generates *saṁskāras,* albeit benign in nature.[96] As usual, these *saṁskāra*s are also imprinted on the *karmāśaya,* the reservoir of *karmas*.[97] The *karmāśaya* is a subtle organ in the internal instrument (*antaḥkaraṇa*) of the subtle body. The *saṁskāra*s produced by the *ṛtambharā prajñā* antagonise and uproot the other types of *saṁskāra*s that already lie in the *karmāśaya*.[98] The other types of *saṁskāra*s are rooted in the five *kleśa*s (*avidyā, asmitā, rāga, dveṣa, abhiniveśa*). Thus the *kleśamūla saṁskāras* are erased and their place is occupied by the *ṛtambharā prajñā saṁskāra*s.

Through sustained practice of the higher type of *samādhi,* the *yogī* develops *vairāgya* (freedom from worldly passion; freedom from all worldly desires) and *anāsakti* (non-attachment). This results in the complete erasure of all traces of the *ṛtambharā-prajñā saṁskāra*s. Thus the *citta* has neither seeds

---

96. *PYD*, I.48 (*ṛtambharā tatra prajñā*).

97. *PYD*, II.12; *SPS*, II.42.

98. *PYD*, I.50.

nor roots of *vṛttis* (whirls). This *samādhi* is *nirbīja* (seedless).[99] This is the culminating state of *yoga,* in which the *yogī*'s *puruṣa* (self) is detached from *Prakṛti* (the Primordial Nature) and attains *kaivalya* (the liberated state of isolation).[100]

### Saṁyama

The yogic processes of *dhāraṇā, dhyāna* and *samādhi,* done together at a time, is known as *saṁyama.*[101] This *saṁyama* is very important in *yoga.* In most cases, it is *saṁyama* that a *yogī* practises instead of *dhāraṇā, dhyāna* or *samādhi,* practised separately.

---

99. *PYD,* I.51.

100. *PYD,* III.50.

101. *PYD,* III.4.

# 2.9

## Equanimity: Contradictions Dissolved

THE *Bhagvad-Gītā* prescribes unattched actions and rejects renunciation of actions. No individual and no society can exist without actions. Even the non-living world always performs actions. A piece of stone, stationary in a particular locality, seems to be at perfect rest. This apparent obeservation, however, is not correct. The stone is made up of molecules, atoms, sub-atomic particles and micro-particles. Not a single particle can exist without motion. Matter is always in motion. In the micro-world, motion of micro-particles is random and bizarre. They run about and dash against one another. They appear, dance, collide and disappear. In the macro-world, galaxies, stars, planets and satellites are always in motions. Stars are nuclear furnaces. The rest-mass of a particle is an intrapolatory or extrapolatory mass and not one which is actually determined. No particle can exist without motion, and hence the actual determination of the rest-mass of any particle is impossible. The Vedānta says that the whole universe and everything of the universe are constantly in motion. Hence the Sanskrit word for the universe is *jagat* (*gam* + *kvip*), meaning that which is in motion. Only *Brahman* is at absolute rest and nothing else. Even God (*Īśvara*), *Brahman* with attributes and functions, cannot be conceived to be in absolute rest. Hence renunciation of work by man cannot be recommended. Every man should work for his own good and for the good of the soceity.[102] Everybody should work for God, that is, for the

102. *BG*, III.4-8; III.19-24; V.2; V.6; V.11.

creation of God.[103]

**Pairs of opposites**

Life is full of contradictions, of pairs of opposites (*dvandva*). Each brick of the edifice of the universe is constituted by a pair of opposites. There is no physical entity (matter or energy) which is an exception to the general principle of the pair of opposities. Contradictions are accentuated in working. Life, busy in work, is full of joy and sorrow, pleasure and pain, agony and ecstasy, likes and dislikes, love and hatred, friendship and enmity, ups and downs, profit and loss, success and failure, hopes and despairs, fortune and misfortune, praise and blame, fame and ill fame, meet and separation, affluence and poverty, and the like.

The *Bhagavd-Gītā* advises to get rid of all pairs of opposites by transcending them (*dvandvātīta*).[104]

> Be contented with whatever gain comes to you as such. Transcend all pairs of opposites. Forsake jealousy. Be equal-minded, that is, maintain equanimity, in success and failure. If work is done by maintaining these standards, the self is not bound thereby.

A state neutral to pairs of opposites (*nirdvandva*)[105] is befitting to a *yogī*.

We desire everything good for us. We desire more wealth, more power, more fame, more luxury and comforts, and more of sensual gratification. At the same time, we become jealous of other persons' happiness and prosperity. But all things do not happen as we desire. We get both success and failure in

103. *BG*, XI.55.

104. *BG*, IV.22.

105. *BG*, II.45; V.3.

our work. Similar things also happen for others. We become overjoyous with our success. We are seized with extreme grief with other persons' success. Due to desire (*icchā*) and enmity (*dveṣa*), we create pairs of opposites (*dvandva*) and we are deluded with them. We can be free from this delusion if we transcend pairs of opposites.[106]

## Stay in Brahman

Pertinent questions are often asked: Is it a practicable proposition to renounce desires ? Is it possible to be I-less (*niraham*) and myless (*nirmama*) ? Where is 'I' with 'my', there sprouts desire. The *Gītā* has a satisfactory answer to such questions. It is *brāhmī sthitiḥ* (stay in *Brahman*).[107] The *yogī* stays in the Full (*Pūrṇa=Brahman*) and thereby takes the role of a full sea into which water of many rivers enters.[108] It is a state of fully satisfied desires into which desires of rivers flow.

Śrī Kṛṣṇa did not promise Arjuna that the latter would win victory in the Mahābhārata War. He did not give any assurance. He said:

> If you are killed in the War, you will go to the heaven for having done your duty. If you win, you will enjoy the kingdom.[109]

There are chances of either success or failure, of either profit or loss. Arjuna was advised to equalise happiness and sorrow, profit and loss and victory and defeat.[110]

---

106. *BG*, VII.27-28.
107. *BG*, II.72.
108. *BG*, II.70.
109. *BG*,II.37
110. *BG*, II.38.

### Karmayogī

Confusion prevails over the use of the word *karmayogī* in popular literature on *yoga*. The performance of any action is not *yoga*. A farm worker, a factory labourer, a business executive or any Army General may do hard and sincere work and still is not necessarily a *karmayogī*. A political leader may strive hard throughout his life and still may not be a *karmayogī*. Who is a *karmayogī* then? Work done without attachment (*āsakti* or *saṅga*) to the fruits thereof is *karmayoga*.[111] 'It is my duty to do this work and so do I work'. This is the sole motto of a *karmayogī*.[112]

### Buddhiyoga

The *Bhagavad-Gītā* has used the term *buddhiyoga* a number of times.[113] Much has not been elaborated on this *buddhiyoga* in yogic literature. One who constantly fixes one's intellect on God and who has grasped the knowledge on *Brahman* is a *buddhiyogī*. *Buddhiyoga* is nearer to *jñānayoga*, but not identical to it. A *jñānayogī* realises the non-duality of *Brahman* and his identity to *Brahman*. There is very little need of work when one attains the state of a *jñānayogī*. But a *buddhiyogī* has still the need of becoming a *karmayogī*.

A *buddhiyogī*'s internal instrument (*antaḥkaraṇa*) becomes purified (*cittaśuddhi*). He develops equanimity of mind. His mind becomes neutral to success (*siddhi*) and failure (*asiddhi*). While united to God, he works for Him (for His creation), and that too is done without being attached to the fruits of actions or any return from God. A *buddhiyogī* attains his mind's equalness (*samatvam*) in both success and failure.[114]

---

111. *BG*, II.48; III.19; XI.55.

112. *BG*, III.8 (*niyataṁ kuru karma tvam*); III.19 (*kāryaṁ karma samācara*).

113. *BG*, II.49; X.10; XVIII.57.

114. *BG*, II.48.

Action without attachment to desires for fruits thereof is called *niṣkāma karma* (desireless action). Its opposite is *sakāma karma* (action with thirsty desires). A *buddhiyogī* performs actions, but desireless actions. The *Gītā* advises to take refuge in *buddhiyoga.*[115]

The *Bhagavad-Gītā* declares: '*Yoga* is skill in action'.[116] Here the word *yoga* contextually means *buddhiyoga.* There are chances of success or failure in every action. Actions are generally accompanied with good and bad effects. The effect of an action may be good for some and bad for others; may be good for some purpose and bad for some other purpose. There is hardly any action that is absolutely good. One can be free from the contradiction of good and bad by *buddhiyoga* (the *yoga* of equalness, the *yoga* of equanimity). Hence it is said : '*Buddhiyoga* is skill in action'.

Many interpreters of the *Gītā* have sown a weed in explaining the statement — '*Yoga* is skill in action'. They explain the sentence, 'skill in action is *yoga*'. A factory-worker may show skill in his action. A secretary may be very efficient in working. An engineer may be ingeniously skillful. A mechanic may show extraordinary skill in his work. Still these skillful and efficient workers are not *yogī*s. Thus it is not correct to say that skill in action is *Yoga.*

The sentence '*A=A*' or 'Man is man' is an identity statement. Here the subject and the predicate are identical. One can reversibly express the subject and the predicate without alteration of meaning. This is, however, not true for non-identity statements. 'All tigers are animals'.'All animals are tigers'. The second sentence does not convey a correct meaning. An animal may be a cow, a horse, a dog or a cat. '*Yoga* is skill in action'. But the reverse is not true. Skill in action is not *yoga.*

---

115. *BG,* II.49.

116. *BG,* II.50.

Simple mechanical meditation, without *buddhiyoga*, can hardly bring peace to a person. The *yogī* has to get rid of contradictions and pairs of opposites. He has to practise detachment (*anāsakti*). He has to develop his equanimity of mind. If he unites his *antaḥkaraṇa* with God while doing any work, his *buddhi* (intellect in his *antaḥkaraṇa*) is purified, and thereby he becomes detached and neutral to pairs of opposites. Thus he attains equanimity of mind.

# 2.10

## Universal Love

*Maharṣi* Patañjali, in one of his aphorisms, has stressed four characteristics of a *yogī*. These are: (1) friendship and love (*maitrī*), (2) compassion (*karuṇā*), (3) joy over others' happiness (*muditā*) and (4) ignoring the defects in others (*upekṣā*).[117] Gautama Buddha has also advised to develop these traits in order that one would be a good man and one would get bliss in life.

### Maitrī

Simple meditation, as a mental exercise, would bear little fruit if one develops enmity with others. Enmity disturbs mental peace. And so does the *Bhagavad-Gītā* advise to get rid of enmity (to become *nirvaira*), to develop benevolence (*maitrī*) and to give up ill will.[118]

*Maitrī* (friendliness, benevolence) is established by universal love. It should start at home. Love between wife and husband, among parents and children and among brothers and sisters makes a home sweet. If love is stifled at home and strife and hatred mar the home life, in that unfortunate situation, meditation proves to be of little value.

Enmity in public life is a potent factor that seriously disturbs peace. One should be benevolent to one's neighbours and people in general in the society.

---

117. *PYD*, I.33.

118. *BG*, XI.55 (*nirvairaḥ sarvabhūteṣu*); XII.13 (*adveṣṭā sarvabhūtānām; maitraḥ*) ; XII.15.

Sometimes one does not create enmity from one's own side; others create enmity for their own interest or for their bad nature. In such situations, one should try to soften the matter and solve the problem amicably. If the *yogī* can love his enemies from the core of his *antaḥkaraṇa* (heart), in spite of existing differences in opinion, he does a very good job. He should not hate his enemies although he should not yield to their misdeeds and should not succumb to their misdemeanour.

The *yogī* loves everything and everybody created by God. He loves human beings, animals and birds. He loves trees, creepers, foliage and flowers. He loves the sky, stars in the sky, the moon-lit night, the rising sun, the rainbow in the sky and everything of Nature. He loves the singing spring, the waterfall, the river, the sea, the lake, the green meadow and the green woods. He loves the creation of God; he loves God.

## Karuṇā

*Karuṇā* is the Sanskrit word for 'compassion'. Cruelty is inimical to *yoga*. The *yogī* should be compassionate to the suffering and the distressed human beings. He should be compassionate to the suffering animals and birds. No cruelty to any living being — humans, animals, birds, insects, worms, microbes — should be the motto of the *yogī*. He should be compassionate to the plant-kingdom too. The *Gītā* advises to be compassionate (*karuṇā*).[119]

## Muditā

The word *muditā* has been derived from the Sanskrit verb-root *mud*, meaning 'to be glad, to be happy, to be delighted'. The contextual meaning of *muditā* in *Pātañjala Yoga* or Buddha's teachings is 'the feeling of joy over others' happiness'. It is a

---

119. *BG*, XII.13.

general, social courtesy to congratulate somebody on the occasion of his/her success, achievements, victory, awards, auspiciousness, etc. Occasionally, our congratulation is a mere formality. We do not really rejoice the occasion. In some occasions, we feel unhappy and malicious over the other person's success. Notwithstanding our inner bitterness, we verbally express our feign joy and pretended felicity. The *yogī* should not do that. His *muditā* should be genuine. It should come from the core of his heart.

### Upekṣā

Here the contextual meaning of *upekṣā* is 'indifference'. It is indifference towards others' negative traits and weaknesses. It is not the lack of cognisance of others' faults. It is the action of ignoring the faults of others. It is also not the action of ignoring the injustice and wrongs done by others. Arjuna was not advised to yield to injustice done by the Kauravas. To tolerate injustice is not good. Injustice must be fought against. What is the exact nature of *upekṣā* then?

All of us have divine (*daiva*) and demoniac (*āsura*) qualities. Among the common men, there is hardly anybody who is purely divine, and hardly anybody who is purely demoniac. We are usually blends, varing in quantities above zero and below 100 per cent. *Daiva* predominates in those who have less of *āsura*. Conversely, demoniac predominates in those who have less of *daiva*. Blends are many in number since the variation is continuous. The sixteenth chapter of the *Bhagavad-Gītā* has been devoted to the *daiva* and *āsura* qualities of man.[120] The fourteenth chapter of the *Gītā* describes the three strings (*guṇas*) of which the Primordial Nature (*Mūlaprakṛti*) is constituted.[121] We all are made up of these three strings. They

120. *BG*, XVI.

121. *BG*, XIV.

are: *sattva, rajas* and *tamas. Sattva* is in the right side, in the positive extreme of the swing of the pendulum, whereas *tamas* is in the left side, in the negative extreme. *Rajas* occupies a middle position. These three strings, by permutations and combinations and by different proportions, give rise to a large number of blends. Each of the blends is a personality type in the language of Sāṅkhya-Vedānta. Each of these types has been assigned to one of two groups, namely, *daiva* or *āsura.* This is an over-simplification of the numerous personality types; but this has been done for clarity and convenience.

Only the *jīvanmukta* (librated, although living) transcends the three strings — *sattva, rajas* and *tamas.* He becomes free from the three *guṇa*s (strings), or in Vedāntic language, becomes *nistraiguṇyaḥ.*[122] Barring the *jīvanmukta*s, we hardly come across a person who has no minus points. Of course, the degree of negativity varies. We do not categorise an individual as *āsura* (demoniac) unless he has a preponderance of minus points.

Coming to the original issue of *upekṣā,* a *yogī* should show indifference towards the minus points of a person. He should not be fault-finding and discard people because of their faults. This does not mean that the *yogī* should eulogise the faults of people. He should ignore the faults and show benevolence towards these persons. He should not hate persons because of their faults.

Forgiveness (*kṣamā*) is a noble quality which a *yogī* should cherish. This quality is implied in *upekṣā.* The *Bhagavad-Gītā* has spoken high of forgiveness.[123]

The *yogī* loves God and loves God's creation. He loves all — human beings, animals and plants. He loves Nature — living and non-living. His love is universal.

---

122. *BG,* II.45.

123. *BG,* X.4; X.34; XII.13; XVI.3.

# 2.11

# A Dedicated Life is Yoga

THE best *yogī* is he who lives a life dedicated to the cause of the universe. The best *yogī* is he who performs all actions at all moments while united with God (*yagastha*).[124] The best *yogī* is he who makes everything of his and every occasion of his an offering to God.

## Work for God

In the concluding verse of the eleventh chapter of the *Bhagavad-Gītā*, Śrī Kṛṣṇa advises Arjuna to work for God.[125] This advice is to be correctly interpreted. God has no need for anything. He does not need any service for Himself. He has no desire to be fulfilled. What is the meaning of 'Work for God' then?

God has created the world. He is not only the Creator, but also the Sustainer. He maintains the world. For the maintenance of God's creation, every human being should help God and thereby he serves God. If man does this service, he works for God. In the *Mahābhārata War*, God desires that Arjuna should fight against the Kauravas. Arjuna worked for God by doing his duty.

## Dedicate your life

Anybody who has been born has to live and he works to

---

124. *BG*, II.48 (*yogasthaḥ*); V.6-7 (*yogayuktaḥ*); VI.29 (*yogayuktātmā*); VIII.27 (*yogayuktaḥ*).

125. *BG*, XI.55 (*matkarmakṛt*).

sustain his life. Man works for himself. He earns a living. He works for comforts in his life. He works in order to be rich. He eats, sleeps and indulges in sex. He produces children and works for them. He works for acquiring power and for getting fame. He is afraid of calamities. He is afraid of enemies. He works for his safety and protection. These actions are not proscribed and condemned, if done within limits and not at the cost of the society. Some of these actions are essential for one's survival, and they are to be done without harming others. Nevertheless, yogic actions are different. They are dedicative.

'One for one' is the slogan in individualism. A *yogī* rejects this slogan. 'One for all, all for one and all for all' is the slogan for the theory and practice of a *yogī*. He lives an altruistic life. He dedicates his life to the cause of humanity, to the cause of all animals and plants, to the cause of the non-living world and to the cause of the entire universe. In the language of the *Bhagavad-Gītā,* the *yogī* dedicates himself to the cause of the welfare of all beings (*sarvabhūtahite ratāḥ*).[126] Here the word *bhūta* has a wider connotation. It includes all created entities, both living and non-living.

The *yogī*'s life constantly adheres to altruism. Daily he prays: Let all be happy. Let all be healthy. Let all see what is good and benign. Let not anyone suffer.[127]

### Enjoy self-denial

The *White Yajurveda* has a *mantra* which has also been given *in*

---

126. *BG,* V.25; XII.4.

127. *sarve bhavantu sukhinaḥ,*
*sarve santu nirāmayāḥ,*
*sarve bhadrāṇi paśyantu,*
*mā kaścid duḥkhabhāg bhavet.*

*toto* in the *Īśopaniṣad*.[128] The *mantra* says: 'Enjoy by self-denial, self-abnegation or renunciation (*tena tyaktena bhuñjīthā*)'. It is not simply a prescription for renunciation. 'Enjoy by renouncing'. One may renounce, but may not renounce and enjoy simultaneously. One must attain to a higher level of life by the ascension of the spiritual ladder so that one may enjoy self-abnegation. An adept in *yoga* can do it. He really enjoys by seeing others happy if his self-abnegation brings about peace and prosperity for others.

## Make your life an offering

Out of faith and devotion, the *yogī* offers little things to God. It may be a green leaf, a fresh flower, a ripe fruit or a handful of water; it is devotionally offered to God.[129] Whatever work he does, whatever he eats, whatever he oblates, whatever he donates and whatever austerities he makes, he first offers all those to God.[130]

Anything you begin — the construction of a house, living in a new house, the establishment of a school, a hospital, a factory, or any other institution — first offer that to God. Any new work you begin in your life or the life of any member of your family, do that by offering to God. You wear a new cloth; you write a new book; you paint a scenery; you sing a song; do that by offering to God. You marry; you start your sex-life; do that by offering to God. You observe your birthday or the birthday of your wife or children; do that by offering to God. The *yogī* divinises all his life and all his activities.

---

128. *YV*, 40.1; *IU*, 1.

129. *BG*, IX.26.

130. *BG*, IX.27.

### In constant communion

Everybody, including a *yogī*, has to do work. Problems crop up during working. A work may not satisfy all. A work may not be free from blemish. The effects or products of a work may be beneficial to some and harmful to others. Crises in judgement and crises in making a decision (*dharma-saṅkaṭa*) may stand on the way. What is the solution then ?

The solution may be had if the mind keeps contact with God while working. The *Gītā* advises: 'Work while united with God (*yogasthaḥ kuru karmāṇi*)'.[131] It further says: 'Be always united with God.'[132] This union is not a one-way traffic. It is communion. Once the intellect (*buddhi*) establishes contact with God, blessings of God shower on *buddhi* that is purified as a result of illumination. This is called *buddhiyoga. Buddhi,* thus enlightened and purified, can take a proper decision. The good results that accrue to one from *buddhiyoga* have been stated in the last chapter of the *Gītā.*[133]

The illumination of the *antaḥkaraṇa,* especially the *buddhi,* by *Brahman,* the pure Consciousness, has been mentioned here. This doctrine of reflection is known as *citchāyāpatti* (the falling of the shadow of Consciousness), *caitanyādhyāsa* (the super-addition or super-imposition of Consciousness) or *cidāveśa* (the possession of Consciousness). The *antaḥkaraṇa,* by nature, is insentient. It is rendered sentient by the reflection of the *Puruṣa,* the sentient Being. The *Puruṣa* is inactive and indifferent. Due to the proximity of the *Puruṣa* and the *Prakṛti* and the reflection of the former on the latter, induction of consciousness in the latter takes place, and the latter assumes

131. *BG,* II.48; V.6-7; VIII.27.

132. *BG,* VI.10; VIII.14; VIII.27; IX.14; X.10;XII.1;XVIII.57.

133. *BG,* XVIII. 57-58.

the role of agency.[134] The *antaḥkaraṇa,* that is grossly called the mind (constituted of *buddhi, ahaṅkāra* and *manas*), unreflected by the *Puruṣa,* is insentient and, when reflected, is sentient. It is the *antaḥkaraṇa* that is the doer in an individual body and that possesses properties.[135] The Sāṅkhya asserts that it is the *ahaṅkāra* that is the agent of actions, and not the *puruṣa* (self).

The *Gītā* advises to work and not to renounce work. At the same time it advises to dedicate the work to God and, at the mental level, to be constantly united with God.[136] Thus the *yogī* lives a dedicated life.

---

134. *SPS,* I.96; I.99; I.164; II.35; *SK,* 20.

135. *SPS,* V.25; VI.64; *BG,* III.27.

136. *BG,* XVIII.56-57.

# 2.12

## A Yogī's Vision — All in One, One in All

YOGA philosophy, in original, has accepted the metaphysics of Sāṅkhya with the single exception that it has recognised the existence of God (*Īśvara*),[137] who is not the creator of the universe, but a special *puruṣa* (sentient being) unconnected with hindrances (*kleśa*), karmic *saṁskāras* (*karma*), the fruition of *karma* (*vipāka*) and the reservior of karmic impressions (*āśaya* or *karmāśaya*) unlike the other *puruṣa*s that are individual selves.[138] Thus the *Yoga* philosophy does not establish any identity between the individual selves and the Universal Self. We do not get the Vedāntic concept of *Brahman* in Patañjali's philosophy of *Yoga*.

Most Indian *yogī*s, however, follow Yoga-Vedānta rather than Sāṅkhya-Yoga with special reference to the metaphysics. They accept the theory and practice of *Yoga*, as prescribed by Patañjali, but they superimpose the Vedāntic metaphysics on it. They accept *Brahman* as the absolute Reality and God or *Īśvara* as *Brahman* with attributes (*saguṇa brahma*) or as *Brahman* with *Māyā* as limiting adjunct (*upādhi*) or as *Brahman* reflected on its own Power *Māyā* (*Māyā-Śakti*). Unlike the yogic concept of liberation (*kaivalya*)[139] which is separation of the *puruṣa* (self)

137. *PYD*, I.23 (*īśvarapraṇidhānād vā*).

138. *PYD*, I.24 (*kleśakarmavipākāśayairaparāmṛṣṭaḥ puruṣaviśeṣa īśvaraḥ*).

139. *PYD*, IV.34 (*puruṣārthaśūnyānāṁ guṇānāṁ pratiprasavaḥ kaivalyaṁ svarūpapratiṣṭhā vā citiśakteriti*).

from *Prakṛti* (Primordial Nature), the concept of liberation (*mokṣa*) in the Advaita Vedānta is the re-establishment of identity of the individual self and the Universal Self, consequent upon the removal of ignorance (*ajñānam*) and the realisation of the identity. The Advaita Vedānta speaks of *brahma-nirvāṇa*,[140] a complete merger of the individual self in the Cosmic Self with the concomitant loss of identity of the former.

Here we may quote some statements given in the Upaniṣads which establish the identity of the selves (*jīvātmās*) with the Self (*Brahman*): 'Thou art that (*tat-tvam-asi*)'.[141] 'I am Brahman (*ahaṁ brahmāsmi*)'.[142] 'I am He (*so'hamasmi*)'.[143] This self is *Brahman* (*ayamātmā brahma*)'.[144] 'All this verily is *Brahman* (*sarvaṁ khalvidaṁ brahma*)'.[145] 'Here is no diversity whatsoever (*neha nānāsti kiñcana*)'.[146]

The *Puruṣa-Sūkta* of the *Ṛgveda* unequivocally states that 'All this (the whole universe) verily is *Brahman*'.[147] Whatever was in the past, is at present, and will be in the future is nothing other than *Brahman*. *Brahman* is both immanent and transcendent. One-fourth of *Brahman* is manifested and its three-fourths still remain as the Unmanifest.[148] The *Yajurveda*

---

140. *BG*, II.72; V.24-26.
141. *CU*, VI.8.7; VI.9.4-VI.14.3.
142. *BU*, I.4.10.
143. *CU*, IV.11.1.
144. *BU*, II.5.19.
145. *CU*, III.14.1.
146. *BU*, IV.4.19; *KTU*, II.1.11.
147. *ṚV*, X.90.2.
148. *ṚV*, X.90. 3-4.

and the *Īśopaniṣad* also state that *Brahman* pervades everything.[149] The whole universe, micro- and macro-, is pervaded by *Brahman* that becomes the substratum (*adhiṣṭhāna*) of the biggest and the smallest entity of the universe. By the mind's eye (the third eye), the *yogī* can see or feel the presence of the all-pervasive *Brahman*.

The attributeless *Brahman* or *Brahman* with attributes (*Īśvara*) is not altogether extra-cosmic. The universe is not likened to a chair and *Brahman* to a carpenter. It is not the relation of the maker and the made, the creator and the created, and the subject and the object. The subject and the objects are identical. He wanted to be many and He became many.[150] The many are not *essentially* different from the one.

The *Bhagavad-Gītā* presents the *yogī*'s vision of all in One and One in all. It is a divine vision. The *yogī,* with full knowledge on *Brahman,* sees Vāsudeva (God) in all.[151] He sees God everywhere and sees all in God.[152] He has equality in vision and thus becomes a *samadarśī*. He sees his self in all beings and all beings in his self.[153] With knowledge and humility, he develops equal vision among spiritually learned men, cows, elephants, dogs and dog-eaters.[154] There is no created entity in which the *yogī* does not see God.[155] He sees all in the One and the One in all.

---

149. *YV*, 40.1; IU, 1.

150. *TU*, II.6 (*so'kāmayata bahu syāṁ prajāyeyeti*).

151. *BG*, VII.19.

152. *BG*, VI.30.

153. *BG*, VI.29.

154. *BG*, V.18.

155. *BG*, VI.31.

# 2.13

## The Root of Evil

SOME glimpses of the metaphysics of Yoga-Vedānta have already been given. *Īśvara* (God) or *Brahman* with attributes wanted to be many and became many. Before the creation began, *Brahman* had been one alone, of course, with its Power (*Śakti*) *Māyā,* which was not a second to the former. The creation is not really *de novo;* it is anew not from nothing. It is an instance of emanation, something coming out of an already existing source. The Sanskrit word *sṛṣṭi* (*sṛj* + *ktin*) has been derived from the verb-root *sṛj*. One of its meanings is 'to emit from one's self'. The Vedāntic creation is manifestation from the Unmanifest (*prakaṭa* from *aprakaṭa, vyakta* from *avyakta*). Thus, the whole universe is *essentially Brahman.*

In this context, we ask a pertinent question: 'What is the root of evil ? God is Existence (*Satya*), Good and Benign (*Śiva*) and Beautiful (*Sundara*). God is Existence (*Sat*), Consciousness (*Cit*) and Bliss (*Ānanda*). If we accept these statements, we have to explain the origin of what is bad, ugly, insentient, sorrowful, cruel, selfish and all such attributes for which we use the group word 'EVIL'. How and wherefrom does evil originate ?

The problem of suffering and evil has been one of the subject-matters of the *Brahmasūtra.*[156] Here it is said that the differences in the individual selves are due to their merits

156. *BS,* II.1.34.

and demerits. There are also other scriptural texts in support of this view.[157]

The Upaniṣads tell us that 'In the beginning there was being alone, one without a second.'[158] This being accepted, there could be no *karma* which had to be taken into account before creation. At least for the first creation, all created individuals should have been free from inequalities and should have been free from merits and demerits.

The *Brahmasūtra* says that there was nothing like a first creation and that the world is without a beginning.[159] Accordingly, *karma* and inequality are like seed and sprout. They are caused as well as causes.

On the supposition of a beginningless universe, the *Brahmasūtra* explains individual inequalities.[160] It pleads that no one, without *karma,* can come into existence and that *karma* cannot be formed without coming into existence. Other scriptures affirm the beginninglessness of the universe too.[161] In order to explain this topic, we may dilate it further. Every unliberated *ātmā* or self remains in a dormant, potential condition in *Māyā,* the Power of *Brahman,* after a dissolution and before the subsequent creation. In this potential state, all the karmic impressions in the *karmāśaya* of the individual persist to stay in a dormant condition. When the next creation ensues, different *ātmās*, with different *karma* types, get embodied. Thus inequalities in individuals continue due to inequalities in *karma* and beginninglessness of creations.

---

157. *BU,* III.2.13.

158. *CU,* VI.2.1 (*sadeva saumya idamagra āsīd ekamevādvitīyam*); VI.2.2.

159. *BS,* II.35.

160. *BS,* II.1.36.

161. *Ṛ V,* X.190.3; *CU,* VI.3.2; *BG, XV.3.*

The notion that *avidyā* (ignorance) is the cause of evil, suffering and inequalities has also been refuted since it is held that *avidyā* is common to all selves. *Māyā,* the power of *Brahman,* devoid of the reflection of the light of Consciousness of *Brahman,* is insentient. By such a consideration, *Māyā* may be said to be insentient. But *Māyā* is a metaphysical entity, the Power (*Śakti*) of *Brahman,* both the Power and the Possessor of Power not being different. If *Avidyā* is the total ignorance of the universe, or the individual ignorances, it does not concern *Māyā* at all. Thus the ignorance of an individual is not *Māyā.* Hence it is not understood how ignorance is common to all individual entities. Consciousness varies from individual to individual. Hence ignorance should vary in a converse way.

Cycles of creation are to be admitted. The beginninglessness of the cycles is also to be admitted. This, however, does not explain the existence of evil. If one *Brahman* became many, even in the repeated cycles of creation, *Sat, Cit* and *Ānanda* could have continued as such, and *śiva* (good) and *sundara* (beautiful) could have continued without being *aśiva* (bad) *asundara* (ugly).

We may search for a suitable, convincing explanation instead of being satisfied with the traditional one, just mentioned. The sole purpose of God for creating a universe is His sportive play (*līlā*).[162] But no *līlā* is possible in the presence of Pure Consciousness (*Viśuddha Cit*) only, and in the absence of ignorance (*avidyā*). For *līlā* to be operative, whatever was created by *Māyā* was covered by ignorance. This covering was free from partiality and discrimination. Thus it is said that *avidyā* was and is common to all created entities.

The doctrine of limitation is applicable to the Cosmic Mind (*Virāḍ* or *Mahat*). Any micro- or macro-entity that is created

---

162. *BS,* II.1.33.

becomes a limiting adjunct (*upādhi*) for *Brahman* and also for *Virāḍ*. As *upādhi* for *Brahman*, it embodies the individual self (*ātmā*). As *upādhi* for *Virāḍ*, it embodies the individual *buddhi* (intellect). *Ahaṅkāra* (Ego) evolves from *buddhi* and *manas* (mind) evolves from *ahaṅkāra*. The light of consciousness of the self, reflected on the *buddhi* makes the latter sentient. Thus *buddhi* gets induced consciousness. The self does not work. It is *buddhi* along with *ahaṅkāra* and *manas* (the top trio of the *antaḥkaraṇa* or internal instrument) that works. This trio has the freedom in working. It is this freedom that may generate merits or demerits differentially. The freedom of each individual *buddhi* is responsible for inequalities.

*Saṁskāra*s and *vāsanā*s (*vāsanā*s are special *saṁskāra*s) are imprinted on the *buddhi*. Thus the *karmāśaya* (the reservoir of *karma*s) is formed. The *buddhi* of each individual independently acts and each individual's *karma*s are separate from those of others.

The common cover of ignorance which was originally cast by *Māyā* made the Cosmic *Buddhi* translucent. Thus, from the beginning, the Cosmic *Buddhi* lost its transparency. Bad *karma* of an individual renders his *buddhi* more translucent or even opaque. This happens in the analogy of a mirror that loses its reflecting power due to differential deposits of dirt on it. The more dirty it becomes, the less light it reflects. When it becomes fully dirty due to a thick deposit, it completely ceases to reflect any light. Thus is explained the inequality in the ignorance of individuals. The more ignorant a person, the more evil he creates. For this purpose, 'ignorance' does not mean 'lack of informational knowledge'. It really means 'lack of knowledge on *Brahman*'. One may be highly intelligent, qualified and informed; but spiritual wisdom (*prajñā*) may be lacking in him.

The *yogī*'s duty is to clean the mirror of his mind. Once the dirt is removed, he is liberated (*mukta*). This is the concept of liberation (*mokṣa*) of Yoga-Vedānta. There are many scribblings on his *buddhi;* there may be clear written lines and paragraphs on it; the printed matter may be jumbled up and very illegible; the whole surface of the *buddhi* may be disfigured; the pages of the deeper layers of the *buddhi* may be full of deep impressions. It is the duty of the *yogī* to erase all the pages of the *buddhi* — both surface and deeper. If and when he does this erasing work, he attains *mokṣa* (liberation). Once the karmic impressions are totally erased, then ceases the metempsychosis — process of reincarnation.

On the earth, we get water or, chemically speaking, $H_2O$. Water in the sea, in the river, in the spring and fall, in the stagnant pool, in the factory-effluent, in the sewerage pipe and in our urine, faeces and blood is $H_2O$, mixed with dirt, poison and filthy, obnoxious gases, or mixed with useful minerals and tasteful gases. On the acquisition of foreign materials, water acquires colour, odour and flavour. If it acquires medicinal principles, it improves our health. If it acquires toxic materials, it tells upon our health. Water of any source can be filtered and can be distilled and redistilled to restore its purity. It has to be made $H_2O$ by the purificatory processes. *Yoga* provides the purificatory processes to purge all foreign materials from the *buddhi.* An individual *buddhi,* without karmic impressions, becomes non-different from the Cosmic Mind — *Buddhi, Mahat* or *Virāḍ*. On the occasion of the Cosmic Dissolution (*Mahāpralaya*), the Cosmic *Buddhi* dissolves in *Māyā* or the *Mūlaprakṛti* (Primordial Nature).

The individual self (*ātmā*) and the Cosmic Self (*Paramātmā* or God) are not essentially different. The individual self remains hooked up with *buddhi* and *ahaṅkāra* and with the *saṁskāra*s and *vāsanā*s imprinted in the *buddhi.* This hooking up or binding is the bondage (*bandhana*) of the *ātmā.* In the binding process, no change takes place in the *ātmā.* It always remains pure. *A* (*ātmā*) is bound to *B* (*buddhi*) by the valency of *karma.* With the *karma* erased, the binding vanishes, and *A* becomes free (*mukta*). Once the self becomes free, it loses its individual identity and re-establishes its identity with the Great Self or *Ātmā* (God). The Great Self is not extra-cosmic. It is all-pervasive and pervades the individual body too. Both the Great Self and the individual self inhabit the body, the former without eating the fruits and the latter enjoying the fruits of life and experiencing both pleasure and pain.[163] On attaining liberation, the *ātmā* is not to make a long and upward sojourn to reach the *Paramātmā.* In reality, there are no up and down. These concepts are valid with reference to the gravity of our earth while we are on this planet. The *Paramātmā* is right by the side of the *ātmā.* The language 'by the side of' is totally inadequate. We have to express the inexpressible by language and our language for such a purpose is bound to be inaccurate. It is the Great Self, present in our body as the operator of our body machine, that induces *Māyā* to stir the machine to revolve. The individual self, also sitting on the same machine, experiences the swinging of the revolving machine.[164] As long as the self is bound to the *buddhi* and the *ahaṅkāra,* it maintains its individuality and separateness. On the severence of the bond, the self merges with the Great Self and thereupon there is no way to identify the self that had been bound previously and was subsequently released.

Our gross body (*sthūla śarīra*) of matter and energy has come from the parents[165] (through an egg and a sperm and the genes contained therein) and has subsequently grown through assimilation of nutrients. This body is decomposed on death.

---

163. *R̥V,* I.164.20; *KTU,* I.3.1; *MUU,* III.1.1; *ŚU,* IV.6-7.

164. *BG,* XVIII.61.

165. *SPS,* III.7.

Each individual person has a subtle body (*sūkṣma śarīra*) and a causal body (*kāraṇa śarīra*) that survive death.[166] The self (*ātmā*) inhabits the causal body. In the same causal body is located the *karmāśaya* (reservoir of *karma*s) that is the causal agent of rebirth. The gross body is the material sheath (*annamaya kośa*).[167] The causal body is the blissful sheath (*ānandamaya kośa*).[168] In addition, there is a subtle body (*sūkṣma śarīra*) that is constituted of three sheaths, namely, the vital sheath (*prāṇāyama kośa*),[169] the mental sheath (*manomaya kośa*)[170] and the intellectual sheath (*vijñānamaya kośa*).[171] The vital sheath encases the five subtle organs of action (*pañca karmendriya*) and the five *Prāṇa*s (*prāṇa, apāna, vyāna, udāna, samāna*). The mental sheath encases the *manas* (mind) and the five subtle organs of perception (*pañca jñanendriya*). The intellectual sheath encases the intellect (*buddhi*) and the ego (*ahaṅkāra*).

These sheaths (*kośa*) are not concentric spheres. One sheath does not encase another sheath. Being subtle and not being gross, they pervade the whole body. There is no special location in the body in which a sheath is placed and other locations in which a particular sheath is absent. 'Sheath' may be considered, for this purpose, as a subtle container and not a limiting holder. The whole body, each organ of the body, each tissue of each organ, each cell of each tissue, and each sub-cellular entity of each cell contain all the five sheaths.

The sequence of evolution has been presented in the

---

166. *SPS*, III.12; *SK*, 39, 40 & 42; *CU*, III.14.2; *CUŚB*, III.14.2.

167. *TU*, II.2.1; III.2.1.

168. *TU*, II.5.1; III.6.1.

169. *TU*, II.2.1; II.3.1; III.3.1.

170. *TU*, II.3.1; II.4.1; III.4.1.

171. *TU*, II.4.1; II.5.1; III.5.1.

Sāṅkhya philosophy.[172] *Ahaṅkāra* evolves from *buddhi. Manas,* the five subtle organs of perception, the five subtle organs of action and the five *tanmātra*s (subtle fields) evolve from *ahaṅkāra.* The process of involution is just the reverse of that of evolution. The evolute is reconverted into its respective evolvent. Thus, in the process of involution, all the subtle structures are reconverted into *ahaṅkāra* which, in turn, is reconvented into *buddhi. Prāṇa* is not an evolute of *ahaṅkāra* or *buddhi.* It is an evolute of the Primordial Cosmic Fluid (*Āpaḥ*) which is all-pervasive, and which, on getting a limiting adjunct, becomes the vital energy of a particular entity. It is in the same analogy of the Cosmic Mind (*Virāḍ* or *Mahat* or *Buddhi*) that becomes individual *buddhi* on getting a limiting adjunct (*upādhi*). *Āpaḥ* or the Primordial Cosmic Plasma evolves from *Virāḍ.* In the final process of involution, *Virāḍ* or *Mahat* goes back to the state of the Primordial Nature (*Mūlaprakṛti* or *Māyā*).

It may be mentioned here that the Saṅkhya-Yoga accepts the doctrine of transformation (*pariṇāmavāda*) whereas this doctrine is rejected by the Vendānta that holds either *vivartavāda* or *adhyāsavāda. Vivartavāda* is the Vedāntic doctrine that maintains the development of the universe from *Brahman* which is the sole real entity, the phenomenal world being held to be a mere illusion or *Māyā.* We do not accept *vivartavāda* and do not take *Māyā* as a synonym of illusion. *Māyā* is the Power (*Śakti*) of *Brahman* and is a metaphysical entity not second to *Brahman.* The Power (*Śakti*) and the Possessor of Power (*Śaktimān*) are one and the same. Secondly, we do not consider the universe as nothing and as a mere mental illusion. Of course, we do not subscribe to realism. In this regard, we agree with Śaṅkara who advocates the doctrine of *adhyāsa.* He accepts *Brahman* as the absolute reality (*pāramārthika satya*)

172. *SPS,* II.10; II.17; II.18; II.42; *SK,* 22-26.

and the phenomenal universe as the empirical and relative reality (*vyāvahārika* and *āpekṣika satya*).[173] The universe is not as real as *Brahman*. The universe of multiple appearances is the appearance of a single, non-dual reality that is *Brahman* which is the substratum (*adhiṣṭhāna*) of all appearances. We see *B* (*Brahman*) as not-*B* or as *C, D, E, F,* etc., but not as *B*. This illusory appearance is due to *avidyā* or ignorance, which can be corrected by *vidyā* (*Brahma*-knowledge and *Brahma*-realisation). This is the doctrine of *adhyāsavāda* expounded by *Śaṅkara*.[174]

We have rejected the beginninglessness of the cycles of the universe *as an explanation* for the existence of evil. (We have not rejected the beginninglessness of the cosmic cycles, of course). Now we would reject another traditional concept that tries to explain the endlessness of metempsychosis due to the infinite number of selves and the beginninglessness of the cosmic cycles. We reject the explanation only; at the same time, we accept the endlessness of metempsychosis. For this purpose, we do provide an alternate explanation. According to the Bible, a soul is created by God for an individual person, to be born, at the time of conception in the mother's womb. The Bible further says that souls are created out of nothing and only for human beings. The Vedānta conceives of selves (*ātmās*) for every created entity — living and non-living. It is *jīvātmā* for the living being and *bhūtātmā* for the non-living entity. The self is never created. The eternal and timeless *Brahman* is the Self. The all-pervasive Self, within a limiting adjunct, becomes the self (*ātmā*). Without the self which is

---

173. *TUŚB*, I.6 (*ekameva hi paramārthasatyaṁ brahma. iha punarvyavahāraviṣayamāpekṣikaṁ satyam*).

174. See *BSSB*.Introduction, *Adhyāsa Bhāṣyam: atasmiṁstadbuddhiḥ*.

pure consciousness, no particle, no atom, no molecule and no star can function. But their functioning is mere mechanical and law-abiding. No *saṁskāra* traces are left on them. In the evolutionary ladder, the apparatus of the *cit* or *ceta*s evolves, but the *cit* itself does not evolve; as the components of the *citta* or the mind evolve, they become more complicated; and the individual entity gets more freedom in acting. The more evolved the internal instrument (*antaḥkaraṇa*), the more use and abuse of actions and the more intense are the feelings. Hence, unlike the non-living entities and the lower living entities, *saṁskāra*s and *vāsanā*s are printed on the *antaḥkaraṇa*s of higher-evolved animals and especially of human beings. The concept of *karma* is more relevant to humans than to others, if we restrict our discussion to the earth only and exclude probable exobiology. It may not be wrong to suppose that many selves might have been liberated in the past, are being liberated at present and will be liberated in the future. If liberation is a continuous process, the number of unliberated selves may be zero sometime. If that happens, metempsychosis would come to an end point. The concept of an infinite number of selves may save this situation. It is an easy solution and we are not convinced with it.

We rather say that infinite number of *empirical* selves is a possibility and a practicality. Any newly created entity acts as a limiting adjunct (*upādhi*) in which *Brahman* inhabits. Thus not only empirical selves came into being, but also are coming into being and will be coming into being. But all of them will not be bound. In the course of mental evolution, with *buddhi* imprinted with *saṁskāra*s, the question of the empirical bondage of the self arises. Without karmic impressions, no self is bound. With karmic impressions, the self is bound. Without *karma,* there is no transmigration of the self. Thus we present a theory which keeps the number of bound, empirical selves always open.

The *yogī* has been born. His present transmigration has been possible for his past karmic impressions. It is possible for him to prevent the generation of future (*āgāmī*) *karma*s and to erase all the accumulated (*sañcita*) *karma*s (may not be possible to erase the already initiated or *prārabdha karma*) and thus terminate his transmigratory existence after the death of the present body.

# 2.14

## A Flame without Flicker

To control the mind is an important feature of meditation. But mind is always in motion. Calmness and stillness are not the usual properties of mind. Mind moves in straight lines, in curved lines, in a zig-zag way, perpendicularly, vertically, horizontally, in vortices, like whirlpools and like whirlwinds. It seems almost impossible to calm the mind.[175] But it is possible for a *yogī* to yoke the mind and bring it under control. It can be done through practice (*abhyāsa*) and dispassionateness (*vairāgya*).[176]

A lamp in a windless place does not flicker. Similarly a *yogī* who is united with God and whose mind has been controlled remains calm.[177] *Samādhi* is a technical word in *yoga*. The word has two prefixes, namely, *sam* and *ā*. It has been derived from the verb-root *dhā*. It literally means 'to unite', 'to hold together'. In *yoga*, it is the eighth limb, in which the *buddhi* is completely absorbed in *puruṣa* or individual self (according to Patañjali), or in the Great Self (according to the Vedānta). The *yogī*, sitting in *samādhi*, by intently fixing his *buddhi* on the Self and by a complete absorption of the *buddhi* in the Self, keeps his mind motionless.[178]

---

175. *BG*, VI.34.

176. *BG*, VI.35.

177. *BG*,VI.19.

178. *BG*, II.53.

The *yogī* becomes a *sthitaprajña*.[179] Before we state the symptoms of a *sthitaprajña,* we would like to analyse the meaning of the word etymologically. It is a compound word formed by the combination of two words, namely, *sthita* and *prajñā*. The former word has been derived from the Sanskrit verb-root *sthā,* meaning 'to stand'. The latter word has been derived from the Sanskrit verb-root *jñā,* meaning to 'know'. This verb-root has the prefix *pra*. *Prajñā* literally means 'wisdom'. According to Śaṅkara, one whose wisdom is firmly established in the concept that one is the Supreme *Brahman* is *sthitaprajña*.[180]

A *sthitaprajña* purges all desires from his mind. He can differentiate self from non-self. He remains contented in his self by his self. He plays with his self (*ātmakrīḍā*); he finds delight in his self (*ātmārāma*).[181] His mind remains untroubled in the midst of sorrows. He remains free from eager desires amid pleasures. Passion, fear and anger pass away from him.[182] He does not rejoice when he gets something good and does not loathe as he obtains evil.[183] Like a tortoise that draws in its limbs into its shell, the *sthitaprajña yogī* draws away his senses from all sense-objects.[184] Even after drawing away the senses from the sense-objects and after renouncing the sense-objects, one may still be mentally attached to the pleasure contained in them. When the *yogī* has the full realisation that

---

179. *BG*, II.54.

180. *BGŚB*, II.54.

181. *BG*, II.55.

182. *BG*, II.56.

183. *BG*, II.57.

184. *BG*, II.58.

he himself is *Brahman*, he becomes free from any type of passion and attachment.[185]

One may strive for ascending the ladder of *yoga* by controlling one's mind. But the impetuous senses are very forceful. Forcibly they carry off the mind and attach the mind to the sense-objects. In spite of the distractions of the senses, the *sthitaprajña yogī* brings all his senses under his control. In the language of poet Kālidāsa, the *yogī*'s mind is not disturbed even when the sources of disturbance are present.[186] The questions are: 'How can the *yogī* bring all his senses under his control when the latter are uncontrollably forceful? What is the technique for it ?' The *yogī*'s *buddhi,* when completely absorbed in the Self (*Brahman,* Vāsudeva or God), cannot be forcefully won over by the senses that are rather brought under control. He remains united with God, and that union is so strong that the forces of the senses are too feeble to break the bond. The senses yield; they are tamed; they are controlled. The wisdom of such a *yogī* is firmly established. It stands on *Brahman;* it is rooted in *Brahman;* it is absorbed in *Brahman.*[187]

We have already given the etymological meaning of the word *sthitaprajña.* It literally means 'one whose intellect is firm, whose decisions are unwavering'. This is, however, not the contextual meaning of the word in the *Gītā.* According to the literal meaning, Napoleon, Hitler and historically famous persons like them were persons of firm intellect and strong determinations. But they were not *sthitaprajña* of the *Gītā.* Here we would like to refer to the *Māṇḍūkyopaniṣad.*[188] In the said *Upaniṣad,* the word *Prājña* stands for God (*Īśvara*), the third

185. *BG,* II.59.

186. *Kumārasambhava,* I.59.

187. *BG,* II.60-61,

188. *MAU,* 11.

state of *Brahman* in each of us (*Brahman* in the state of deep sleep). The *yogī* who stays in *Prājña* and firmly stays there is *sthitaprajña*.

A person whose *buddhi* is not constantly united with *Prājña* cannot get any true spiritual knowledge on *Brahman*. Such a person's *buddhi* will be opaque rather than transparent. He cannot get knowledge on the self or the Self (*ātmajñāna*). And a person, without knowledge on the Self, cannot get peace.[189]

The *sthitaprajña* state has also been named as the *brāhmī sthitiḥ* (stay in *Brahman*) by the *Gītā*.[190] The forceful and moving mind of a person who is not firmly anchored in *Brahman* drifts his *buddhi* away from the Self and takes towards sense-objects like a boat drifted away by strong winds from the destination towards other places[191].

Stay in *Brahman* (*brāhmī sthitiḥ*) is a supersaturated state. We may take a simile of a glass of water into which salt has been added. More and more salt is added until the solution gets supersaturated. After the state of supersaturation is reached, the water in the glass will dissolve no more salt. The desire of the *yogī* is to reach the state of *brāhmī sthitiḥ*. That is a supersaturated state. It is likened to the mass of water in a sea. The sea is full of water. Any further entry of river-water does not make the sea fuller. The sea is undisturbed. So is the mental state of a *sthitaprajña yogī* into whom desires enter without causing any disturbance therein. The *yogī* has already full peace, which is not going to be fuller.[192]

After attaining the *brāhmī sthitiḥ*, the *yogī* is not shaken

---

189. *BG*, II.66.

190. *BG*, II.72.

191. *BG*, II.67.

192. *BG*, II.70.

even by the heaviest sorrow, and he thinks that there is no greater gain beyond it.[193] At this state, he abandons all desires and acts free from longing. Becoming I-less and my-less, he attains to peace.[194]

---

193. *BG*, VI.22.

194. *BG*, II.71.

# 2.15

## Yoga for Peace

PEACE is disturbed at the physical level. Peace is disturbed at the mental level. Sometimes Nature becomes violent and agitated. This happens is Space, in intergalactic, interstellar and interplanetary space. This happens inside stars, planets and our planet — the earth. Water in the sea and rivers may be agitated. Air may develop low pressure and localised vacuums. Whirlwinds and cyclones may disturb the air-mass. Disturbance of peace may be observed in the plant kingdom and also in the animal kingdom. We do not know if these components of Nature are *mentally* disturbed. Traditionally, the word 'mind' has been hardly applicable to them, although the Vedānta holds that everything, living or non-living, other than *Brahman,* has a mind. Physical disturbance is not uncommon in Nature.

*Homo sapiens* (the human species) occupies a special position on the earth. This is due to the evolution of the human brain. We have maintained that mind (a subtle micro-structure with various micro-components too) is different from the brain which is part of the gross body. We have further maintained that the brain is the apparatus of the mind. According to our theory, every created entity — macro or micro, gross or subtle and living or non-living — has a mind. This is true irrespective of the possession or non-possession of a brain by an entity. The electron, the proton or the neutron has a mind although none of these entities has a brain. There is no created entity without the possession of consciousness. Of course, the exhibition of the symptoms of consciousness varies in a long range due to the variation in the apparatuses of minds. The human brain, an apparatus of the human mind, is the most evolved one among the living species on the earth. Hence human consciousness has reached the zenith when we consider the terrestrial existence. For most purposes, peace is a word that is relevant to mental phenomena. Hence we gave a short description of the controversial issue of brain-mind identity *versus* brain-mind distinction.

Physical agitation and violence do produce disturbance in the mind and thus disturb mental peace. Any simple ailment in any part of the body may seriously affect the mind. A physical event that is unfavourable to the normal functioning of the body may be a potent source of discomfort to cause peacelessness. But mental factors are different from physical ones in the genesis of peace-disturbance. One's peace is disturbed when one does not get success in a competitive examination. One may be disappointed in love-affairs. The death of a kith and kin may be shocking to one. One may be terribly upset in hostilities. Anger may produce serious disturbance in the peace of the mind. In the disturbance of peace, mental factors generally play a more pernicious and a more profound role than physical factors.

In physics and physical chemistry, there are three laws of thermodynamics. The second law contains the concept of 'entropy'. This word was first introduced in 1850 by the German physicist Rudolf Julius Emmanuel Clausius. Entropy is a measure of the degradation of energy. The more energy degrades, the higher the level of entropy. Otherwise speaking, entropy is a measure of the disorder of a system. The more the disorder, the more the entropy.

*Brahman* which is absolutely motionless, functionless and attributeless is absolutely devoid of entropy. The state of

*Brahman* is the state of *ṛta* (perfect order). With the appearance of the Cosmic Egg and its explosion, with the beginning of space and time and with the progress of cosmic activity, disorder (*anṛta*) has been gradually increasing. The increase in disorder is the same as the increase in entropy.

Some scientists are of the opinion that entropy is the arrow of time. Entropy tends to increase and finally will become maximum. Synchronising the maximum disorderliness and the maximum entropy, equalisation of temperature (isothermic condition) will take place. In that condition, without difference in temperature, the whole universe will stop working. First, maximum entropy and zero available energy go together. Second, work is not possible in an isothermic universe. This is the supposed heat-death of the universe. The universe would remain in that non-functional condition for eternity.

We do not agree to the concept of the heat-death of the universe. The presently expanding universe will stop expansion and will start contracting. Finally, the volume of the contracting universe will be zero, with the total dissolution of the universe in *Māyā,* the Power of *Brahman.* Entropy will be zero consequent upon the total dissolution of the universe. There would be no adequate negentropy in the contracting phase to counterbalance entropy quantitatively. Negentropy does occasionally function in both the phases — expanding and contracting, but, quantitatively, entropy processes are far in excess of negentropy ones. Entropy will still increase in the phase of contraction. But the entropy will never reach its maximum stage with the concomitant zero available energy even at the maximum time (the time of dissolution). Contraction is also a work and no work can be done without available energy.

The hypothesis of a non-functional universe existing for eternity goes with the concept of the heat-death of the universe.

Such a hypothesis is untenable, however. Time is not a physical entity. It is a mental construct only. There cannot be time without work and events of work. Hence 'eternity' is meaningless in the absence of work. We use the word 'timelessness' with reference to *Brahman* without a universe. Secondly, both the micro- and the macro- structures of the universe spend energy for maintaining their form and position. This involves expenditure of energy. That the universe will stay without the expenditure of energy is not a valid proposition. Thirdly, no particle and no celestial body can exist without motion. And no motion is possible without expenditure of available energy.

We took a sidewalk to encounter the issue of entropy. This issue is very important in philosophy, especially in the philosophy of cosmology. The source of the spring of disorder is absolute order. Only *Brahman* is in the state of perfect order. From order emanates disorder. From Pure Existence of no form, no attributes and no actions, emanates empirical existence of forms, attributes and actions. The former is devoid of entropy. The latter develops entropy that grows and continues to grow. When the empirical universe is dissolved in the Power of Pure Existence, Consciousness and Bliss, entropy also dissolves.

In the state of no entropy, there is Perfect Peace (*Praśānti*). That Perfect Peace is Bliss (*Ānanda*). It is not really joyfulness which is an attribute, whereas *Brahman* is attributeless (*nirguṇa*).

The production and the growth of entropy in the universe from its birth to its death is a natural phenomenon. It cannot be prevented. We associate entropy with disorder. We associate peacelessness with disorder. Logically we can associate peacelessness with entropy. Hence it is natural for us to infer that peace in the total universe has a tendency to decline. We cannot do anything about it.

Let us now confine our discussion to the prospects of the promotion of peace by *yoga*. To achieve the end, we do not have a single technique which can do the miracle. Most of the things we have discussed in this second part of this book are to be made use of for getting peace in life.

We have to get rid of the six *ripus* (foes), namely, desires and especially sensual desires (*kāma*), anger (*krodha*), greed (*lobha*), delusion (*moha*), pride and arrogance (*mada*) and malice (*mātsarya*). We have to observe the six *yamas*, namely, non-violence, truthfulness, non-stealing, celibacy or abstention from sexual excess and immoral sex-indulgence, and non-acceptance of unearned wealth and non-accumulation of wealth. We should accept the five *niyamas*. Our body, mind and words should be clean. In spite of our utmost efforts and honest and benign strivings, we may not get what we expect. We should be contented with whatever we get irrespective of our expectations. We should be prepared for any suffering if that becomes necessary for a good cause. We should study good scriptures and get good knowledge on *Brahman*. We should dedicate all our work to God and take refuge in Him. Complete surrender to God purges all worries from the mind and saturates the mind with peace.

Meditation renders the mind peaceful. It makes the mind calm and removes all types of agitations from it. It quietens the mind. If one sits in meditation at least twice a day (in the morning and in the evening), one's mental whirlwind will subside and mental disturbances will be quietened. Meditation stills the mind. Stilling the mind brings peace.

Meditation culminating in *samādhi*, the eighth and last limb of *yoga*, anchors the *yogī*'s *buddhi* in God. When it is done, the *yogī* becomes a *sthitaprajña*. He stays in *Brahma* (*brāhmī sthiti*). After attaining to this state of *yoga*, the *yogī*'s life is filled with peace.

Some persons and some societies in the modern age live in affluence, material affluence. But there is a vacuum of peace in their mind. The affluent modern man, with plenty of wealth, with plenty of comforts and luxury, and with plenty of sensual gratification, commits suicide out of complete disgust in life. He has everything except peace. He is alienated from the Self. He identifies himself with matter. His body is all that he is. He is the body-machine. He wants sensual pleasure. He gets it and gets plenty of it. Still he is not satisfied. He is frustrated. He lives a meaningless life. He craves for peace. He does not get it. He shall get it if he lives a yogic life.

The *Bhagavad-Gītā* has rightly given emphasis on peace (*śānti*) in a number of places.[195] The water of a river in spate has whirlpools here and there. With that type of agitation continued, the river-water cannot be calmed. Whirlwind is caused by low pressure that creates partial vacuum. Cyclones and tornados are caused by low pressures in the atmosphere over the sea. A tempestuous atmosphere with a violent storm over the ruffled sea that is tumultuously agitated cannot be calmed unless the cause is removed. The *Gītā* advises to uproot the causes of mental agitation and prescribes techniques to still the mind. In order to be united with the Cosmic Self, the *yogī* has to become a *praśāntātmā* (with a serene and tranquil self).[196] A peaceful mind becomes a prerequisite for advanced yogic attainments.

The Vedic seer foresaw this predicament of *Homo sapiens*. Daily he prayed for peace.

> Let there be peace in the heaven; peace in space; peace on the earth; peace in water; peace in medicinal plants;

---

195. *BG*, II.66; II.70-71; IV.39; V.12; V.29; VI.15; IX.31; XII.12; XVI.2; XVIII.53; XVIII.62.

196. *BG*, VI.14; VI.27.

peace in the plant kingdom; peace for all gods; peace for the whole universe; peace for all. Peace. Peace. Peace.[197]

197. *YV*, 36.17; 30.3

# 2.16

## A Middle Path in Yoga

THERE is a general belief that *yoga* prescribes severe austerities to torture the body and the mind. Such a notion is not true, however. Lord Gautama Buddha prescribed a middle path in conduct. *Yoga* also prescribes a middle path. Unnecessary self-denial and mortification are contraindicated in *Yoga.* The body and the mind are necessary vehicles by which one must travel to reach the spiritual destination. These are not unwanted vehicles. No yogic progress can be made with a sickly weakling. The body must be healthy for doing *yoga.* The mind must be healthy for the practice of the higher limbs of *yoga* (especially *dhyāna, dhāraṇā* and *samādhi.*) Neither too much indulgence nor too much mortification is conducive to *yoga.*

### The middle of the pendulum

The *Bhagavad-Gītā* says: 'Do not adopt extreme steps. Don't reach the left or the right extreme. Stay in the middle'. Neither fasting nor over-eating is good for *yoga.* One should not sleep too long. One should not give up sleep altogether.[198] The *yogī* is temperate in food habits. He takes the right quantity and quality of food. He does not overfeed him and does not undernourish him. He is temperate in exercise, recreation and rest. He does not over-exercise and does not under-exercise. Too little or too much of recreation is not good for him. Too little or too much of rest is not advisable for him. He should not overstrain himself in working. He should not idle away

198. *BG,* VI.16.

his time by working little. His sleep and waking are regulated. His sleeping and waking should be temperate in quantity with punctuality in time. Such disciplined practices in life destroy all sorrow.[199]

## The food and drink of a yogī

Before we proceed on this topic, we would like to etymologically analyse the meaning of the word *śraddhā* which is *śrad-√dhā. Śrat* or *śrad* means 'truth, faithfulness'. The Sanskrit verb-root *dhā* means 'to hold, to have'. Thus the word *śraddhā* means 'faith, trust, confidence, truthfulness, belief in'. It has not an exactly equivalent word in English. We may take a statement and explain its connotation. 'A person *X* practises *yoga* with *śraddhā*'. This statement means that *X* has strong faith in *yoga,* that he has *niṣṭhā* in *yoga,* that is, he steadfastly adheres to it, that he is very sincere in practising it, that he has reverence for it, that it is very dear to him, and that he is determined to go along with it.

The *Gītā* says that *śraddhā* is of three kinds, namely, *sāttvika, rājasika* and *tāmasika*.[200] The first one is good and benign; the second one is passionate; and the third one is inertial, lethargic and dull. These three types take their shapes in accordance with the *svabhāva* (own nature) of a particular person. The *svabhāva* is a collective word which stands for the sum total of the *saṁskāra*s (karmic impressions), built up in the past lives, to which those of the present life are added cumulatively.

The food which promotes longevity, vitality, strength, health, joy, and cheerfulenss is *sāttvika.* This food is nutritious, soft and non-irritant, non-disturbing to the system, and agreeable to the body.[201]

---

199. *BG,* VI.17.

200. *BG,* XVII.2.

201. *BG,* XVII.8.

The *rājasika* food is bitter, sour, saltish, very hot, pungent, harsh and burning. It produces pain, grief and disease.[202]

The *tāmasika* food is spoiled due to long standing, poor in nutrients, putrid, stale, refuse and unclean.[203]

It is desirable that the *yogī* does not eat meat, fish, eggs, and any such food that directly or indirectly involves violence. Man has no right to kill animals and birds. Think of a situation in which man is killed as a food-animal by some species stronger and cleverer than man. What would be the feeling of man in that situation ? Non-violence is the *yama* of priority for *yoga* to be effective. Violence and *yoga* should not go together.

What has been said in the foregoing paragraph concerns the moral aspect. There is the health aspect too. Food of animal origin is generally rich in cholesterol. In contrast, food of plant origin does not contain cholesterol. It is a fact that cholesterol is required by the body. It is a constituent of the brain tissue. It is a precursor material for the biosynthesis of steroid hormones (including the sex hormones). But this requirement can be met with from the source of the endogenous origin. Common food like rice, wheat, oil, etc., is catabolised in our body-cells where acetyl-CoA is a metabolic product. Cholesterol is synthesised by the body cells from this acetyl-CoA. Excess of cholesterol is harmful to our health. It forms an ester in the body. The cholesterol-ester is deposited in the interior wall of blood vessels (arteries) of the heart and brain. As a result, the calibre of blood vessels becomes narrower and the vessel-wall is hardened. This pathological process is known as atherosclerosis. This condition causes stroke in the brain, cardiac disease and hypertension. To counteract the issue of the violence involved in killing animals, some persons

---

202. *BG*, XVII.9.

203. *BG*, XVII.10.

plead for eating vegetarian egg (infertile egg; egg produced by hens without being crossed by cocks). Egg-yolk is very rich in cholesterol (egg-white is albumin which is a protein; it does not contain cholesterol). Although it is rich in nutrients like vitamins and minerals, its cholesterol is the incriminating factor in producing atherosclerosis. In addition to the harmful effects of excess of cholesterol contained in foods of animal origin, such foods sometimes contain some carcinogens (cancer-producing substances). Epidemiological studies have indicated that the incidence of cancer is more among non-vegetarians than among vegetarians.

Sex-abstinence or regulated sex is *brahmacarya* which is one of the five *yama*s of *yoga*. Food of animal origin has the general property of being sex-stimulant (if not aphrodisiac). This is partly due to cholesterol and partly to richness in protein. Over-stimulation of the sex-organs disturbs and distracts the mind. Mental concentration is interfered with. Some sexually over-stimulated persons, when not in their control, resort to abnormal sex practices and may be tempted towards unsocial and criminal acts like rape. It is not a fact that vegetarians are completely free from such offences. But it is to be admitted that vegetarianism is more conducive to *yoga*.

It may not be wrong to infer that non-vegetarian food makes one's psychology more violent and aggressive. We may compare the psychological behaviour of the tiger or the lion with that of the rabbit, the cow, or the deer. It may be difficult to decide which is the cart and which is the horse. The necessity of eating, leading to the catching of prey, may be the cause of showing aggressive behaviour and non-vegetarian food may not be the cause. The organs of the gastro-intestinal tract might have evolved to eat flesh rather than grass. Animals evolved to belong to the family *Canidae* are to live on flesh and, in order to live, they are to be violent and aggressive.

The argument can swing to the other side also. The mental trait of violence has induced the carnivorous animal to eat animals, and this has influenced evolution to structure the body-organs accordingly. The evolved anatomy has also a parallel physiology. In this short discussion, we are not able to draw valid conclusions for the hypothesis that food of animal origin makes the psychology violent and aggressive. But the observed data from the study of Nature are more in favour of this hypothesis.

We do not contend that a non-vegetarian person cannot practise *yoga*. He/she can practise and can get the benefits thereof. The ideal condition of 100 per cent success is rarely obtained. Some percentage of attainment is always more desirable than no attainments at all. We only prescribe vegetarianism for *yoga*-practice. If individual aptitude is contrary to it, one may continue to be a non-vegetarian and practise yoga at the same time. Still we would advise to be moderate and selective. One may avoid eating excess of meat, fish and eggs. One may prefer lean meat to red meat, fish to meat, and small fish to big fish.

The traditional Indian opinion gives a clean chit to milk as a diet. It was regarded as *sāttvika* without conditions. But it is far from truth. Milk, especially mother's milk of the own species, is good for the suckling young. Milk is secreted from the mammary gland for that purpose only. It is not a natural diet for the adults. If adults take milk, the quantity they take should not be in excess. After all, milk is a food of animal origin. It is secreted by the alveolar cells of the mammary gland from the raw materials present in blood. The habitual intake of an excessive quantity of milk fat for a prolonged period makes a person vulnerable to diseases due to the excess of cholesterol and also due to the probability of obesity. Milk-fat is rich in cholesterol. All saturated fats, if taken regularly in excess, are hazardous for health. Of course, milk-fat, due to its content of some unsaturated fatty acids and low-chain fatty acids, is comparatively safer than many other animal fats. But it is not completely safe. Habitual taking of ice-cream, butter and ghee is contraindicated. Lacto-vegetarianism is a classical Indian concept. Some strict vegetarians avoid milk and milk-products from their diets. Butter-milk and curd prepared from separated milk are good for health. Other animal-fats such as beef-fat, lard, pork-fat, and fat from the body of sheep, goats and broilers are very harmful to health. They should be avoided. Hydrogenated fat, although made from vegetable oils, is as bad as animal fats, and may be worse too.

Eggs are not natural foods for human beings or for animals. Mammals are viviparous whereas avians are oviparous. All fertilised eggs contain a fertilised ovum with some degree of cell-division and cell-multiplication. The human foetus or to speak generally, the mammalian foetus, grows in the mother's womb and is nourished by getting nutrients from the mother's blood through the umbilicus. That does not happen with the avian embryo that grows inside the egg when incubated naturally or artificially. The nutrients stored in the egg are meant for the avian embryo. Birds synthesise vitamin C and they don't need it from the diet. Eggs do not contain vitamin C. Inner egg-contents hardly contain any calcium. But it is necessary for bone-growth and also for other physiological processes. And so is the egg-shell made up of calcium carbonate. Eggs we eat are food-packets provided by God (not by Nature) for the nutrition of the would-be avian embryo. No eggs of birds are meant to be foods for human beings.

One vegetarian adult, without taking even milk, can maintain good health. (This statement, however, does not apply to growing children, pregnant and lactating mothers and old persons.) Animal protein is not indispensable in the diet of an adult human. It is a fact that animal proteins have higher biological values than plant proteins. The biological value of the protein of the whole egg is 94, that of milk is 85, of whole wheat is 67 and of cooked navy beans is 38. This picture holds good for growing children, lactating mothers and patients in convalescence. A healthy human adult requires protein for maintenance only. He needs about one gramme of protein for every one kilogram of body weight. Out of this amount of protein, one-third of it is traditionally recommended to come from animal sources. If he takes a variety of plant-proteins, he will have no problems. Lysine and methionine are the limiting amino acids in the diet for humans. But sulphur-containing methionine, because of its higher content in feathers and hairs, is more critical in rats and chicks than in man. Our experimental results have been based on research work conducted on rats and chicks. The human body, in the course of evolution, has lost most of the hairs. And hence is the difference. Lysine, the other limiting amino acid, can be had in required quantity if a variety of protein sources of plant origin are included in the human diet. In Asia and Africa, protein-hunger among people is more of a quantitative nature than of a qualitative nature. The inclusion of more of legumes in the cereal-rich diet would provide the solution. Moreover, in nutritional experiments on animals, growth, based on body-weight, has been the criterion for assessment. In the human species, leanness may be a more desirable health characteristic. Thus we conclude that the *yogī* does not need extra protein supplementation, in quality or quantity, for his practice of *yoga*.

It is very often thought that all vegetarian diets are *sāttvika*. This is the notion especially in India. It is, however, not correct. An imbalanced diet, deficient in some nutrient(s) and excessive in some other(s), is not *sāttvika*. The food that is too greasy, too much over-cooked, badly cooked so as to be deprived of its own nutrients, badly processed with loss of nutrients and with added deleterious substances, is not *sāttvika.* The food that contains an excess of spices and condiments and that is hot with excessively added chillies is not *sāttvika.* A food overstayed in a putrid condition or contaminated with pathogens is harmful to the health and hence is not *sāttvika.* A food cooked and kept in unhygenic conditions cannot be called *sāttvika.*

The tradition of some religious sects in India prohibits eating vegetarian substances such as onions, garlics, some species of legumes and some species of vegetables. It is believed that these food substances or condiments are stimulants and especially sex-stimulants. First, being foods of plant origin, they are genuine constituents of vegetarian diets, and the killing of animals is not an issue in eating them. Second, if stimulant spices are eaten by vegetarians, there is no reason why to avoid onions and garlics that contain some medicinal principles too. Of course, raw and freshly cut onion is irritant and an excess of garlic is stimulant to the gastro-intestinal tract. But the excess may be avoided. Boiled onion is no longer irritant. It has been proved that raw garlic reduces the concentration of cholesterol in blood.

In addition to the quality of food, its quantity becomes also important for *yoga.* The *yogī* should avoid over-eating as well as under-eating. Obesity (adiposity) is contraindicated in *yoga.* Eating calories more than the necessary amount enhances adiposity. Of course, genetic factors and lack of exercise are contributing factors too. But dietatic control with some amount of exercise (*yogāsana*s or otherwise) ameliorates the genetic predisposition. One-half of the stomach should be filled with food. One-quarter of the stomach should be filled with water. The rest one-quarter of the stomach should be empty. Instead of overloading the stomach through two or three meals, it would be better to eat more number of times (say four times) and eat less quantity of food at a time. Plenty of green and salad vegetables would be good for health. Some food with fibre would be useful. Natural fresh foods would be better than artificially processed foods. More refined, calorie-rich food, fat-rich food and sugar-rich food should be minimised.

The *Gītā* has not issued commandments to eat this and not to eat that. For any action to be done, the *Gītā* prescribes: 'Without attachment, do what should be done'.[204] It does not specify and spell out that which should be done. Any such issue is open for the present and the future. Further investigations and discoveries should be able to update human knowledge, and thus there are always chances for correction and improvement. Three verses of the seventeenth chapter of the *Gītā* with reference to food have already been quoted.[205] In none of them, there is such commandment as 'Eat this and don't eat that'. The fundamental principles and working guidelines have been given. It is man who is to find out what is good and what is bad.

Intoxicants are to be avoided if *yoga* is to be practised. One cannot be a drug-addict and a *yogī* simultaneously. Intoxicating agents exert profoundly adverse effect on the nervous system and on the mind. They are harmful to the body. They are habit-forming. An intoxiated person cannot control his own faculty; he cannot discriminate good from bad; no crime is bad for him since he is not in his sense. He ruins his health, both physical and mental; he ruins his economic condition; he spoils his family relations; he spoils

---

204. *BG*, III.19 (*tasmādasaktaḥ satataṁ kāryaṁ karma samācara*).

205. *BG*, XVII.8-10.

his conduct and behaviour; he spoils his character. He degrades himself to sub-human levels or to sub-bestial levels. He becomes a big liability on his family and on the society. The intoxicant may be opium or opium-products, may be *gāñjā* (marijuana) or *bhāṅga* (leaves and flower-tops of Indian hemp) or may be any alcoholic drink; it should be avoided for getting success in *yoga*. Alcoholic drinks have been very common in the society. Some *yoga-guru*s advise to be moderate in taking alcohols. We are, however, reluctant to be permissive to this extent. *Yoga* and intoxication should not go together.

In addition to food and drink, the *yogī* is to follow the middle path in many other activities of life. We categorise three types of *yogī*s. The mendicant monks belong to the first type. They live on alms. They have completely renounced the world. Salvation or spiritual liberation is their only goal in life. In traditional Indian system of life, this is the fourth and last *āśrama* (the last quarter of the expected life-span of one hundred years; a hermit's dwelling place) of a person. The ancient Hindu sages or saints (*ṛṣi*s), belonging to the second type, were living in *āśrama*s (hermitage; a hermit's dwelling place), far away from the hubnub of the crowd, generally located in the outskirt of forests. They were generally married. They lived with their families and disciples. They did not possess property. They avoided sensual indulgence and luxury. They had moderately restricted, regulated sex-life. They dedicated all their actions to the spiritual welfare of the universe. These sages were the second type of *yogī*'s (here 'second' is not used in the sense of grading). The third type of *yogī*s are the householders who practise *yoga*. This book is primarily meant for the householder (*gṛhastha*) *yogī*s. They should follow the middle path. We do not recommend self-abnegation for them. Neither do we recommend indulgence. They may marry and live a regulated sex-life. We prohibit extra-marital sex-relations. Some money, a house, some household articles and some other facilities are necessary for life. They should earn *enough* to get the optimum facilities for life. This earning should not be immoral. They should avoid accumulation of wealth (*parigraha*). For the householder, *yoga* is the art of living. This art shows a direction in life, gives peace and tranquillity to life, and makes the life contented and full.

# PART 3
# BENEFITS FROM MEDITATION

# 3.1

# Psychosomatic and Somatopsychic Effects

## Cartesian dilemma

THE word 'psyche' means 'soul', 'spirit' or 'mind'. Etymologically it has been derived from a Greek word meaning 'soul', 'life' or 'breath'. The classical Western thought on mind has been hinging on this Greek idea which equated mind and soul. René Descartes, the seventeenth-century French philosopher and mathematician, established his theory of dualism (body-mind dischotomy) which influenced Western philosophy, psychology and science to a great extent. Cartesianism steadfastly held the idea that God created minds and bodies, that mind is non-material whereas body is material, and that mind and body cannot influence each other.

The Cartesian dichotomy of mind and body had its full sway on Western thoughts for about three and a half centuries. It was discarded in the twentieth century in which the dominant view went in favour of brain-mind identity. The brain being matter, the distinction between matter and mind was no longer held to be tenable.

With the acceptance of Cartesianism, the exclusiveness of the mind-body dualism posed a problem. If soul (mind) and body are utterly unlike, it is impossible to explain how their interaction occurs. Occasionalism of the same seventeenth century brought about a pseudo-solution to the pseudo-problem. It is a theory that God is the intermediary between soul and body. On each occasion of the soul's consent to a given action, God moves the body. It is God, too, who delivers to the soul the awareness of any physical modification of the body.

We reject Cartesian dualism and also occasionalism. We do not accept the modern view of mind-body identity. To clarify the controversial issue, we would present a short description of the Vedāntic view of mind. Although we do not prove the truth of our claim in this brief description, we present our concept on mind which is at variance with the Western concept.

### Vedāntic concept of mind

The individual self (*ātmā*) is not *essentially* different from the Great Self (*Paramātmā*). *Brahman* and *ātmā* are identical. Thus we do not sustain the idea that soul and mind are non-different.

*Brahman* is the Fundamental Consciousness and Pure Consciousness. Matter as such is insentient. Matter, on getting the reflection of the Fundamental Consciousness, acquires sentience. Each created entity, micro or macro, is conscious. This consciousness of matter is induced.

The first manifested evolute in the long sequence of creation was *Virāḍ* or *Mahat* (*Buddhi* or Cosmic Mind). *Virāḍ* evolved from *Mahāmāyā,* the Power (*Śakti*) of *Brahman* and everything else of the universe evolved from *Virāḍ. Virāḍ* or *Buddhi* may be considered as the first empirical consciousness. If mind is considered as empirical consciousness, it is not different from *Buddhi.* We use *Buddhi* for the Cosmic Collective Mind and *buddhi* for the mind in each manifested entity which functions as a limiting adjunct (*upādhi*) by encasing the Cosmic *Buddhi.* Thus each *buddhi* of each created entity is its primary mind. The Sāṅkhya School of Philosophy holds that *ahaṅkāra* is an evolute of *buddhi* and that *manas* is an evolute of *ahaṅkāra.* The Vedānta School has assigned no place to *manas* in its evolutionary chronology or sequence. Of course, the *Vedānta manas* is not the same as the Sāṅkhya *manas* whose function is restricted to receiving sensations from the five subtle organs of perceptions and issuing direction to the five subtle organs of actions. The Vedānta uses the word *manas* for the agency of sentient activities in general and refers primarily to *cit* or induced consciousness which does not evolve. Its subtle *upādhi* (limiting adjunct or embodying container) evolves. We use the word *antaḥkaraṇa* (internal instrument) for this *upādhi.* In the language of the Sāṅkhya, the *antaḥkaraṇa* is made up of *buddhi, ahaṅkāra, manas,* five subtle organs of perceptions and five subtle organs of actions. Pātañjala *Yoga* uses the word *citta* which, being a component of *buddhi,* plays the role of the thinking substance. The five *kośa*s (sheaths), the seven *cakra*s, some additional minor *cakra*s, the prāṇic channels or *nāḍī*s and the *karmāśaya* (reservoir of *karma*s) are components of the subtle and the causal bodies, which may not be strictly called the *antaḥkaraṇa.* It is the *antaḥkaraṇa* which is popularly known as mind.

We referred to the mental *upādhi* (*antaḥkaraṇa*) which is different from the mental apparatus. The brain, the spinal cord and the peripheral nerves constitute the apparatus or the instrument of the mind. The Vedāntic doctrine of mind rejects the notion of the brain-mind identity and asserts that the mind uses the brain and the gross organs of perceptions (gross visual, auditory, olfactory, gustatory and tactile organs) as its instruments.

The subtle body has seven *cakra*s, namely, *mūlādhāra, svādhiṣṭhāna, maṇipūra, anāhata, viśuddhi, ājñā* and *sahasrāra,* with interconnecting subtle channels (72,000 in number) for the flow of the prāṇic energy. The five subtle and gross organs of perception and the five subtle and gross organs of action are regulated by the five lower *cakra*s. The *mūlādhāra* controls the nose, the excretory organs and the *apāna vāyu*. The *svādhiṣṭhāna* controls the taste buds, the reproductive organs and *vyāna vāyu*. The *maṇipūra* controls the visual organs, the locomotor organs and the *samāna vāyu*. The *anāhata* controls the tactile organs, the hands and the *prāṇa vāyu*. The *viśuddhi* controls the vocal organs, the auditory organs and the *udāna vāyu*. The *ājñā* is the seat of the principal *antaḥkaraṇa* consisting of *buddhi, ahaṅkāra* and *manas*. The *sahasrāra* is the supreme controlling authority of all the subtle and gross organs.

There are two minor *cakra*s known as *hr̥daya-puṇḍarīkam* and *bindu*. The former is in the chest in between the *anāhata* and the *viśuddhi*. The latter is in between the *ājñā* and the *sahasrāra*.

Long-term memory has no location in the brain-tissue or anywhere in the nervous system. The memory store is in the subtle body. It is in the *ājñā*. In addition to the memory pertaining to the present life, the karmic *saṁskāra*s of the past lives which have not yet been fructified have also been recorded and stored in the *buddhi* located in the *ājñā*. This karmic reservoir is known as *karmāśaya*. Some *saṁskāra*s and *vāsanā*s are stored in the deeper layers of the subtle body. They may be concerned with the present life or the past lives. This deep storage is the Unconscious. Easy retrieval is done from the conscious, but not from the Unconscious. If the Conscious and the Unconscious make a total of one hundred, the former is only about 10 per cent and the latter is about 90 per cent.

All the subtle entities that have been described with reference to the individual empirical consciousness combinedly constitute the *antaḥkaraṇa* (inner instrument) that forms the micro-apparatus of the mind. This micro-apparatus uses the brain and its related nervous system as the macro-apparatus.

The Fundamental Consciousness (*Cit* or *Brahman*) is not material. According to Sāṅkhya, even *buddhi* is material, although it is the subtlest matter. Since *Mahat* or *Virāḍ* or *Buddhi* is the first evolute from the *Mūlaprakr̥ti* or *Māyā,* and *buddhi* is *Buddhi* encased in an created entity, *buddhi* is regarded as the subtlest form of matter. The micro-apparatus which is the *antaḥkaraṇa* is material, albeit very subtle. Hence, for the Vedānta, the Cartesian problem of the interaction between matter and spirit (body and mind) does not exist. The interaction between body and mind is that between matter and matter.

### Phychosomatic effects

The word 'psyche' is retained, although its ancient meaning has been discarded. At present, it simply means 'mind' irrespective of the diverse interpretations of the concept of mind. It has been well recognised that mind exerts its influence on the body. This phenomenon is known as psychosomatic effect.

There are a number of psychosomatic diseases. Bronchial asthma, eczema, peptic ulcer and ulcerative colitis are some such diseases. At least one of the aetiological factors of bronchial asthma is mental allergy. There is something disagreeable to the mind. This results in the exhibition of typical symptoms of asthma in the lower respiratory passages. The root is in the mind; the fruit is in the body. The most common cause of eczema is allergy. The allergen may be a physical agent, a chemical agent or a dietetic factor. It may also be an unpleasant mental factor, deeply buried in the Unconscious. Peptic ulcer (stomach ulcer or duodenal ulcer) may primarily be a genetic predisposition. The acid (HCl)-

secreting cells in the stomach wall may be present in higher number. The vagus-supply to the stomach may be more irritated by higher rate of neuro-electrical stimulation from the central origin in the medulla oblongata in the brain. *Helicobacter pylori*, a pathogenic bacteria, may attack the mucous membrane of the stomach or the duodenum and may be the aggravating and complicating factor. Over and above all these causal factors, it is also to be recognised that prolonged worries, stress and strain or mental tension may produce hyperacidity and peptic ulcer as a sequel to the acidity. Ulcerative colitis is a disease of the colon, with ulcerative lesions in its mucous membrane. In the mild form of the disease, it may be an irritable colon; in its moderately severe form it may develop as mucous colitis. In the highly severe form, it is ulcerative. The symptoms may be exhibited by recurrent episodes of diarrhoea preceded or followed by constipation. This disease usually occurs after some specific emotional conflict. Do emotional disturbances directly produce the disease? Are they only the precipitating factors for the onset of the disease, caused by some other specific agent? Disputes prevail over the issue of the primary cause *versus* the secondary cause of ulcerative colitis. In this regard, Prof. Dr. K.N. Udupa (M.D.) of Banaras Hindu University remarks: 'We are convinced that this disease is caused by intense psychological trauma'.[1]

## Somato-psychic effects

When we use the term 'psychosomatic interaction', it conveys a two-way meaning. Mind influences the body and the body influences mind. 'Psychosomatic disorders or diseases', however, conveys a one-way meaning. It states that mind can cause disorders in the body. The concept of psychosomatic disorders has been well established in medical science and

1. Udupa, K.N., 1985, p. 266.

psychology. This is, however, not the case with 'somato-psychic disorders'. In such cases, the stimulus is in the body and the response is in the mind. Any serious and prolonged disorder in the body may cause disorders in the mind. The mental disorder may be mild in nature or may take a serious form.

## The source of stimulus for the cerebral cortex

There are four sources of stimulus for the cerebral cortex. These are: Environment, body, conscious mind and unconscious mind. The first two sources are generally recognised; the last two sources are hardly accepted.

The environment may favourably or unfavourably influence the cerebral cortex. Sometimes an unfavourable environment may be seriously traumatic to the cerebral cortex. The five sense-organs, namely, eyes, ears, nose, taste-buds and skin, are the connecting links between the cerebral cortex and the environment. These are the exteroceptors.

The interoceptors are embedded in the internal organs of the body such as the viscera, endocrine glands and blood vessels. They have three parts: (a) peripheral division, (b) intermediate division that is the conducting pathway up to the subcortical level, (c) cerebral division consisting of nuclei in the cerebral cortex. The interoceptors keep on informing the cerebral cortex about their respective organs.

The third source of stimulus for the cerebral cortex is the conscious mind which is only about 10 per cent of the total mind. The conscious mind wills and that will is translated into action by the cerebral cortex. It is the *ahaṅkāra* that wills. If willing is in the form of a strong resolve (*saṅkalpa*), it evokes response in the cerebral cortex.

The fourth source of stimulus for the cerebral cortex is the Unconscious which constitutes about 90 per cent of the total mind. It is the cumulative deposit of mental impressions through past lives including the present life. New additions are made to the mental reservoir. Old impressions, on fruition, are subtracted from the mental reservoir. The total deposit existing at any particular time is the *saṁskāra-piṇḍa.* The mental reservoir is known as *karmāśaya.* Mental impressions of strong emotional attachments are *vāsanā*s. All *vāsanā*s are *saṁskāra*s, but all *saṁskāra*s are not *vāsanā*s. *Vāsanā*s are embedded in the deeper layers of the Unconscious. The reservoir of *vāsanā*s is known as *vāsanāśaya. Saṁskāra*s and *vāsanā*s of the Unconscious bubble up from below and unconsciously affect the conscious mind that ultimately influences the cerebral cortex.

The cerebral cortex, on receiving information from any of the four sources, informs the prefrontal area of the cerebrum. This area sends efferent impulses to the hypothalamus through the limbic system. It is the hypothalamus that activates the autonomic nervous system and the pituitary.

### Holistic constitution

From the foregoing discussion, it becomes obvious that body and mind are not two separate entities of an individual. They are not two entities insulated from each other. They are not independent of each other. If one is affected, the other is also affected. They are interrelated in a reversible way. They work integrally for the interest of the holistic individual.

# 3.2

# Physiopathology of Stress Disorders

THAT stress causes physiological disorders and serious pathology in the system has been confirmed by empirical observations. There is no doubt in the observations. The question is: What is the mechanism of action? How do we explain the fact scientifically? First we may present a brief note on the relevant nervous system.

## Divisions of the nervous system

The nervous system has two divisions, namely, central nervous system and peripheral nervous system. The brain inside the cranium and the spinal cord inside the vertebral column constitute the central nervous system (CNS). Both these structures are continuous. Nerves that originate from the CNS to innervate various organs and tissues in the body belong to the peripheral nervous system (PNS). The peripheral nerves branch and rebranch before they reach the farthest tissues of the body. A schematic diagram of the peripheral nervous system has been presented in *fig*. 3.1. The human body has 12 pairs of nerves that originate from the brain and connect the organs such as eyes and ears directly to the brain. These are called cranial nerves. Spinal nerves are 31 pairs in number. They branch out from the spinal cord to reach organs and tissues of the body. The cranial and the spinal nerves belong to the PNS. The PNS has two types of neurons (nerve cell = neuron; a nerve cell has a cell-body consisting of a nucleus and protoplasm, surrounded by a cell wall, and a fibre of varying length that transmits electrical impulses), namely, sensory neurons and motor neurons. The sensory neurons transmit messages from the body and senses to the CNS. The motor neurons transmit impulses of work-order from the CNS to the peripheral organs and tissues. The sensory pathway is known as afferent and the motor pathway efferent.

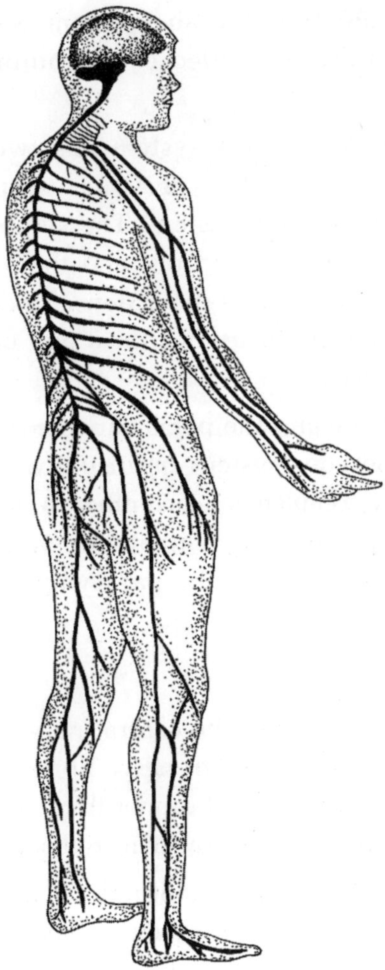

*fig.* **3.1 A schematic diagram of the peripheral nervous system**

The motor nerves belong to two different systems, namely, somatic or skeletal system and autonomic system. Motor neurons of the somatic system control voluntary muscle movements. Motor neurons of the autonomic system regulate involuntary muscle actions. The beating of the heart, the normal breathing movements, the gastro-intestinal muscle movements, the muscle movements of the blood vessels, etc., go on without our thinking about them. Such actions are involuntary and are controlled by the autonomic nervous system.

The autonomic nervous system has two sub-systems, namely, the sympathetic nervous system and the parasympathetic nervous system. The sympathetic system accelerates (speeds up) the actions and the parasympathetic system retards (slows down) the actions. To cite an example, sympathetic nerves speed up heartbeat and parasympathetic nerves slow it down.

The sympathetic and the parasympathetic sub-systems of the autonomic nervous system *apparently* work against each other. They really complement each other in normal situations. In stressful conditions, the sympathetic system dominates. During times of relaxation, the parasympathetic system is dominant.

## Spinal cord

The spinal cord belongs to the central nervous system. It is basically a transmission cable of nerve fibres lying within the vertebral column (backbone). It cannot think. However, it does have some decision-making power in reflex actions.

The spinal cord is an important reflex centre. Reflex action may be better explained by an example. One's hand touches a hot iron. A sensory nerve from the skin sends a message to the spinal cord immediately. Without taking time, the spinal cord sends its order through a motor nerve to pull one's hand away. This is a reflex action. For such emergency actions, the spinal cord takes its own decision without waiting for the command of the brain. Of course, the spinal cord informs the brain about the incidence. But it takes action before the brain feels the pain and before the brain sends some order.

**The cerebral cortex of the brain**

The brain is located inside the cranium. Our thinking, decision-making, feeling, creative work, intelligence and all such mental activities are done by the brain. The outermost and uppermost part of the brain is the cerebral cortex. It is a folded and refolded structure abundantly rich in nerve cells. it is the 'thinking brain'. The human brain has a much greater size of the cerebral cortex, compared to animal brains. The more evolved the animal, the greater the size of its cerebral cortex. The cerebral cortex does not have direct nerve-connections with the internal organs. In contrast, the brain stem has direct connections with all the internal organs through the medulla oblongata and the spinal cord. Parts of the frontal and temporal lobes of the cerebral cortex constantly communicate and interact with limbic structures. The cerebral cortex makes its contact with the internal organs of the body through various subcortical structures.

The cerebral cortex is divided into four lobes, viz., frontal lobe, parietal lobe, temporal lobe and occipital lobe. These lobes have been illustrated in *fig*. 3.2. The ophthalmic (vision) centre, situated in the occipital lobe at the extreme back of the brain, receives and interprets visual signals. The temporal lobes, named for their location at the temples, are involved in hearing and memory. Nerves from both ears go to each temporal lobe in which our hearing centres are located. The limbic system is responsible for our love, hatred, fear, anger, lust, greed, emotion, delusion and jealousy. The temporal lobe, through its links with the limbic system, affects these behavioural qualities. The parietal lobes are located at the back top half and sides of the brain. They are just to the rear of the frontal lobes. The frontmost portion of the parietal lobe is the somatosensory cortex. The rearmost portion of the frontal lobe is the motor cortex. The Broca's area (identified by Paul Broca), located in the left frontal lobe, controls muscles that produce speech. The Wernicke's area (identified by Karl Wernicke), present on the left temporal lobe, is a centre for understanding speech. Four senses (visual, auditory, gustatory and tactile) have areas of the cerebral cortex devoted to them. The olfactory sense is a notable exception. Each primary receptor cell, present in the mucous membrane of the nose, is connected to a nerve fibre which runs without interrruption to the olfactory bulb which is the enlarged distal end of the olfactory lobe. This olfactory lobe is on the lower surface of the brain's frontal lobe. It is responsible for the sense of smell. The olfactory lobe is better developed in many animals (especially species of the canine family — dogs, foxes, jackals, wolves) than in man.

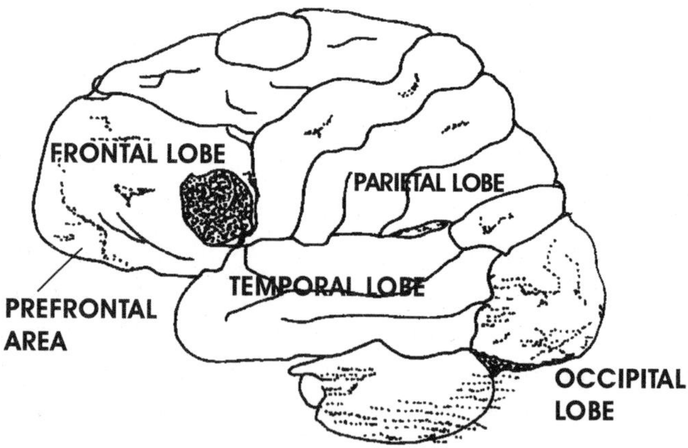


*fig.* **3.2 The four lobes of the cerebral cortex**

## Three divisions of the cerebral cortex

The human cerebral cortex may be divided into three areas, namely, the sensory area, the motor area and the associated area. The cerebral centres for senses other than the tactile have already been mentioned.

The somatosensory cortex receives signals from touch receptors. In addition, it responds to heat, cold, pain and body position. The more sensitive a body part is, the more space the somatosensory cortex devotes to it. The hands and fingers, the teeth, lips and tongue owe their higher sensitivity to the huge amount of brain tissue devoted to them.

The motor cortex extends across both the cerebral hemispheres like the somatosensory cortex which is behind the former. The motor cortex controls the voluntary muscles of the body. Specific regions of the motor cortex are devoted to movements of specific parts of the body. Nerve fibres are sent from these regions to the brain stem and the spinal cord, which in turn make appropriate synaptic connections to send nerve-impulses through specific peripheral nerves to the muscles.

The cortical regions that are not concerned with sensory and motor activities are the *association areas.* The term does not correctly convey the functions of the areas which are involved in complex psychological functions such as the production and understanding of language, thought, memory, imagery, creativity, intelligence, wisdom and any such higher mental activity.

## Psychic centre

We have already mentioned the frontal lobe of the brain. It is the anterior part of either of the two hemispheres of the cerebrum. The prefrontal cortex is the anterior portion of the frontal lobe. It is this prefrontal area which is the psychic centre.

The posterior part of the frontal lobe is the motor cortex. The rest of the frontal lobe and especially the prefrontal area are not concerned with sensory and motor activities. This front part of the brain is the third eye of Śiva. It is the psychic centre, the centre of intuition, intellection and creativity. It is the seat of conscience that discriminates good from bad, right from wrong and moral from immoral.

If we consider the evolution of the brain, the cerebral cortex is ill-developed in avians and hardly developed in still lower species. Among mammals, the human species has the most developed cerebral cortex. Furthermore, the prefrontal area is much more developed in the human species than in other mammals.

The focus of *dhāraṇā* in meditation is the prefrontal area. It is *locationally* related to the *ājñā-cakra*. Here a note is necessary to expel confusion. Many modern authors have tried to identify the subtle organs such as *cakra*s and *nāḍī*s with the gross organs. The *ājñā* has been wrongly identified with the pituitary gland, or pineal gland, or the prefrontal area. Similarly, the *suṣumṇā nāḍī* has confusedly been identified with the spinal cord or the central canal in the spinal cord. The structures of the subtle body are distinct from those of the gross body. Even the electron microscope has not been able to detect the subtle body which is too subtle to be detected even by such sophisticated apparatus. We used the term 'locationally related' to bring about any relation between the prefrontal area and the *ājñā-cakra*. It is a question of reference point for description. Identification is totally ruled out.

The psychic centre is well informed through nerve connections. It is the executive head of the body. Exteroceptors send messages to the ophthalmic centre in the occipital lobe and the auditory centre in the temporal lobe. With reference to stressful stimuli, only the visual and the auditory receptors play important role. The vision centre and the hearing centre keep on informing the psychic centre. Interoceptors present in the internal organs and tissues of the body send stressful stimuli to the subcortical brain that relays the message to the specific cerebral centres (the cerebral cortex has no direct nerve connection with the internal organs and tissues of the body). All these messages ultimately converge on the psychic centre. In stressful situations, the psychic centre provides defence mechanism to the body. It regulates the basic excitation and inhibition balance of the brain. The inhibitory mechanism is usually more upset than the excitatory mechanism in the state of prolonged and profound stress. When the mental trauma is too serious and stressful stimuli operate for a prolonged period, the defence mechanism usually fails and the person's capacity to fight against the stress breaks down. It is meditation that prevents this condition through its favourable influence on the psychic centre. We will dilate this topic later.

**Left and right cerebral hemispheres**

Some individuals are more logical, rational and scientific. Some other individuals are more artistic, emotional and intuitive. Why is this difference ? All the exact answers are perhaps not available with us. There may be structural differences between the left brain and the right brain. There may be structural differences in the limbic system. We will take up the limbic system a little later. Here we propose to present a brief description of the left and the right brains.

The brain is divided down the middle into two hemispheres, the right and the left. The corpus callosum is the main connecting link between the right and left hemispheres. The left hemisphere is more logical. It is the mathematical, scientific and rational brain. The right hemisphere is more creative. It is the artistic, emotional and sentimental brain.

Persons whose left brain is more dominant have better aptitude for mathematics and science. Persons whose right brain is more dominant have better fascination for fine arts, poetry, and the like; they are more imaginative. There are rare persons whose left and right brains are equally developed. They are good in both science and art. What has been said here is on the mental aptitude. The two hemispheres control our body differently too. The left half of the brain controls the right side of the body and the right half of the brain controls the left side. Notwithstanding the differential patterns of the two halves of the brain, the hemispheres of a normal brain hardly exist in total isolation. Between them runs the corpus callosum which is packed with innumerable nerve fibres. This corpus callosum is not a mechanical partitioner; it is an interbrain connector.

### The secretary of the executive head

The thalamus consists of two oval-shaped lobes. It lies at the core of the brain, beneath the cerebrum and above the brain stem. It functions as the secretary of the cerebral cortex. It is mostly a multi-relay-centre. It is a key communication link between the cerebral cortex and the other parts of the brain and between the cerebral cortex and the organs and tissues of the body. Almost all the afferent nerve-pathways of the body terminate in the thalamus. It is the thalamus that informs the cerebral cortex about what happens in different parts of the body. The thalamus is well connected with the frontal lobe by afferent and efferent pathways.

The thalamus receives incoming signals, determines their source and evaluates their importance before passing them on to the cerebral cortex. It receives outgoing signals from the cerebral cortex and passes them on to the other parts of the brain, to the spinal cord and to the organs and tissues of the body.

In addition to the secretarial work done by the thalamus, it registers signals from pain receptors and labels them painful. Pain-receptors transmit pain signals to the thalamus via two main nerve pathways. The express pain route is made up of large nerve fibres that allow pain messages to be transmitted at about 354 km per hour. The slower pain pathway is made up of small nerve fibres that transmit dull throbbing sensation. After receiving the pain message, the thalamus routes it to the cerebral cortex, near the front of the brain.

## The limbic system

There is no scientific agreement about the nomenclature of 'the limbic system'. Anatomically speaking, it can hardly be said where this system starts and where it stops. Some scientists are in favour of discarding the usage of 'limbic system'. Notwithstanding this controversy, the limbic system may be considered as a functional unit (if not a structural unit). Three structures of the brain are the *main* components of this unit. They are: the hypothalamus, the amygdala and the hippocampus. This unit is our emotional switchboard. *Fig.* 3.3 illustrates the location of the thalamus, the hypothalamus, the amygdala and the hippocampus.

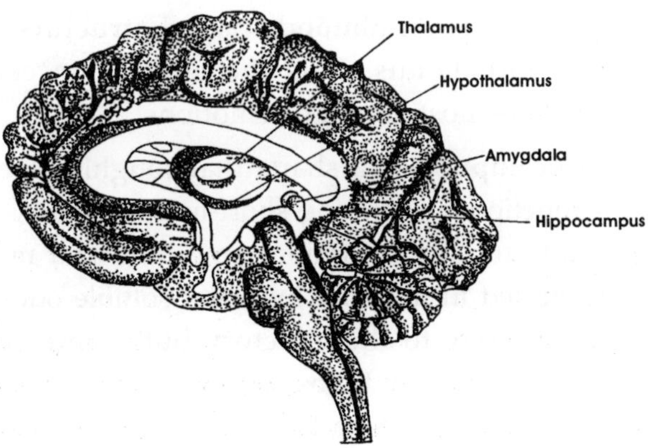


***fig.* 3.3 The locations of the thalamus, the hypothalamus, the amygdala and the hippocampus**

The hypothalamus is situated below the thalamus. It is a small-sized structure whose weight hardly exceeds fifteen grams. By the hypothalamus, we feel and express our emotions. It is the hypothalamus that regulates the autonomic nervous system. The thirst centre, and the appetite centre (feeding centre and satiety centre) are situated in the hypothalamus. The body has a thermostat in the hypothalamus. It regulates the body temperature. The hypothalamus regulates the pituitary gland which is the master endocrine gland in the body. The pituitary, in turn, regulates all the other endocrine glands of the body. Thus the hypothalamus exercises its control over the hormone-production in the body by its direct effect on the pituitary and indirect effect on the other endocrines. The hypothalamus does not transmit any electrical message to the pituitary through any nerve pathway. It sends a chemical message to the pituitary gland through blood. On receiving the chemical message, the pituitary gland secretes trophic hormones such as gonadotrophic hormones, corticotrophic hormones, thyrotrophic hormones, etc. The hypothalamus is said to contain a 'sex nucleus' through which the emotionality in sex-life is influenced.

The amygdala is an almond-shaped structure situated below the hypothalamus. It is the aggression centre. Its stimulation causes hostile, angry emotions.

The hippocampus has a shape that roughly resembles a seahorse. It functions in forming short-term memory. Through this organ, odours stir sensation, emotions and memories. Impulses generated in the nose by water-soluble odouriferous materials go directly to the olfactory bulbs and the limbic system. The two olfactory bulbs are extensions of the brain's limbic system; they are lima-bean-sized organs behind the bridge of the nose. From these organs smell signals move to the hippocampus of the limbic system. Through the hippocampus, certain smells can arouse emotions and can recall old memories. Through it, smell is also involved in arousing sexual urges.

The smell areas in the limbic system in animals, especially in dogs, cats, tigers, etc., are more developed than in humans.

**Brain stem**

The base of the human brain lying beneath the cerebrum and the cerebellum is the brain stem (*fig*. 3.4). It consists of the midbrain (mesencephalon), the pons and the medulla oblongata. It connects the spinal cord with the forebrain. The medulla oblongata is located at the top end of the spinal cord. It consists of nerve fibres and nerve centres. Many areas in the reticular substance of the medulla, pons and midbrain as well as many special nuclei in the hindbrain (the back part of the brain is known as the hindbrain which includes the cerebellum, pons and the medulla oblongata) control a number of autonomic functions such as arterial pressure, heart rate, glandular secretion mainly in the upper gastrointestinal tract, gastrointestinal peristalsis, the degree of contraction of the urinary bladder, and many others. The medulla oblongata contains the cardiovascular regulatory centres that regulate the arterial pressure and the heart rate. Closely associated with the cardiovascular regulatory centre in the medulla is the medullary centre for the regulation of respiration. Although the respiration-regulatory centre is not an autonomic function, it is one of the many involuntary functions of the body. The autonomic control centres of the brain stem have been illustrated in *fig*. 3.5.

The autonomic control centres in the hindbrain are not fully autonomic. They have autonomy, but have no sovereignty. Signals from the hypothalamus and even from the cerebrum can affect the activities of the autonomic control centres in the hindbrain.

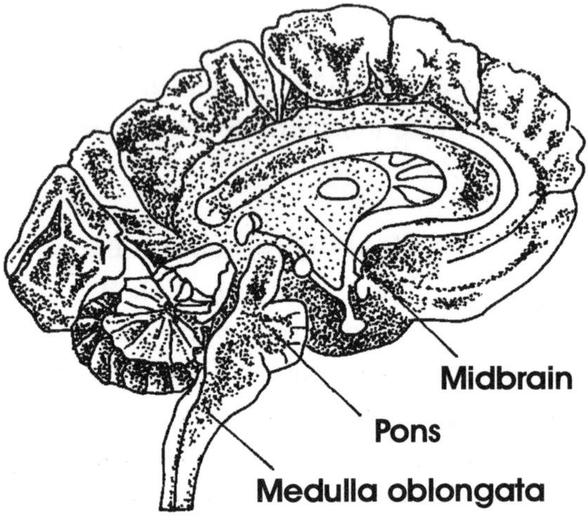


*fig.* 3.4 The brain stem : midbrain, pons and medulla oblongata

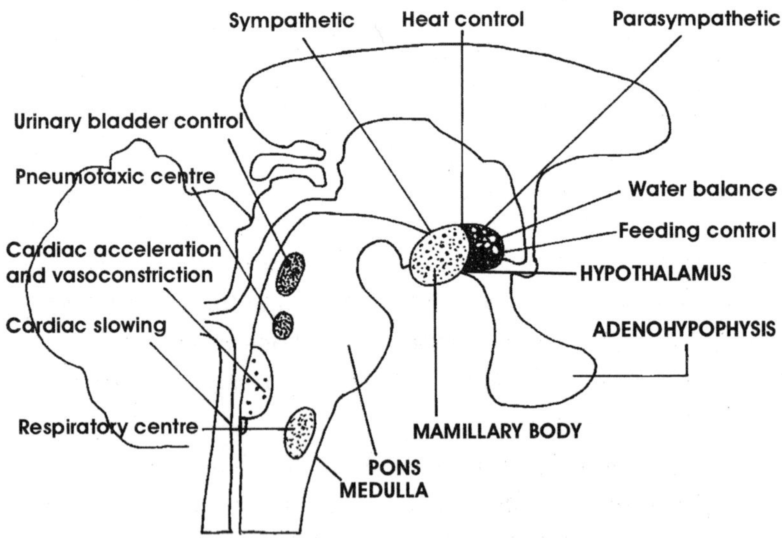


*fig.* 3.5 The autonomic control centres of the brain stem

## Paul MacLean's concept of reptilian brain

Neuroscientist Paul MacLean sees the human brain as really three brains. The first is the reptilian brain. Structures at the very top of the spinal cord, including portions of the brain stem, resemble the total brain possessed by reptiles and hence is the name. It is mainly devoted to life support, such as the regulation of respiration and heartbeat. According to MacLean, the limbic system is the core of our second brain. This is the mammalian brain. It regulates our behaviour involving complex emotional responses. This mammalian brain is not so well developed in reptiles. The third brain, as seen by MacLean, is the reasoning brain of man. It is composed of the outer bulges of the cerebrum and the overlying cerebral cortex. This is the latest addition to the central nervous system in the course of evolutionary ascent. Paul MacLean's thought on the three evolutionary brains has some truth in it, although his three divisions are not 100 per cent correct, when considered analytically from the point of view of evolution.

## Transmission of signals through synaptic junctions

A neuron or a nerve-cell has a cell-body containing the nucleus, and usually several dendrites and a single axon. Neurons are impulse-conducting cells of which the brain, the spinal cord and nerves are composed. A nerve impulse is an electrical transmission of a special type. A signal may travel through a nerve-fibre as rapidly as 200 metres per second. A neuron has been diagramatically presented in *fig*. 3.6.

In most cases, a signal travels to the effector organ through a number of neurons arranged one after another in the route. For this purpose are synaptic junctions across which electrical transmission is not possible. The picture of a synapse has been given in *fig*. 3.7.

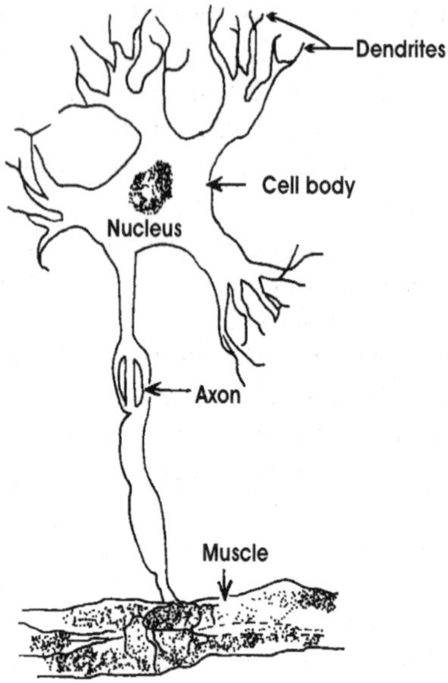


*fig.* 3.6 A neuron

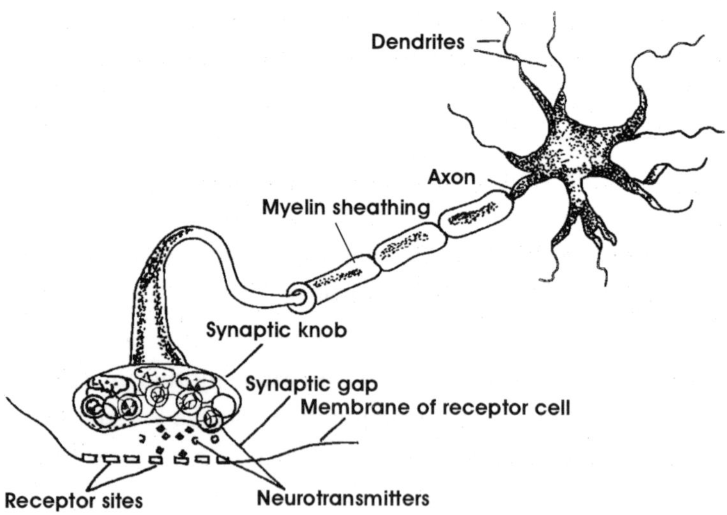


*fig.* 3.7 A synapse

The nervous system of the body contains more than ten billion neurons, most of them being in the brain. A single neuron of the cerebral cortex may be so interconnected as to influence the behaviour of a hundred other cell bodies. Thus interconnections between neurons are too many, the total number being one trillion (1000 billion).

Here the question arises: How does a signal travel across a synaptic gap? Here the transmission is chemical rather than electrical. An electrical impulse, travelling down an axon, causes the release of neurotransmitter molecules from the synaptic knob into the synapse or synaptic gap. The neurotransmitter then traverses the gap. In this process, an electric charge, or signal, is generated. This signal passes on to the receptor cell.

## Neurotransmitters

A neurotransmitter is a substance that transmits impulses between nerve cells. It carries a signal across the gap between two neurons. It is otherwise called a neurohumour or a neurohormone. The nervous system secretes a number of neurohumours. The main neurohumours are listed below.

### ACETYLCHOLINE

Acetylcholine is a chemical substance secreted at the ends of nerve fibres of the somatic and parasympathetic nervous systems, closely associated with the transmission of nerve impulses in the body. Acetyl-CoA and choline are the precursors for the synthesis. Choline acetylase is the enzyme that catalyses the synthetic reaction. Cholinesterase is the enzyme that degrades acetylcholine.

### CATECHOLAMINES

Catecholamines are a group of amines that act as neurotransmitters. There are three important catecholamines in the body, namely, noradrenaline (norepinephrine), adrenaline (epinephrine) and dopamine. Noradrenaline is liberated by the nerve-endings of the sympathetic system. The adrenal medulla secretes adrenaline and also some amount of noradrenaline. Adrenergic tracts are also present in the mid-brain. Dopamine is another neurotransmitter, mainly localised in the nerve tracts in the brain. Its precursor is the amino acid tyrosine. Dopamine is the precursor of noradrenaline. In addition, it has also its own function as a neurotransmitter from the presynaptic axon to the postsynaptic nerve cell through the synaptic cleft.

In the synthesis of catecholamines, tyrosine is converted into dopa by the enzyme tyrosine hydroxylase. Dopa is then changed into dopamine by the enzyme dopa decarboxylase. With the help of the enzyme dopamine-B-hydroxylase, dopamine is transformed to noradrenaline.The adrenal medulla changes noradrenaline to adrenaline with the help of the enzyme phenyl-ethanolamine-N-methyl transferase. All these enzymes are present in the sympathetic nerve terminals and also in the adrenal medulla.

Two enzymes are involved in the degradation of catecholamines. The first one is catechol-o-methyl transferase. The second one is monoamine oxidase (MAO).

SEROTONIN

Chemically, serotonin is 5-hydroxytryptamine. Its precursor material is the amino acid tryptophan. It is formed within some brain-neurons. It is involved in the transmission of impulses between nerve cells. It causes blood vessels to constrict. It stimulates smooth muscles. The enzyme tryptophan hydroxylase catalyses the synthesis of serotonin. It is degraded by the enzyme monoamine oxidase (MAO).

GAMMA-AMINO-BUTYRIC ACID (GABA)

GABA is an inhibitory transmitter in the vertebrate central nervous system. It is formed from L-glutamic acid, being catalysed by the enzyme L-glutamic acid decarboxylase. It is degraded by the enzyme GABA transaminase.

HISTAMINE

Histamine is a neurohumour. It is found in significant concentration in the brain and extra-cranial nerve-tracts. The main source of histamine outside the central nervous system is the mast cell. Mast cells, with granular cytoplasm, are present in the connective tissues. These granules are associated with the release of histamine. The general distribution of histamine in the brain is like that of other biogenic amines such as noradrenaline and serotonin. Histamine is formed from histidine with the help of the enzyme histidine decarboxylase.

Is histamine a neurotransmitter ? It might not be. What is the exact function of histamine in the central nervous system? It is closely associated with catecholamines. Catecholamines are vasoconstrictive whereas histamine is vasodilating. The vasoconstrictive action of noradrenaline in the brain for a prolonged period would be very harmful. Histamine may be functioning as a safety measure by preventing vasoconstriction. In the pathology of allergic conditions, the concentration of histamine in the tissue increases.

## Psychogenic control of endocrine glands

Endocrine glands are otherwise known as ductless glands. They secrete hormones directly into the blood or lymph. The hormone is carried by blood to the target organ, tissue or cell on which the hormone acts.

The human body has a number of endocrine glands. A schematic diagram of their locations in the body has been presented in *fig*. 3.8. The thyroid and the parathyroids are located in the neck region. The pancreas, situated in the duodenal loop inside the abdomen, is both an exocrine and an endocrine gland. Its islet cells are endocrine; they secrete the hormone insulin that is necessary for the metabolism of glucose by the body cells. The adrenal (suprarenal) glands are a pair of ductless glands, situated on or near the upper part of the kidneys. The outer wall or cortex of the gland secretes corticosteroid hormones. The inner part or medulla of the gland secretes adrenaline and noradrenaline. The gonads (ovaries and testes), in addition to their ovogenic and spermatogenic activities, function as endocrine glands.The ovaries secrete estradiol (estrogen) and progesterone; the testes secrete testosterone (androgen). Inside the cranium, there are two endocrine glands, namely, the pituitary gland and the pineal gland. The positions of these two glands inside the cranium in association with the brain have been shown in *fig*. 3.9. The pineal gland is a small, somewhat conical structure, present in the brain of all vertebrates having a cranium. It secretes the hormone melatonin. It functions as a light-sensing organ, as a biological clock or as a ductless gland whose secretions regulate the activity of sex glands. It has a role in sexual development and menstruation. The pituitary gland is a small, oval endocrine gland that is situated at the base of the brain in most vertebrates, in a cavity of the sphenoid bone. It has two sections: the anterior lobe or adenohypophysis and the posterior lobe or neurohypophysis. The anterior lobe secretes several hormones, namely, growth hormone (GH), prolactin, adrenocorticotrophic hormone (ACTH), follicle-stimulating hormone (FSH), luteinising hormone (LH) and thyroid-stimulating hormone (TSH). The posterior lobe secretes the hormones oxytocin and vasopressin. The anterior pituitary is called the master gland since it regulates all the other endocrine glands of the body.

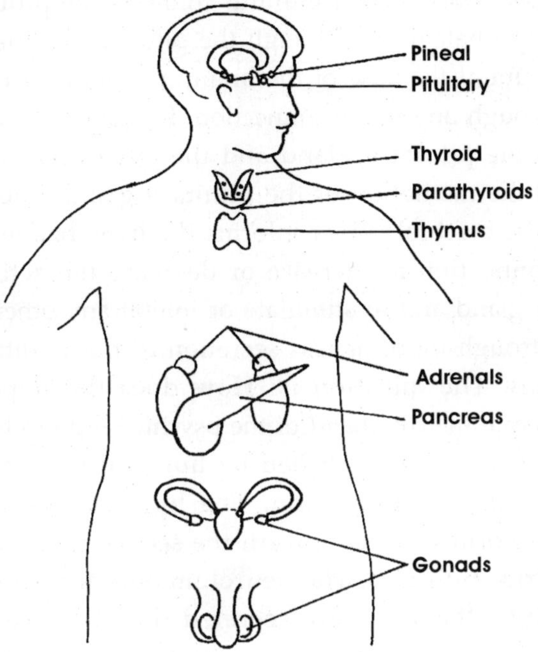


*fig.* **3.8 The locations of the endocrine glands in the body**

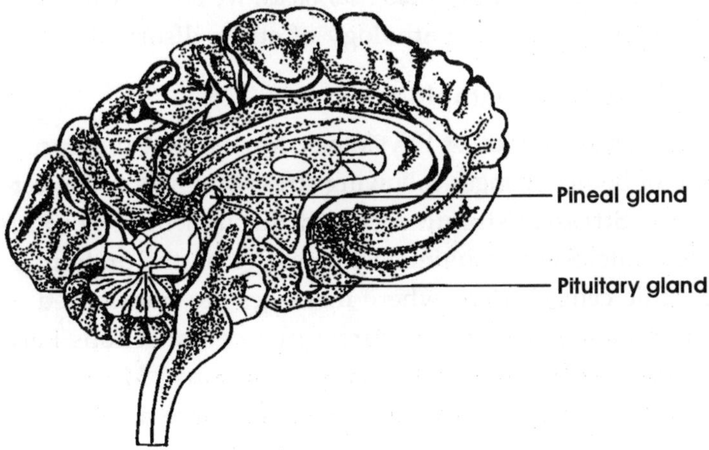


*fig.* **3.9 The pituitary and the pineal glands inside the cranium in association with the brain**

A short stalk (infundibulum) connects the pituitary gland to the hypothalamus. Although the pituitary is situated inside the cranium at the base of the brain, it is not controlled by the brain through any nerve-connection. In spite of this fact, mind controls the pituitary gland and the other endocrine glands through the mediation of the pituitary gland. The prefrontal lobe of the cerebral cortex informs the hypothalamus through nerve connection to increase or decrease the activity of the pituitary gland and to stimulate or inhibit any other endocrine gland through more or less secretion of the pituitary trophic hormones. The question is: How does the hypothalamus communicate the command of the psychic centre to the pituitary gland ? This is accomplished by humoral transmission, but not by neural transmission. The hypothalamus produces releasing hormones that govern the secretion of hormones by the anterior pituitary. The neurohumours that are produced by the hypothalamus are secreted directly into the blood vessels flowing in the narrow stalk that connects the hypothalamus to the pituitary.

With this much physiological basis, we are now in a position to explain the physiopathology of stress disorders.

## Psychosomatic pathology

The Russian School of Physiology for the first time proposed that all bodily changes following stress originate in the cerebral cortex. Stressful stimuli received through the exteroceptors or the interoceptors ultimately converge on the prefrontal area (psychic centre), from where messages are transmitted to the hypothalamus. There are direct nerve-connections between the frontal lobe and the hypothalamus. Most of these connections are two-way and bilateral. There are also indirect nerve-connections between the hypothalamus and the cerebral cortex through various subcortical structures — corticothalamic and thalamohypothalamic nerve fibres. The hypothalamus functions through the autonomic nervous system and the neuroendocrine apparatus.

The neuroendocrine apparatus has already been described. The hypothalamus secretes corticotrophic releasing factors that stimulate the anterior pituitary to secrete more of ACTH. This in turn stimulates the adrenal cortex to pour out excess of corticosteroids. Excess of steroids cause all the bodily changes in stress.

The hypothalamus is connected with the sympathetic nervous system. Stimulation of the hypothalamus activates the sympathetic nerves, resulting in the liberation of excess of noradrenaline.

The adrenal medulla receives stressful stimuli through the neural pathway. Stimulation of the adrenal medulla causes an initial secretion of adrenaline, with some amount of noradrenaline, into the blood. In the presence of an excessive quantity of plasma corticosteroid, the secretion of adrenaline and noradrenaline by the adrenal medulla becomes copious.

## General adaptation syndrome

Hans Selye termed the body's response to stressors the general adaptation syndrome.[2,3] This syndrome consists of three stages, namely, (1) the alarm reaction, (2) the stage of resistance, and (3) the stage of exhaustion.

### ALARM REACTION

The emergency response of the body is called alarm reaction. Many of these prompt responses are mediated by the sympathetic nervous system. They prepare the body to cope with the stressor here and now.

---

2. Selye, H., 1956.
3. Selye, H., 1976.

STAGE OF RESISTANCE

If the stressor persists in spite of the alarm reaction, the stage of resistance begins. In this state, the body resists the effects of the continuous stressor. However, resistance to new stressors is impaired during this stage. On the perception of the stressor, various parts of the cerebral cortex of the brain send signals to the prefrontal area (psychic centre) that in turn activates the hypothalamus through neural pathways. The hypothalamus secretes corticotrophin-releasing factor (CRF) which is transported to the anterior pituitary through a specialised system of blood vessels. The anterior pituitary secretes adrenocorticotrophic hormone (ACTH) that is carried by blood to the adrenal cortex. The adrenal cortex secretes cortisol and other corticosteroid hormones. During the stage of resistance, the corticosteroid hormones function so as to allow the body to deal adaptively with the stressors. This process goes on for long periods of time. But the continuance of the action of a high level of corticosteroid hormones becomes harmful to the body. A few harmful effects may be mentioned here. Corticosteroids promote neoglucogenesis, that is, they induce the formation of glucose from fats and proteins, especially from proteins of endogenous source. In the short run, this is adaptive and helpful. Muscles and nerves need glucose from blood to work. It is their fuel from which they get energy. If the breakdown of the tissue-proteins is prolonged, old cells cannot be maintained and new cells cannot be formed due to the paucity of protein supply. As a result, the body decays. White blood cells (leucocytes) are crucial for fighting infection. They have a short lifetime and need be replaced continually. Proteins are needed for the formation of white blood cells. If they are in short supply due to their diverted function as fuel, they cannot be made available for the formation of the white blood corpuscles. As a result, the defence of the body is weakened. In addition, there is shrinkage of the tissue that manufactures white blood cells due to the same reason of protein-deficit. Antibodies are special proteins that fight infection. Corticosteroid hormones exert inhibitory action on the formation of the antibodies. Thus high levels of corticosteroid hormones for a prolonged period impair the defence mechanism of the body, resulting in failure to fight infection. Prolonged elevation in the level of cortisol has also other harmful effects such as rise in blood pressure.

STAGE OF EXHAUSTION

This is the final stage of the general adaptation syndrome. In this stage, the body's capacity to cope with the continuing and fresh stressors is lost. As a result, the body succumbs and collapses. The body is no longer able to ward off infection. Death may be due to any infectious disease that cannot be cured by medicine if the defence system fails. Because of stressor-induced hormonal effects, the affected person may get peptic ulcer, diabetes, skin disorders, asthma, high blood pressure, increased susceptibility to cancer, or a host of other diseases.[4,5]

### Pathogenesis of stressful disorders

We have not yet pinpointed the pathogenesis of stress. What is the exact mechanism of the genesis of pathological lesions in an organ? Tension induces the hypersecretion of catecholamines by the sympathetic nerves and the adrenal medulla. Adrenaline causes vasodilation in the cardiac and skeletal muscles. More blood is shifted from the stomach and intestines to the heart, brain and skeletal muscles. Simultaneously adrenaline causes vasoconstriction in other organs and tissues. As a result of this vasoconstriction,

4. Allen, R.J., 1983.

5. Selye, H., 1976.

disturbance in the microcirculation in the organs takes place. When the stress is mild and temporary, acetylcholine is secreted by the parasympathetic nerves to cause vasodilation and thus the vasoconstrictory action of catecholamines is antagonised. In due course of time, normal circulation in the blood vessels is restored. When the stress-stimulus is severe and prolonged, blood vessels in the organ remain in a constricted state. The cells in the locality do not get enough blood. This condition is known as ischaemia. The cells are deprived of nutrients and oxygen and hence they die. This process is known as infarction.

Some organs fight the severe and prolonged vasoconstriction brought about by catecholamines. The local liberation of histamine antagonises the vasoconstriction and produces marked vasodilatation, leading to severe vascular engorgement, oedema and swelling in the region.

Here we may take the example of peptic ulcer to describe the role of stress in the pathogenesis of a non-cardiac organ. As a result of stress-exposure, the cerebral cortex releases an excess of acetylcholine. This neurohumour activates the subcortical centres, especially the hypothalamus. The hypothalamus, in turn, activates the sympathetic division of the autonomic nervous system and the adrenal medulla and simultaneously activates the pituitary through its releasing factors. The pituitary secretes more of ACTH that stimulates the adrenal cortex to secrete more of corticosteroids. The adrenal medulla, being informed by the subcortical brain through the neural pathway and synergised by the corticosteroids secretes excessive quantity of adrenaline. The excess of adrenaline produces vasoconstriction in the wall of the stomach or that of the duodenum. Lack of adequate blood supply to the cells in the affected area for a prolonged period culminates in the death of the cells (infarction). This triggers off the development of autoimmune phenomenon in the organ, finally resulting in a chronic inflammatory process in the mucous membrane of the organ. If the stressful situation subsides and a favourable state is restored, the inflamed tissue is healed up by fibrosis. If the stressful situation persists and aggravates, a breakdown of the process takes place, and the end result is ulceration.

In the causation of peptic ulcer, persistent hyperacidity, bacterial infection, hereditary predisposition and many other directly or indirectly causal factors may play their roles. However, only the psychosomatic pathogenesis has been discussed here.

It has already been stated that catecholamines (especially adrenaline) dilate the coronary vessels in the heart. Hence microcirculation in the blood vessels of the myocardium due to the actions of catecholamines cannot be the cause of heart diseases. In addition to the vasodilatory effect on the coronary artery of the heart, catecholamines accelerate the heartbeat and pulse rate, increase the blood pressure and increase the rate of respiration. It is an well established fact that stressful trauma causes cardiac diseases such as coronary insufficiency, angina pectoris and myocardial infarction. What is the exact pathogenesis?

The heart is well connected with the hypothalamus (emotional switch-board) through the sympathetic and the parasympathetic nerves. The former nerve accelerates the heartbeat wehreas the latter (vagus nerve) retards it. Catecholamines are liberated by the stimulation of the sympathetic nerve and that of the adrenal medulla. How stress brings it about has already been described. Catecholamines accelerate the heartbeat without the corresponding increase in the oxygen-supply to the myocardium. This leads to insufficiency to coronary circulation giving rise to angina pectoris. Usually catecholamines are degraded by specific enzymes and antagonised by acetylcholine. If stress is severe and prolonged, the excess of catecholamines cannot be degraded and antagonised quantitatively. In such a situation, the person develops the clinical features of coronary insufficiency which ultimately leads to angina pectoris.

An excess of catecholamines (adrenaline and noradrenaline) may be the cause of coronary vascular (artery) disease. Catecholamines and corticosteroids increase glycogenolysis in the liver and gluconeogenesis (production of glucose as a result of the degradation of body proteins). They also increase the serum cholesterol level. They increase the intimal absorption of lipids, leading to the damage to the vascular tissue. They favour the deposition of cholesterol ester (a cholesterol molecule combined with a fatty acid with the elimination of one molecule of water) in the intima of arteries. The subintimal deposition of the cholesterol ester in the blood vessels of the heart and the brain poses serious health hazard. The lumen of the coronary artery in the heart gradually gets narrowed down. In due course, the cholesterol deposit becomes calcified. Chronic emotional stress leads to the development of arteriosclerosis (atherosclerosis) in the coronary arteries of the heart and the blood vessels in the brain. Arteries of the body in general are affected by this condition. The arterial wall is hardened; the arterial lumen is narrowed; the blood pressure is increased.

A branch of the coronary artery in the heart may be partially or fully blocked. If this happens, the cardiac tissue distal to the block becomes deprived of blood-supply, oxygen-supply and nutrient-supply. As a result, the affected tissue dies. This dead tissue is the myocardial infarct.

Stress increases the viscosity of blood and decreases its coagulation time. Hence a prolonged stress may lead to the development of an arterial thrombosis. A number of precipitating factors, namely, atherosclerosis, higher dietary intake of fat, excessive smoking, hypertension and diabetes mellitus, may facilitate the pathogenesis of coronary thrombosis.

The neurohumours are constantly produced and constantly destroyed. In this process, a balance is maintained with a net amount of the neurohumour to do the right job. The initial reaction to a psychic trauma results in an enhanced liberation of acetylcholine in the cerebral cortex. This chemical causes excitation in the cortical synapses and in the post-ganglionic endings of cholinergic fibres. In normal conditions, acetylcholine, after its release into synaptic cleft, is rapidly broken down by the enzyme cholinesterase. This does not happen so if the stimulus is very strong or repetitive in nature. In a condition of severe psychic trauma, there is always a decrease in the formation of cholinesterase at the synapses. As a result, the excess of acetylcholine cannot be destroyed. Thus is the accumulation of acetylcholine in the synaptic cleft. This is the initial biochemical condition that causes stress disorder.

What has been said about cholinesterase holds good for the other enzymes that destroy other neurohumours. Psychic trauma decreases the activity of cholinesterage, monoamine oxidase and histaminase in the brain-tissue. As a result, there occurs an excessive accumulation of acetylcholine, catecholamines, serotonin and histamine in the various centres of the brain. In addition, there occurs an accumulation of cyclic AMP.

The cerebral cortex controls the subcortical centres through its excitatory and inhibitory functions. Following a psychologic stress, the accumulation of acetylcholine causes exhaustion of the inherent excitatory and inhibitory functions of the cerebral cortex. Especially, the exhaustion of the inhibitory function of the cerebral cortex becomes more critical. The subcortical centres receive some excitation with little inhibition. As a result, they become hyperactive. They excessively excite themselves and their linked systems — the neuroendocrine system and the autonomic nervous system. Both these systems ultimately excite all the organs and tissues of the body.

## Psychopathology

It is not the intention here to give the details of the pathology of all mental diseases. Neither is it possible due to the paucity of knowledge obtained so far. That some mental problems may be due to the excess or the deficiency of some neurohumours is indicated here.

In our opinion, the brain is the apparatus of the mind. The apparatus becomes topsy-turvy in the preponderance or deficiency of some brain-chemicals. Once the brain-apparatus is disturbed, the mind goes out of order.

Neuro-scientists have enough data to establish a link between brain-chemistry and depression. In persons suffering from depression, three neuro-transmitters, namely, dopamine, noradrenaline and serotonin, appear to stop functioning at full strength.

Research on brain-biochemistry suggests that schizophrenia is linked to biochemical imbalances in the brain. Many schizophrenics seem to have elevated levels of dopamine, one of the neurotransmitters.

## Individual susceptibility to stress

Susceptibility to stress varies from individual to individual. Some individuals can withstand stress whereas some others easily succumb to it. Again, those who can withstand may not be able to do so if the stress is too severe and too prolonged.

The nature of stress is also a deciding factor.

Susceptibility varies from genotype to genotype. The genetic constitution of a person is his genotype. Deoxyribonucleic acid (DNA) is the chemical nature of genes. Every human being inherits 23 chromosomes (a chromosome is a strand carrying genes) from the mother and 23 from the father. Genes regulate the synthesis of proteins. All enzymes are proteins, and they are rate-limiting too. All neurotransmitters are synthesised with the catalytic help of enzymes. The destruction of neurotransmitters is also catalysed by enzymes. By the variation in the quantity of the enzymes, genes may be deciding the susceptibility of an individual to stress.

Environment and education may nurture the capacity of an individual to withstand stress. It is a fact that stress is caused by unfavourable hostile environment. But it is also a fact that education and training help to fight stress. If a person is brought up in a family and a society where people do not fall easy victim to stress, he builds up his mind not to yield to stress so easily. The type of education a person gets from his parents, teachers and the society to which he is exposed exerts tremendous influence on his mind to fight stress.

Personality type is another factor that influences the susceptibility of an individual to stress. E. Kretschmer in 1925 and W.H. Sheldon in 1954 have classified individuals into personality types on the basis of body build. A short, plump person is said to be sociable, relaxed and even-tempered. He belongs to the endomorph type. A tall, thin person is characterised as restrained, self-conscious and fond of solitude. He belongs to the ectomorph type. A heavy-set, muscular individual is described as noisy, callous and fond of physical activity. He belongs to the mesomorph type.

Personality-type theories have also been based on purely psychological characteristics. The Swiss psychiatrist Carl Jung has divided all personalities into two types — introverts and extraverts (extroverts). Introverts have a tendency to withdraw into themselves, particularly in times of emotional stress and conflict; they are generally shy; they do not talk much; they prefer to work alone. Extroverts are more talkative; they seek the company of others; they are more sociable. Introverts are more susceptible to stress disorders than extroverts.

Psychologists have divided persons into two types, *A* and *B*, with reference to their susceptibility to heart disease. Type *A* persons are hard-driving and competitive. They are ambitious. They seek recognition and social eminence. They live under constant pressure, largely of their own making. They engage themselves with multiple activities with deadlines to meet. In stressful conditions, they become impatient, hostile, anxious and disorganised. In contrast, type *B* persons are quite the opposite. They are easy-going, non-competitive, placid and unflappable. They seem to be a little dull in comparison with type *A* persons. Type *A* persons are more susceptible to heart disease. Type *B*'s are likely to live longer. Type *A*'s are more susceptible to stressful disorders.

There is one of the major problems of type theories, however. Typologies, based on physical or psychological characteristics, involve a continuum of individual differences rather than discrete types. Every dimension of personality is distributed according to a normal bell-shaped curve. On most human characteristics and especially psychological characteristics, people tend to cluster near the middle of the range (mode), and only a few stand out at the extremes. Hence it is futile to assign a type to every person — either introvert or extrovert and either *A* or *B*.

In ancient India, three major psychological types were recognised, namely, *sāttvika, rājasika* and *tāmasika.*[6] It was also recognised that the distribution of *sattva, rajas* and *tamas* was continuous rather than discrete. There is hardly any person who is purely *sāttvika* or *rājasika* or *tāmasika.* Every individual has a mixture of these three, varying, of course, in proportion. A type is assigned to a person on the basis of the dominance of the attribute — *sattva, rajas* or *tamas.*

A *sattva*-dominant person is a serene, calm, contented, peace-loving, altruistic and idealistic individual. A *rajas*-dominated person is an over-active, restless over-ambitious, competitive, power-loving, dominating and egoistic individual. A *tamas*-dominated person is a lethargic, inactive, idle, non-competitive and inertial individual.

An individual's personality is very much influenced by his past *saṁskāras*, recorded in his mind's *karmāśaya* (reservoir of *karmas*) in the past lives. Continual additions to the *karmāśaya* are made through fresh recording of *saṁskāras*. Subtractions from the *karmāśaya* are made through the fruition of *saṁskāras*. The *vāsanā*-type of *saṁskāras* are especially more potent in shaping the personality of an individual.

*Sāttvika* persons are good for themselves, for the family and for the society. They are kind, affectionate, liberal, rational, progressive, forgiving, active for the sake of duty, committed to ethical and moral life, calm and serene. Someone who is *sāttvika* is not disturbed by opposites like success and failure. His mental condition is steady in opposing circumstances and he is ever contented although his contentment never leads to inactivity. Generally *sāttvika* persons remain free from worries, anxiety and mental tension.

*Rājasika* persons desire more and more. They want social

6. *BG*, XIV; XVII; XVIII. 7-9; 20-28; 30-35; 37-39.

prominence, more wealth, more power, more prestige. They refuse to be lead. They aspire for leadership. They are over-active, over-ambitious and always dissatisfied. They are restive and rarely calm. They are ordinarily victims of worries, anxiety and tension.

*Tāmasika* persons are slothful. They are reluctant to make any effort. Due to their inertial nature, they are in the habit of *status quo*. They are pessimistic rather than optimistic. They are very often melancholic.

The *Bhagavad-Gītā* has also typed persons as divine (*daiva*) and demoniac (*āsura*).[7] Persons with *daiva* qualities are *sattva*-dominated. The *sattva* qualities have already been described. Persons with *āsura* qualities are *tamas*-dominated. In addition to their inertial and slothful nature, they are pernicious and malignant to others. It may be pointed out here that no common individual is fully *daiva* or fully *āsura*. There are many blends in varying proportions. *Daiva* persons are calm, serene, undisturbed and unworried. *Āsura* persons create running spots of whirlwind for themselves and there they swirl with tension and anxiety.

That *saṁskāra*s influence the personality of an individual has already been stated. Some *saṁskāra*s germinate intense, insatiable desires (*kāma*). In some others, the ego has patches of low pressure and vacuum; their ego remains in irritable condition. Anger is a commonly exhibited quality with them. The *saṁskāra*s of some persons favour the dominance of covetousness in them. Some others are easily deluded. There are others who are too much proud; they always rate themselves as superior to others. They, by virtue of their power and wealth, tyrannise over others. There are persons in whom jealousy is excessively manifested. Persons whose *saṁskāras*

---

7. *BG*, XVI.

breed any one or more of these qualities become inimical to themselves. They remain in vicious circles and fall easy vicitim to anxiety and tension.

**Role of emotion in the etiology of psychosomatic diseases**

Persons with specially developed right brain are more emotional. Their limbic system is hyper-active and more responsive. In contrast, persons with dominant left brain are less emotional and sentimental; they are more logical and apt to be materialistic. They weigh profit and loss and always tilt at the former.

A number of physiological changes take place during emotional arousal. Some of the salient changes are the following:

1. Rapid heart-beat and increase in blood pressure.
2. Rapid respiration.
3. Increased perspiration.
4. Decreased secretion of saliva and mucus and dryness of the throat and mouth.
5. Dilatation of the pupils of the eyes.
6. Increased muscle tension.
7. Trembling of the extremities.
8. Increase in the blood-sugar level.
9. Quick clotting of the blood in case of wounds.
10. Decrease in the motility of the gastro-intestinal tract.
11. Diversion of blood from the stomach and intestines to the brain and skeletal muscles.
12. Erection of hairs on the skin.

These physiological changes result from activation of the

sympathetic division of the autonomic nervous system to prepare the body for emergency action. The sympathetic system gears the organism for greater output of energy. In contrast, the parasympathetic system is the energy-conserving system. As the emotion subsides, the parasympathetic system takes over and brings the organism back to its normal state.

We have a tendency to think that bodily changes that occur in response to stress are caused by emotion. Emotions vary in intensity. The more intense ones manifest the typical bodily changes already described. The milder affective states may be called emotional *feelings*. They do not exhibit the symptoms typically. But emotional feelings do activate the sympathetic system in an occult way. Unpleasant emotions such as anger, fear, agony are apt to create stressful disorders. Pleasant emotions such as joy, love, ecstasy are not harmful, although emotionlessness is the ideal yogic state. States of agony are the worst emotional states to cause severe stressful disorders.

More emotional and sentimental persons are more susceptible to cardiovascular diseases and other psychosomatic diseases such as ulcerative colitis, diabetes mellitus, migraine, etc. How does emotion cause ischaemic heart disease, diabetes or some such disease? This question has already been answered with reference to ischaemic heart disease and peptic ulcer. A few more pathological conditions are briefly discussed here.

Intense emotion, leading to agonising experience, activates the cerebral cortex, especially the prefrontal area, to release more of acetylcholine. This neurohumour stimulates the nerves that connect the prefrontal area and the hypothalamus. The hypothalamus activates the sympathetic sub-division of the autonomic division to release more of noradrenaline and adrenaline. The adrenal medulla gets message through the nerve-pathway to secrete more adrenaline. The concentrations of these neurohumours become much more than those of their corresponding enzymes that could destroy them. An excess of adrenaline working for a prolonged period causes vasoconstriction in the arteries and arterioles of the organs and tissues other than the cardiac and the skeletal muscles. There is also a second pathway through which the hypothalamus works. It is the neuro-endocrine pathway. The hypothalamus, through its *specific* releasing factor, can stimulate the pituitary gland to secrete more trophic hormones that stimulate the *specific* endocrine glands to secrete their hormones. By this technique, the hypothalamus can make any endocrine gland secrete more of its hormone. With special reference to the adrenal cortex, more corticosteroid hormones are secreted. They stimulate the adrenal medulla to pour out more adrenaline. They also work on various organs directly.

The role of sustained emotion on the causation of diabetes may be outlined here. The corticosteroid hormones increase the glucose-concentration in blood through enhanced glycogenolysis and gluconeogenesis. The pancreas gets a generous supply of nerve-fibres, both sympathetic and parasympathetic. The beta-cells present in the islets of Langerhans in the pancreas secrete the hormone insulin. Sympathetic stimulation leads to decreased insulin secretion and increased glucagon secretion (glucagon is a polypeptide hormone secreted by the alpha-cells of the islets of Langerhans and it raises the blood sugar level by stimulating the breakdown of glycogen to glucose). Increased concentrations of catecholamines in the blood due to hyperactivity of the sympathetic nervous system raise the blood glucose level. Adrenaline inhibits the secretion of insulin and stimulates the secretion of glucagon. In contrast, parasympathetic stimulation and cholinergic drugs have a stimulatory effect on the beta cells of the islets; thus they reduce blood sugar by increasing insulin secretion. If a person remains in intense emotional state of agony, fear, rage and anxiety for a prolonged period, his pre-diabetic condition is aggravated to be manifested as an open diabetic disease. His blood sugar level is increased as a result of less insulin secretion and more glucagon secretion. Hyperactivity of the sympathetic nerves, hypersecretion of catecholamines by the adrenal medulla and hypersecretion of corticosteroids by the adrenal cortex are the etiological factors of stress-induced diabetes. It may be pointed out here that diabetes has also etiology other than intense emotion. Heredity plays a crucial role. Viral infection of the pancreas may play an important role in the causation of juvenile diabetes.

Out of the many psychosomatic diseases, here we take up a very small number as representatives. The causation of cancer by agonising emotional experiences would be our last representative. It is a fact that cancer-cells are mutant. Somewhere in their DNA, the base sequence is altered or one base (or more than one) is replaced by another. In genetic language, this is known as mutation. A mutant cell declares 'autonomous' and 'sovereign'. It proliferates without obeying the command of the Ego (*ahaṅkāra*). This is the fundamental principle of oncogenesis. There are a number of mutagens — physical, chemical, microbial, etc. Agonising emotion is a potent stressor that increases susceptibility to cancer.[8] Hormonal imbalance is one of the many oncogens. Charles Huggins demonstrated the role of hormones in the development of cancer of the prostate and the breast. Nobel Laureate (Sir) Frank Macfarlane Burnet postulated that cancer may be developed as a result of immunological failure. In this context, we would refer to the work of K.N. Udupa[9] who has

8. Quoted by Bammer, K. and Newberry, B.H., 1983.

9. Udupa, K.N., 1985, pp. 340-50.

synthesised a concept that could explain the role of agonising emotion in the causation of cancer.

How agonising emotion disturbs the autonomic nervous system, especially the sympathetic system, has already been stated. Noradrenaline and adrenaline are secreted in higher quantity by the sympathetic nervous system in the state of intense emotionality. The adrenal medulla also secretes higher amount of adrenaline and some amount of noradrenaline in such an emotional state. The prefrontal area informs the hypothalamus that in turn influences the pituitary to secrete more adrenocorticotrophic hormone. As a result, the adrenal cortex secretes more corticosteroid hormone. An excess of catecholamines causes vasoconstriction of a weak organ that consequently suffers from anoxia. Corticosteroids cause immuno-suppression. Both cell-anoxia and immuno-suppression lead to the formation of abnormal and mutant cells which subsequently proliferate to produce benign growth (tumour) or malignant growth (cancer).

**Role of meditation in the prevention of stress-diseases**

Many things have been told on the science of psychosomatic diseases and stress disorders. Whatever may be the mechanism of the causation of these diseases, their prevention or cure by meditation is not mechanism-specific. Meditation guards at the entry-point. Stressful stimuli first affect the cerebral cortex. All the centres of the cerebral cortex inform the prefrontal area (psychic centre) which initiates actions by directing the hypothalamus. On receiving the directives from the psychic centre, the hypothalamus initiates actions through the autonomic nervous system and also through the neuro-endocrine system via the pituitary. Meditation works at the psychic centre.

In the meditator's system, neurohumours (acetylcholine

and catecholamines) are secreted in right quantities and right proportions. The enzymes that synthesise these neurohumours and those that destroy them are synthesised in quantities just enough for the purpose. There is no over-activation and over-stimulation of the adrenal medulla and cortex. The parasympathetic and the sympathetic divisions of the autonomic nervous system function normally without being under-active or over-active. The pituitary gland and the other endocrine glands secrete their hormones in right quantities. There is no hormonal deficiency; neither is there hormonal excess or hormonal imbalance. The system has hormonal balance rather than hormonal imbalance. The immune system (defence system) of the body functions in an active, forceful and vigilant way if regular practice of meditation is done. Thus microbial (viral, bacterial, protozoal) infection is effectively combated by the system of the meditator.

The benefits of meditation are not strictly cumulative. Hence regular practice is necessary. Meditation four times a day (6.00 a.m., 12 noon, 6.p.m., 12 midnight) should be ideally practised. If midnight meditation is not convenient, the schedule of three times a day may be adopted. For the modern, busy person, even noon-time's meditation is not convenient. In that case, meditation may be done both in the morning and evening. Four-O'clock meditation in the morning is better than 6-O'clock meditation.

The psychic centre at the level of the *ājñā-cakra* (prefrontal area) is calmed down by meditation. The longer the period of *samādhi,* the more profound is the calming effect of meditation on the psychic centre. The psychic centre initiates the chain of response-reactions, subsequent to the stimulus caused by psychic trauma. Even in the persistence of psychic trauma, the psychic centre does not respond to the stimulus and hence remains unaffected, without producing response-reactions. If the psychic trauma is too severe and prolonged, some minimal response-reactions may be produced. But such stress-reactions may not be too much damaging to the body.

# 3.3

# Meditation on Psychophysiology and Psychopathology

PREVIOUSLY yogic meditation was the subject-matter of philosophy and religion. In the latter half of the twentieth century, it entered into psychology, physiology and medicine. Many scientists conducted controlled experiments to explore the effects of meditation on health and disease. Now meditation is not confined to religious practices. It is an actively discussed subject of science too.

## The yogī's control of autonomic functions

Living would not be possible, had all actions of all organs of the body been consciously controlled by us. Our breathing becomes more rapid when we do exercise. Our heartbeat increases during exercise and excitement. Our digestive glands do secrete enzymes even during our sleep. Our pancreas goes on secreting insulin throughout the day to meet the varying needs. Our liver, kidneys and immune system function without our conscious knowledge. These are only a few examples. Most of our body-functions are free from our conscious efforts. We do not consciously control them. Had they been under our conscious control, it would have been impossible for us to co-ordinate and regulate the sundry physiological and biochemical functions of all the organs and tissues of the body.

The autonomic nervous system, consisting of the para-sympathetic and the sympathetic subdivisions (*fig*. 3.10), has already been mentioned. The sympathetic nerve fibres

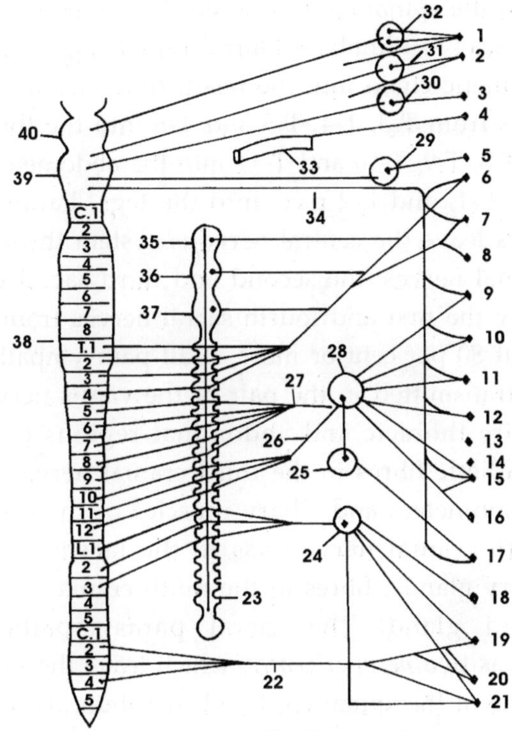


1. Eye
2. Lacrimal gland
3. Submaxillary gland
4. Sublingual gland
5. Parotid gland
6. Heart
7. Larynx,trachea, bronchi
8. Lung
9. Stomach
10. Small intestine
11. Abdominal blood vessels
12. Liver
13. Gallbladder
14. Bile ducts
15. Pancreas
16. Adrenal medulla
17. Kidney
18. Colon
19. Rectum
20. Bladder
21. Sex organ
22. Pelvic nerve
23. Sympathetic chain
24. Inferior mesenteric ganglion
25. Superior mesenteric ganglion
26. Small splanchnic nerve
27. Greater splanchnic nerve
28. Coeliac ganglion
29. Otic ganglion
30. Submaxillary ganglion
31. Sphenopalatine ganglion
32. Ciliary ganglion
33. Carotid artery and plexus
34. Vagus nerve
35. Superior cervical ganglion
36. Middle cervical ganglion
37. Inferior cervical ganglion
38. Spinal cord
39. Medulla
40. Midbrain

***fig.* 3.10 The autonomic nervous system: parasympathetic and sympathetic subdivisions**

originate in the spinal cord between the segments: T-1 and L-2 (T = thoracic; L = lumbar). Fibres from T-1 generally pass up the sympathetic chain into the head; fibres from T-2 into the neck; fibres from T-3, T-4, T-5 and T-6 into the thorax; fibres from T-7, T-8, T-9, T-10 and T-11 into the abdomen; and fibres from T-12, L-1, and L-2 pass into the legs. Parasympathetic nerve fibres leave the central nervous system through several of the cranial nerves, the second and third sacral nerves and occasionally the first and fourth sacral nerves from the spinal cord. About 80 per cent or more of all parasympathetic nerve fibres are transmitted in the pair of the vagus nerve, passing to the entire thoracic and abdominal regions of the body. Parasympathetic fibres in the third cranial nerve flow to the pupillary sphincters and ciliary muscles of the eye; fibres in the seventh cranial nerve pass to the lacrimal, nasal and submaxillary glands; fibres in the ninth cranial nerve pass to the parotid gland. The sacral parasympathetic fibres congregate as two *nervi erigentes,* which leave the sacral plexus on each side of the spinal cord and distribute their peripheral fibres to the descending colon, rectum, bladder, lower portions of the ureters and the external genitalia. The autonomic nervous system controls the visceral functions of the body. It is activated mainly by centres located in the spinal cord, brain stem and hypothalamus. The cerebral cortex can transmit impulses to the lower centres of the brain which in turn can effect the autonomic control. Visceral reflexes often regulate the operation of the autonomic nervous system.

Some important neurohumours have already been referred to. Skeletal nerve endings secrete acetylcholine. The preganglionic neurons of both the sympathetic and the parasympathetic systems and the postganglionic neurons of the parasympathetic system secrete acetylcholine. These nerve fibres are cholinergic because they secrete acetylcholine at their nerve endings. The nerve endings of the majority of the sympathetic fibres secrete noradrenaline and perhaps a slight amount of adrenaline. These fibres are adrenergic. A few of the postganglionic endings of the sympathetic nervous system secrete acetylcholine and the respective fibres are cholinergic.

Let us focus our attention on the secretions of the nerve endings of the postganglionic fibres of both the parasympathetic and the sympathetic system. A basic functional difference between the two systems is recognised. The parasympathetic system secretes acetylcholine whereas the sympathetic system secretes principally noradrenaline. These two systems function in an antagonistic manner. Table 3.1 presents their comparative functions.

**Table 3.1 : Autonomic effects on various organs of the body**

| *Organ* | | *Effect of sympathetic stimulation* | *Effect of parasympathetic stimulation* |
|---|---|---|---|
| Heart: | Muscle | (a) Increased rate<br>(b) Increased force of beat | (a) Slowed rate<br>(b) Decreased force of atrial beat |
| | Coronaries | Dilated | Constricted |
| Lungs: | Bronchi | Mildly dilated | Mildly constricted |
| | Blood vessels | Mildly constricted | Mildly dilated |
| Gut: | Lumen | Decreased peristalsis and tone | Increased peristalsis and tone |
| | Sphincter | Increased tone | Decreased tone |
| | Large bowel | Retention of faeces | Emptying of the large bowel |
| Liver | | Glucose released as a result of glycogenolysis | None |
| Gallbladder and bile duct | | Inhibited | Excited |
| Kidneys | | Decreased output | None |
| Ureter | | Inhibited | Excited |
| Bladder: | Detrusor | Inhibited | Excited |
| | Trigone | Excited | Inhibited |

| | | | |
|---|---|---|---|
| Penis | | Ejaculation | Erection |
| Systemic blood vessels: | Abdominal | Constricted | None |
| | Muscle | Constricted(adrenergic)<br>Dilated (cholinergic) | None |
| | Skin | Constricted(adrenergic)<br>Dilated(cholinergic) | Dilated |
| Arterial Pressure | | Marked increase | Moderate decrease |
| Blood: | Coagulation | Increased | None |
| | Glucose | Increased | None |
| Eye: | Pupil | Dilated | Contracted |
| | Ciliary muscle | None | Excited |
| Glands: | Nasal | | |
| | Lacrimal | | |
| | Parotid | Vasoconstriction | Copious secretion |
| | Submaxillary | | |
| | Gastric | | |
| | Pancreatic | | |
| Sweat glands | | Copious sweating (cholinergic) | None |
| Basal metabolism | | Increased up to 150% | None |
| Adrenal cortical secretion | | Increased | None |
| Mental activity | | Increased | None |
| Piloerector muscles | | Excited (contracts hair follicles) | None |

The two divisions of the autonomic nervous system are apparently antagonistic to each other. The parasympathetic division is associated with relaxation and rest. The sympathetic division functions in emergency situations such as anger, excitement, fear, anxiety, tension, etc. In spite of the *apparent* contradiction, both the divisions of the autonomic nervous system have evolved for a holistic purpose. The body as a whole needs their services as demanded by situations. In the analogy of the micro-universe where the micro-particles are paired and antagonistic to each other, the autonomic nervous system has evolved structurally and functionally as paired opposites for the holistic well-being of the whole body. Problem arises, however, when anxiety and tension create traumatic stress and the stress persists for a longer period. Prolonged over-stimulation of the sympathetic nervous system causes pathology in some organ or the other. In physiological conditions, both the sympathetic and the parasympathetic systems make adjustments for the interest of the whole body.

Those functions of the body which we consciously control as and when we will are voluntary. Body functions done without our consciousness and will are involuntary. The functions of the autonomic nervous system are ordinarily involuntary.

Some *yoga*-practitioners, however, can override the autonomic nervous system during their yogic exercises. Once they stop exercising, the autonomic nervous system regains its own autonomy. The conscious brains of some skilled *yogī*s can override the commands of the autonomic nervous system. They can change their heart rate, bring metabolism to a near halt, lower body temperature, increase or decrease their blood pressure at their will and do many other things which are usually involuntary.

Herbert Benson is a professor of medicine at the Harvard Medical School, Boston, USA. Benson and his co-workers have done controlled experimentation on the effects of *yoga* on psychophysiology and psychopathology.[10-14] Benson uses the

---

10. Benson, H., 1974.

11. Benson, H., 1975.

12. Benson, H., and Klipper, M.Z., 1975.

13. Benson, *et al.*, 1977.

14. Benson, *et al.* in Lipowski, *et al.*, 1977, p., 377.

term 'relaxation response' rather than *yoga*. The summary of the experimental findings of Benson *et al.* is given below:

During meditation, there is slowing down of the heart rate and the breathing rate; the oxygen consumption and carbon dioxide elimination are decreased; the muscle tension is reduced; blood levels of lactate and cortisol, which, respectively, are associated with anxiety and stress, decrease; the skin-resistance to the passage of a weak electric current (otherwise known as the galvanic skin response-GSR) rises; several changes in the electroencephalogram (EEG), such as slowing of the frequency of the EEG with relatively more alpha activity, occur.

Calder has reported the experimental findings on the psychophysiology of a *yogī*.[15] Ramananda Yogī demonstrated the control of vital functions. Transducers were attached to his body for the study of EEGs, heart rate and breathing as he prepared to reduce his oxygen needs while seated in an airtight box.

Although *yoga* has an ancient history in India, scientific experiments were done on it in the 1960s and afterwards. Wenger and Bagchi studied the autonomic functions in practitioners of *yoga* in India.[16] Wenger and co-workers, in their experiments on *yoga* in India, could find that *yogī*s could have volunatry control of their heart and pulse.[17] Datey and co-workers reported the hypotensive effect of *śavāsana*.[18] Although *śavāsana,* by name, is an *āsana,* it is really a kind of meditation in supine pose.

---

15. Calder, N., 1971.

16. Wenger M. and Bagchi, B., 1961.

17. Wenger, *et al.*, 1961.

18. Datey, *et al.*, 1969.

The changed physiological parameters consequent upon meditation persit in experienced meditators even when they are not meditating. Hence the effects of meditation are not transient. Of course, the effects decline in magnitude with the lapse of time after meditation and hence meditation is to be regularly practised twice or thrice a day and daily.

Herbert Benson and his colleagues claim that the same effects will be achieved by the use of relaxation-response technique as by that of yogic meditation. They recommend sitting for 20 minutes or so in a comfortable, relaxed position; progressively relaxing the muscles from feet to head; concentrating on breathing and mentally repeating 'one' after each cycle of breathing in and out, and suppressing unwanted distracting thoughts by thinking 'oh, well' when they occur. They discard the sacredness of any *mantra*. They substitute *AUṀ* with any monosyllabic word such as 'one'.

## Biofeedback

Biofeedback is the technique of using the feedback of a normally automatic bodily response to a stimulus, in order to acquire voluntary control of that response. It is a shorthand term for *external psychophysiological* feedback. The basic idea is to provide individuals with increased information about the physiological processes going on inside their bodies, including the brain. For a historical review of biofeedback and its application, reference may be made to *Biofeedback: A Practitioner's Guide* by M.S. Schwarz and Associates.[19] Instrumental conditioning is involved in biofeedback technique. Mostly electronic instruments are used. Instrumental training can produce increases and decreases in several body responses such as vasomotor responses, blood pressure, salivation, galvanic skin response and cardiac rates

19. Schwarz, *et al.*, 1995.

and rhythms.

Cybernetics is the science of communications and automatic control systems in both machines and living things. It deals most directly with information processing and feedback. One of its basic principles is that one cannot control a variable unless information about the variable is available to the controller. The information provided is called feedback. Another principle of cybernetics is that feedback makes learning possible. From instruments applied to the body, an individual receives direct and clear feedback about his physiology. It may be an EMG (electromyography) instrument, an EEG (electro-encephalography) instrument or any other computerised instrument that can provide information on the physiological parameters such as pulse rate, blood pressure, etc. On receiving the information from the instrument, the individual learns to change the physiological parameter by his thought alone. Biofeedback may be considered as instrumental conditioning of visceral responses. But it is more than that. The important role of cognitive learning operating in the biofeedback technique needs adequate emphasis.

Biofeedback is the 'Yoga of the West' and the 'electronic Zen'. The fundamental principle of meditation has been instrumentalised in what is called 'biofeedback'.

Alpha waves (8-12 Hertz) in the EEG studies are associated with the meditative state and a relaxed but alert state. Before 1969, it was thought impossible to voluntarily control alpha waves. In 1969, Kamiya reported that alpha waves could voluntarily be controlled. Now, with the help of biofeedback technique, it is possible for a trained individual to produce the alpha brain waves.

The EEG theta wave activity (4-7 Hertz) is a slow-wave activity. With the help of biofeedback, a person can voluntarily produce theta brain waves that can be recorded in the electroencephalograph. This can be used in a variety of clinical cases such as epilepsy, drug-addiction and alcoholism.

Patel worked in London on *yoga* and biofeedback.[20-21] He made combined use of these two related techniques for the treatment of hypertension.

The application of biofeedback in the treatment of diseases and self-improvement of health has been widespread especially in the West. Here there is no scope to discuss the topic in greater detail.

## Yoga recognised as a topic of psychology

Before the mid-twentieth century, *yoga* was hardly discussed in psychology. The picture changed in the second half of the said century. Now it has a prestigious position in physiological science, clinical medicine and psychology.[22-23] Morgan and Associates write: 'Take it easy', the yogi says — and now psychologists and physiologists are listening'.

The famous psychologist E.R. Hilgard, while interpreting his research results on hypnosis, recognises a 'hidden observer'.[24-25] He says: 'The subconscious process and the conscious experience go on at the same time'. The former is very like consciousness; but it is not available to the open consciousness. The expression 'hidden observer' is introduced as a metaphor to describe the concealed part that knows things, not present in the person's open consciousness.

---

20. Patel, C.H., 1973.
21. Patel, C.H., 1975.
22. Hilgard, *et al.*, 1979, pp., 171-72.
23. Morgan, *et al.*, 1986, pp., 328-29.
24. Hilgard, E.R., 1973a.
25. Hilgard, E.R., 1977.

Hilgard uses the expression 'hidden observer' for the subconscious. S.R. Dean goes beyond the subconscious and the unconscious and uses the term 'ultraconscious'.[26]

Dean's 'ultraconscious' is the same as our 'Superconscious'.[27] The Superconscious is all-pervasive, homogeneous and unbroken. It is a continuum rather than corpuscular. It need not send information from one locality to another through transmission of signals. Hence it can function without nerve-connections.

## Meditation as a tool for fighting stress

We cannot practically prevent all stresses in life. Especially modern life and stressful situations often go together. Medicine can hardly cure diseases caused by stress. Meditation or related technique such as biofeedback or relaxation response is the only available tool that can prevent and cure stress pathology.

We may take a couple of examples. A person has lost his kith and kin and his property in an earthquake. Another person has lost his only child who died of blood cancer. In these cases, nobody can undo what has already been done. The stress is continuing and hence the effects of stress on the body continue. Only meditation can stop or at least minimise the physiopathological processes.

We do not belittle the beneficial effects produced by techniques such as biofeedback, relaxation response and others. However, we have a conviction that they cannot be placed on par with yogic meditation.

---

26. Dean, S.R., 1970.

27. Panda, N.C., 1996, pp., 547-55.

# 3.4

# Meditation and Psychoimmunology

IT is hardly realised by the common man that the body is a auto-builder, auto-maintainer and auto-defender. At the time of conception in the mother's womb, a sperm fertilises an ovum to form a zygote. The zygote multiplies. Three germ layers, namely, ectoderm, mesoderm and entoderm (endoderm) are formed. Each germ layer is transformed into a set of specific organs and tissues. And so is it said that the body is an auto-builder. The cells of the body and the sub-cellular structures do not stay as such throughout the lifetime. They die, disintegrate and are replaced by fresh ones. This regeneration process goes on throughout the lifetime. It is the physiological process. Pathogenic micro-organisms attack the body and destroy the organs and tissues. The body has the capacity to repair itself. In tissue-injuries and bone-fractures, repair is done, not by the doctor, not by medicines, but by the body itself. As a country has a defence department with army, navy and airforce, so does the body possess self-protection mechanism. It fights against invading pathogens (viruses, bacteria, protozoa and others), toxins and foreign materials and thereby defends the body. When the body's defence system fails, no doctor can save the life of the person.

In this section, we will have a preliminary discussion on the body's defence system and the role of meditation in boosting up the defence activity.

## The military force of the body system

For specific physiological purposes, the body has localised and compact organs such as the heart, the lungs, the kidneys, the liver, etc. However, the defence department of the body is diffuse rather than localised and compact. For example, the expression 'reticuloendothelial system' includes some cells of the spleen, lymph glands, bone marrow and liver. These cells act as scavengers to rid the body of foreign matter and disease germs.

In the human beings, the marrow-function is usually limited to the skull, the vertebral column, the pelvis, the sternum and the proximal ends of the long bones. Erythrocytes (red blood cells), granulocytes, monocytes and platelets are formed in the marrow of the bones. Under conditions of increased demand, the shafts of the long bones may also take up these functions.

The lymphoid cells are formed in lymphatic tissues which are spread widely throughout the body. Lymphatic tissues are found in the mediastinum, the mesentery, along the routes of the great vessels, in the tonsils and Peyer's Patches along the intestine, in the axillae and inguinal regions. Lymphatic follicles are present in the spleen. The bone marrow also contains foci of lymphatic tissue.

The stem cells are the primitive cells that first appear in the embryo. Albeit primitive, they are multipotential. They are the progenitor cells of erythrocytes, leucocytes, platelets and all types of immune cells. They have extensive proliferative capacity. They give rise to differentiated descendants.

The stem cells disperse and seed many organs. After migrating to the bone marrow, they reproduce themselves again and again. They develop into a variety of specialised cells — red blood cells or erythrocytes, platelets or thrombocytes and white blood cells or leucocytes. The leucocytes produced in the bone marrow are the monocytes, neutrophils, eosinophils and basophils.

The original, embryonic stem cells also migrate to the thymus which is a small glandlike organ consisting of lymphoid tissue, found in young vertebrates near the base of the neck. The thymus disappears or becomes rudimentary in the adult. Even though it is absent in the adult system, the cells differentiated in it migrate to the lymphoid tissues and play important roles in immunological reactions throughout the life. Thus, the defence system, otherwise known as the immune system, has its origin from the stem cells in the embryonic life.

First we may have a brief discussion on the white blood cells or leucocytes. They are the soldiers of our body. Unlike the mammalian erythrocytes which are non-nucleated, the leucocytes possess a central nucleus. The blood has two categories of leucocytes — agranulocytes and granulocytes. Lymphocytes and monocytes are agranulocytes whereas neutrophils, eosinophils and basophils are granulocytes.

Small lymphocytes constitute 20 to 25 per cent of the total leucocytes in adult blood. Large lymphocytes are greatly outnumbered by the small lymphocytes. Under physiological conditions (unless a disease is caused by any pathogenic organism), they are largely confined to the lymphoid tissue. The monocyte is the largest leucocyte in the blood, with a single, well-defined nucleus. It comprises about 3 to 8 per cent of the total leucocytes in the blood. Neutrophils are the most abundant leucocytes in the blood. They make up about 50 to 75 per cent of the total number of white blood cells. Of the total leucocytic count (TLC) in blood, eosinophils and basophils constitute 2 to 4 per cent and 0.15 per cent or less, respectively. In physiological conditions, the total number of leucocytes in adult human blood is 5000 to 9000 per cu. mm. of blood.

Neutrophils and monocytes are free lances. They wander from place to place through the tissues. No part of the body is a barrier to them. They are motile and phagocytic. Through one of the joints in the endothelium of the capillary wall, they insinuate a process called pseudopodium from their cell-protoplasm. Then the semifluid substance of their cell-body streams into the pseudopodium. This is how they pass out of the blood vessels. This process is known as diapedesis. After reaching the invading bacteria, they cordon off the threatened area. They ingest the invading, living micro-organisms, kill them and digest them.

Monocytes, with marked phagocytic propensities, join the neutrophils in their massive attack. They engulf and digest microbes. But after their first flooding of the invaded tissue, the number of monocytes comes to rest, and they undergo transformation to fixed tissue macrophages.

Phagocytes are of two types — small and large. Both types are produced in the bone-marrow. Neutrophils, being the small phagocytes, are the microphages. Monocytes are macrophages and the large phagocytes. Neutrophils are short-lived whereas monocytes are long-lived. The phagocytosis of neutrophils is extracellular. Monocytes are intracellular phagocytes.

In the fierce fighting between foreign invaders and leucocytes, some of the latter are killed although the former are also killed. The macrophages secrete powerful toxins that kill micro-organisms. The toxins also kill some white blood cells. The material made up of dead leucotytes, exuded plasma, liquefied tissue cells and a few red blood cells is the pus. The so-called pus cells are dead leucocytes.

Neutrophils, aided by monocytes and other phagocytic cells of the tissues, attack not only micro-organisms, but also any foreign material. The phagocytes elaborate the enzyme protease which hydrolyses proteins. All these cells do scavenging by removing dead, necrotic tissues, blood clots and foreign materials.

The functions of eosinophils and basophils are little known. The eosinophils are not markedly motile and only slightly phagocytic. They perhaps play their role in detoxification and in the disintegration and removal of proteins.

Basophils, like connective tissue mast cells, are found in great number during the healing phase of acute inflammation or in chronic inflammation. Like the mast cells, their metachromatic granules contain heparin, hyaluronic acid and 5-hydroxytryptamine. They probably produce local anticoagulation in inflammation. They are also concerned with the deposition of ground substance, necessary for the repairing of the tissue.

The large, granular lymphocytes are the natural killer (NK) cells. They kill extracellular micro-organisms unlike the macrophages that kill intracellular micro-organisms.

The small lymphocytes may be the B-cell (B-lymphocyte) or the T-cell (T-lymphocyte). They are named so, becuase the B-cell is differentiated in the bone-marrow from the seeded stem cell and the T-cell is originally differentiated in the thymus from the seeded stem cell. The T-cell is distinguished from the B-cell by its relatively smooth surface. The B-cells secrete antibodies whereas the T-cells do not. Both the B-cells and the T-cells migrate to the lymph nodes of the lymphatic system where they settle and multiply.

The bone-marrow produces B-lymphocytes at the rate of about a million a second. Each B-lymphocyte is genetically programmed to make one, and only one, type of antibody. It places this antibody on its outer surface to act as a receptor. About $10^5$ antibody molecules stick out of one B-lymphocyte cell. All the antibodies of a particular lymphocyte cell are identical, although differences do exist from lymphocyte to lymphocyte. It may be noted here that antibodies are formed by the lymphocytes before any antigen is ever seen.

The active site of each antibody on a B-lymphocyte acts as notches on a key whereas each antigen (micro-organism) has an active site which functions as a lock. An antigen binds to that receptor with which it makes a good fit. Upon the fitting of the lock and key, the B-lymphocyte (B-cell) developes into a plasma cell which produces millions of specific IgE (immunoglobulin E) molecules. Gamma globulins or immunoglobulins are the key antibody proteins which are carried in blood plasma. Thus the B-lymphocyte is involved in the production of humoral immunity in contrast to the cellular immunity provided by the other types of leucocytes.

The B-lymphocyte is genetically programmed. Its genetic programme is transferred to its plasma cell. The synthesis of specific immunoglobulins is regulated by the genetic plan. Each immunoglobulin (Ig) is a four-peptide unit. There are perhaps $10^8$ or more types of Ig molecules. Plasma cells are produced as a consequence of the antigen-exposure. The production of immuno-globulins by the plasma cells is also a consequence of the antigen exposure. The genes of the antigen decide the type of the immunoglobulin protein to the produced. This acquired immune response is specific. Each antibody molecule recognises its corresponding antigen. The antigen and antibody fit each other and this combination renders the antigen inactive and inert. The antibody, while recognising its own antigen, distinguishes it from other antigens. The antibody distinguishes the self from the non-self. Hence it does not usually do any harm to the body-cells.

The B-lymphocyte acquires memory. Say, a person suffers from measles, mumps or chicken-pox. The first contact of the B-lymphocyte with an antigen (the specific microbe or any foreign protein) imprints some information in the former. If and when the same antigen attacks the person a second time, the immune system of the body is already prepared to effectively repel the later invasion. The earlier attack has imparted some memory in the B-lymphocyte. This memory of the B-lymphocyte can be transferred from a donor to a recipient.

The T-lymphocytes (T-cells) are involved in defence-operations against intracellular micro-organisms. They can recognise an antigen when it is on the surface of a body-cell. The surface receptors of T-cells recognise the antigen plus a surface-marker. Because of this marker, hetero-transplantation of organs and tissues is rejected. The T-cells produce lymphokine that helps macrophages kill intracellular micro-organisms.

Blood platelets or thrombocytes are fragments of protoplasm, derived from the cytoplasm of the megakaryocytes. They are non-nucleated. They are produced in the bone-marrow. They primarily function in blood-coagulation. Besides this well-known function, they agglutinate into masses and form deposits upon any roughened surface or foregin material. Thus they aid in the body's defence against infective agents. They also play a role in repairing small defects in the endothelial wall of capillaries. They adhere to the defective area and thus seal the leaks.

In normal conditions, the soldiers of the body have normal numbers in the blood, with slight variations around their respective averages. When some pathogenic micro-organism invades the body, the production of the immune cells and the humoral antibodies increases enormously. The type of the specific leucocyte and specific immunoglobulin is also accurately determined. The whole process is intelligently and purposefully planned.

With this much of introductory immunology, we close the discussion on the defence department of the body. The immune system is a wandering system that is always vigilant to the protection of the body that is subject to attack by invaders. Each soldier is a cell such as a monocyte or a lymphocyte, floating and carried away in the blood or the lymph stream. Each is isolated, not connected with the others by any nerve. In spite of this isolated existence, the defence of the body is well designed, efficiently executed and well co-ordinated. We record the facts; but we do not know much about the design, execution and co-ordination.

### The superconscious protector

Now we enter into the territory of metaphysics for which science does not issue a passport. It is not a luxury of speculation and a phantasy for us to trespass on the domain of metaphysics. It becomes an unavoidable necessity in order that we get a holistic explanation for the existence and functioning of the immune system of the body.

We have already mentioned the sudden appearance of the original stem cell in the embryo. Later it disperses to seed other organs. In the bone marrow, the stem cells reproduce themselves again and again and may develop into any type of blood cells — erythrocytes, leucocytes and platelets. The red blood cells (erythrocytes) contain hemoglobin which carries oxygen from the lungs to all cells of the body. The leucocytes or white blood cells have already been discussed. They provide defence to the body. Their shapes and sizes are different. The shapes of their nuclei are different. The cytoplasm of some of them is granular whereas that of some others is agranular. Their functions are different. The platelet is a disc-shaped fragment of cytoplasm, covered with a cell membrane, but with no nuclear component. It is involved in clotting of blood. The question is: Why does the stem cell produce cells of so many types different from itself and still each type being vitally important for the body?

Monocytes develop into phagocytes which are macrophages. They engulf and digest invading microbes and foreign cells intracellularly. This whole process of phagocytosis is not passive and mechanical. It is active, necessitating dexterity, manoeuvres, skill and intelligence. The micro-organism is attracted towards the phagocyte through chemotaxis and is adhered to the surface of the latter. This contact activates the cell-membrane of the phagocyte. It becomes serrated, with the formation of a gulf due to the extension of pseudopods around the invader. The micro-organism falls in the gulf and is subsequently completely enclosed in a vacuole called phagosome. Within a minute's time, granules appear in the cytoplasm of the phagocyte. The granules fuse with the phagosome and discharge their contents around the imprisoned micro-organism. By this mechanism, the micro-organism is killed and digested. Subsequently, the phagosome is opened, the degradation products are released and the phagocyte resumes its normal cellular structure.

The macrophage has no brain. Neither has it any trace of nerve tissue. How has it consciousness and intelligence? Phagocytosis, as briefly described here, is an intelligent activity. Secondly, the macrophage phagocytises invading micro-organisms; it does not phagocytise the body-cells of the host. How does it distinguish the self from the non-self ? Thirdly, it is not connected to the brain or any organ, tissue or other cell by any nerve. Seemingly, it does not receive any command or directive from any source external to itself. For what interest of its own does it remain busy in the scavenger action of phagocytosis ? These questions seem to be odd in science and meaningless in philosophy of science. But, are they really odd and meaningless just because we cannot answer them?

Large granular lymphocytes are the natural killer cells. They kill micro-organisms that are extracellular. They circulate in lymph and blood and thus reach every nook and corner of the body. They do not kill the body cells of the host. About 5 per cent of the total lymphocytes of the body meet their natural death daily. The dead are replaced by fresh production in order that the immune system is effectively maintained. For whose interest does the lymphocyte work? Certainly, it has no interest of its own. If it works for the holistic interest of the body, it must work under the body's directive. But it leaves an isolated life. It has no nerve-connection with anything in the body.

The B-lymphocyte, after being triggered by an antigen, undergoes successive waves of proliferation to produce a large clone of plasma cells. The plasma cells make immunoglobulins (Ig), about $10^8$ or more different Ig molecules. These molecules distinguish the self from the non-self. They do not bind to the cells of the body. Once they meet with an invading micro-organism or a foreign cell, they bind to it, of course, specifically. It is surprising that the B-lymphocyte has memory. It remembers if a person was previously attacked by a virus, say that of chicken-pox, measles or mumps. The science of memory is not clear at all with reference to biological systems with developed brain. The memory of the small lymphocyte is a mystery for us.

All types of leucocytes do not perform the same job. Each type plays a specific role, depending upon the species of the invading micro-organism. Whenever some micro-organism invades certain organ, the relevant leucocyte(s) is (are) produced in abnormally large number and deployed through the blood or the lymph stream to the affected area.

The bone marrow is insentient matter. The lymph glands are insentient too. The stem cells in the bone marrow cannot be said to be the intelligent co-ordinators. Who decides and co-ordinates then? When some virus or bacteria invades the body, the person concerned is not conscious of the infection. No person consciously produces cellular or humoral antibodies. In spite of these negative facts, production and deployment of antibodies are intelligently executed and co-ordinated. Somebody or something must be doing. And that somebody or something must be super-intelligent. Who is the agent?

Does God, sitting in the body, do it ? No, directly He is the non-doer. Does the individual self (*jīvātman*) do it ? The non-dualistic Vedānta asserts that the self is not different from God (*Īśvara*) and *Brahman*. The self does not directly do it. The self or Self that is Consciousness is reflected on the internal instrument (*antaḥkaraṇa*), constituted of three main components, namely, *buddhi* (intellect), *ahaṅkāra* (ego) and *manas* (mind). The *antaḥkaraṇa* which is otherwise insentient is rendered conscious by the reflection of the super-conscious self on the former. Thus it is the *antaḥkaraṇa* that executes and co-ordinates the defence production and deployment. It may be further noted that the brain needs neural connection for action and that the *antaḥkaraṇa* does not need neural connection for communication.

## Meditation influences the immune system

It has already been stated that mental stress, worries and tension first affect the centres of the cerebral cortex of the brain. All these effects converge on the prefrontal area (psychic centre) that in turn activates the hypothalamus through neural pathways. The hypothalamus acts by stimulating the sympathetic division of the autonomic nervous system and also the anterior pituitary. The pituitary secretes more ACTH that activates the adrenal cortex gland to secrete more cortisol and other corticosteroid hormones. More adrenaline and noradrenaline are secreted due to the stimulation of the sympathetic nerves and also the adrenal medulla. Corticosteroids, in association with adrenaline and noradrenaline, have profound immunosuppressive action. If the stress is too severe and if it acts for a prolonged period, the immune system of a person has a total collapse. Meditation stops the chain of reactions by blocking the initial step. The prefrontal area is not adversely affected or is little affected by stress if a stress-affected person regularly meditates. In the first step, usually more acetylcholine is secreted in the cerebral nerves and this neurohumour activates the hypothalamus. The excessive secretion of acetylcholine by the neurons of the cerebrum including the prefrontal area is prevented or drastically minimised by meditation. And hence is the benefit.

What has been said so far is the prevention of immunosuppression. This is the negation of a negation. Meditation has a positive role too. It boosts up the production of more leucocytes in the bone-marrow and the lymphatic system; it accelerates the rate of production of plasma cells from B-lymphocytes and that of immunoglobulin molecules by plasma cells. Meditation can efficiently protect the body against invasion by viruses, bacteria and protozoa by stimulating the antibody production in the body. It promotes the faster production of immune bodies.

How does meditation bring about immuno-promotion? Reference may be made to *saṁyama,* described in the first part of the book. *Dhāraṇā, dhyāna* and *samādhi*, done together, is *saṁyama*. We have a yogic technique known as *saṅkalpāyana*, the practice of which can activate the immune system. The technique is outlined below:

1. Sit in any meditative *āsana* or in a supine pose as in *śavāsana*.
2. Do *dhāraṇā* on the bone marrow and the lymphatic system. Generally *dhāraṇā* is focussed on a spot. But, in this case, a diffuse area is focussed on.
3. Take a long, deep inspiration through both nostrils. While retaining the breath (in *kumbhaka*), mentally repeat the *saṅkalpa* (auto-suggestion). Avoid straining due to long retention of breath. Stop the auto-suggestion and exhale. The *saṅkalpa* should be in the form of a short, imperative sentence with a positive command (for example: Let my immune system be activated). While mentally repeating the *saṅkalpa*, concentrate on the idea. This is a modified form of *dhyāna*.
4. Repeat the *saṅkalpa* in *kumbhaka* several times (about 10 *kumbhaka*s) without counting.
5. Finally, go to the thoughtless state of *samādhi*.
6. After *samādhi*, relax for a couple of minutes and get up.
7. Practise *saṅkalpāyana* two or three times a day two to three hours after full meal.

Strong belief in the technique, and persistence in its practice are necessary for getting success. Immediate results may not be expected. It would take some time (two to three months) for immuno-promotion to be effected. The diet of the meditator should be adequately rich in proteins, vitamins and minerals.

# 3.5

# Meditation on Specific Organs and Functions

FOR the purpose of this section, *saṁyama* and meditation are synonyms. *Saṁyama* is the simultaneous practice of *dhāraṇā, dhyāna* and *samādhi.* We have also described a technique known as *saṅkalpāyana. Saṁyama,* with the insertion of a *saṅkalpa* in it, is *saṅkalpāyana.* By the use of both these techniques, any organ of the body can be corrected and fortified, its disease can be cured, its efficiency can be improved and its functions can be regulated.

We will take a few examples and apply the technique. Once the reader comprehends the principle of the application, he can extend it to the correction of other organs which are not covered here.

## Diabetes mellitus

Diabetes mellitus is a disease condition in which the beta cells of the islets of Langerhans, present in the pancreas, do not secrete insulin or secrete less of the hormone. If all the beta cells are not dead, meditation on the pancreas can cure the disease or can alleviate the symptoms.

Some *āsanas*, *bandhas* and *mudrās* can stimulate the beta cells to secrete insulin. *Prāṇāyāma* can also help. These aspects of *yoga* will not be discussed here. The role of meditation on the secretion of insulin will be the focal point.

The meditator should have a prior, preliminary knowledge

on the location and anatomy of the pancreas which is situated in the abdomen, below the stomach, in the duodenal loop. It is a dual gland — exocrine and endocrine. Its juice containing digestive enzymes is carried through the pancreatic duct into the duodenum (the first of the three parts of the small intestine). The hormone, insulin, is secreted by the beta cells. Insulin is carried directly by blood to different cells of the body.

The meditator does *dhāraṇā* on the pancreas gland. He thinks on the secretion of insulin by the beta cells. He orders his beta cells to secrete enough insulin as and when required by the body cells through a *saṅkalpa* which is to be silently repeated. His *saṅkalpa* may be like this: 'O beta cells of my pancreas, secrete enough insulin as and when required by my body cells'. After repeating the *saṅkalpa* about ten times, the meditator may pass to the state of *samādhi.* The whole process of *saṁyama,* with *saṅkalpa* inserted, is *saṅkalpāyana.* It should be practised 15 to 20 minutes a time and three times a day (a minimum of two times a day — morning and evening).

In addition to *saṅkalpāyana* on the pancreas gland, the meditator may perform the same technique on his *maṇipūra-cakra.*

Depending on the state of the disease and the efficiency of meditation, the prognosis varies. Oral medicine and/or insulin injection may be dispensed with by meditation only, the decision being subject to expert advice after appropriate investigations. Meditation may be complementary to usual allopathic treatment under the supervision of a competent doctor. Yogic *āsanas, bandhas* and *mudrās* would produce synergistic effects. Walking exercise or any other form of exercise would certainly be helpful. Other complementary treatment such as acupressure may give added benefit. What has been said in this paragraph with reference to diabetes holds good, *mutatis mutandis,* for other diseased conditions in principle.

**Hyperacidity and peptic ulcer**

Glands that secrete hydrochloric acid are present in the wall of the stomach. An acid reaction in the stomach is a physiological requirement. When the acid-secretion is excessive and more than normal, the person suffers from hyperacidity. Hyperacidity may be due to excessive stimulation of the acid-secreting glands by stimulants present in food and/or drinks. Excess of spices in the food, regular consumption of sour food in excessive quantities, and consumption of alcohol and tobacco may precipitate the pathological condition of hyperacidity. Some individuals may genetically possess more HCl-secreting cells that predispose them to hyperacidity. Those individuals may be genetically producing more enzymes for the synthesis of hydrochloric acid. More number of neurons may be genetically present in the brain at the root of the vagus nerve (10th cranial nerve) in some individuals. Alternatively, the concerned brain centre may be hyper-irritative. In either of these conditions, the frequency of the nerve-impulses transmitted through the vagus to reach the HCl-secreting cells in the mucous membrane of the stomach may be higher. Finally, hyperacidity may be a psychosomatic disease. The original cause may be mental tension and anxiety. The prefrontal area of the cerebrum activates the hypothalamus which in turn activates the autonomic nervous system and the pituitary gland. The vagus nerve belongs to the parasympathetic system. Its nerve-endings stimulate the gastric glands to secrete more hydrochloric acid. More adrenaline is secreted by the adrenal medulla. More corticosteroids are secreted by the adrenal cortex. These hormones accentuate the secretion of hydrochloric acid by the gastric glands. Worries may be the primary cuase of hyperacidity. They also may be the secondary cause by aggravating the hyper-secretion due to other primary causes.

Over-secretion of hydrochloric acid for a prolonged period may lead to ulceration in the stomach-wall or the duodenal wall. The loss of mucus on the mucous membrane may facilitate the pathogenesis of ulceration. Bacterial infection of the mucous membrane by *Helicobacter pylori* may the cause of gastric or duodenal ulcer. It may be a secondary invader.

The meditator should acquire a gross, preliminary knowledge on the anatomy of the stomach, the pyloric sphincter and the duodenum. This would facilitate the *dhāraṇā* and the *dhyāna.* He should regularly practise *saṅkalpāyana,* as described earlier. The *saṅkalpa* should be specific. It may be like this: 'Let my stomach secrete enough HCl, not more, not less. My peptic ulcer is cured'.

It may be noted that the *saṅkalpa* may be in any language desired by the meditator. It should not contain more than two sentences. Each sentence should be a simple one and reasonably short one. Compound and complex sentences should be avoided. The words used should be well understood by the meditator.

The *saṅkalpa* should be mentally repeated and followed by *samādhi.* It may further be mentioned that the patient's meditation may not be so perfected as to cure the disease by meditation alone. The mental stress may be so massive and prolonged that only meditation by the patient who has not mastered the technique may not fully cure the disease. *Yoga* and doctor's treatment — medical or surgical — are not contradictory. One type of treatment may complement the other.

*Saṁyama* and *saṅkalpāyana* on the *maṇipūra-cakra* would help the treatment of hyperacidity and peptic ulcer. Some *āsana*s, *bandhas* and *mudrās* would also help. Acupressure has beneficial effects, Alcohol, too many cups of tea and coffee, smoking, spiced foods and irritant foods should be avoided. Cold milk and frequent eating of small quantities of bland diet are helpful.

### Hormonal deficiency and imbalance

We have a number of endocrine (ductless) glands in the body. They secrete hormones which are directly absorbed into blood that carries them to the target organs, tissues and cells. The pituitary gland is the master gland in the body. It is situated inside the cranium at the base of the brain. It secretes a number of hormones. Through specific hormones, it controls the other endocrine glands of the body. If *saṁyama* and *saṅkalpāyana* are to be practised on it, *dhāraṇā* is to be done on the *ājñā-cakra* at the spot between the eyebrows.

The thyroid gland and the parathyroid gland are located at the base of the neck. The hormone of the thyroid regulates the basal metabolism of the body. The parathyroid hormone regulates the calcium level in blood and is connected with the metabolism of bones and teeth and that of calcium, phosphorus and vitamin D.

The two adrenal or suprarenal glands are situated anterior and adjacent to the left and right kidneys inside the abdomen. Each adrenal is a composite of two glands. The innermost part is the adrenal medulla and the outermost part is the adrenal cortex. The medulla secretes adrenaline and noradrenaline that are the hormones to meet the emergency situation of the body. The cortex secretes a number of steroid hormones, some of which are the stress hormones.

The pancreas, located in the duodenal loop, is an exocrine as well as an endocrine gland. The exocrine gland secretes pancreatic juice that contains digestive enzymes. The endocrine gland has islets of Langerhans. The beta cells of the islets secrete insulin that is necessary for the utilisation of glucose by the body cells. The alpha cells of the islets secrete the hormone glucagon that raises the blood sugar level by stimulating the breakdown of hepatic glycogen to glucose.

The two ovaries in the female and the two testes in the male are the gonads. One of the ovaries produces usually one mature ovum every month and discharges it sometime in the mid-menstrual period. In addition, the ovaries produce estrogens (estriol, estrone and estradiol) and progesterone, the ovarian hormones. The two ovaries are located inside the pelvic cavity, one on each side. The two testes are located in the scrotum. They produce sperms. They also contain the Leydig cells that produce testosterone, the male hormone.

The anterior pituitary gland secretes a number of hormones. Its growth hormone (GH) accelerates body growth. Prolactin is a pituitary hormone that stimulates the secretion of milk and maternal behaviour. The thyroid-stimulating hormone (TSH) stimulates thyroid growth and secretion. The adrenocorticotrophic hormone (ACTH) stimulates adrenocortical growth and secretion. The follicle-stimulating hormone (FSH) stimulates ovarian follicle growth in females and spermatogenesis in males. The luteinising hormone (LH) stimulates ovulation and luteinisation of ovarian follicles in females and testosterone secretion in males. The effect of the pituitary hormones on the other endocrine glands of the body is not a one-way-traffic. There is feedback effect too. Due to the feedback, the anterior pituitary increases or decreases the quantity of secretion of its regulatory hormones.

The pituitary gland has three lobes. The hormones of the anterior lobe which is the most important one have so far been mentioned. Its intermediate lobe secretes melanocyte-stimulating hormone (MSH) that expands melanophores. Melanin is the black pigment in the skin. It is formed under the influence of this hormone. The posterior lobe of the pituitary gland secretes two hormones, namely, vasopressin and oxytocin. Vasopressin promotes water retention. It is the antidiuretic hormone (ADH) that works through the kidneys. Oxytocin causes milk ejection and the contraction of the uterus at the time of child-birth.

With this much introduction to the endocrine glands and their hormones, we would pass on to meditation for the treatment of hormonal deficiencies and imbalances.

To restore hormonal balance, the affected person should perform three sets of *saṁyama* and *saṅkalpāyana*. The first set should be done on the pituitary at the *ājñā-cakra* (eyebrow centre). The resolve (*saṅkalpa*) may be like this: 'My pituitary, secrete enough hormones for a good hormonal balance'. The second set should be practised on all the endocrine glands from the pituitary above to the ovaries or testes below in succession. The third set should be practised on the endocrine gland specifically known to be deficient. For example, irregular menstruation in a woman may be due to hormonal imbalance and sub-normal functioning of the ovaries. The *saṁyama* and the *saṅkalpāyana* may be performed on the two ovaries. The resolve may be like this: 'My ovaries, secrete enough hormones for good health'.

We may take two examples of the functional states of the thyroid gland (*fig*. 3.11). The name of its hormone is thyroxine. The principal thyroxine is T-4, one molecule of which contains four atoms of iodine. When the thyroid gland subnormally functions, it produces the clinical symptoms of hypothyroidism. The hyper-function of the thyroid gland produces the clinical symptoms of hyperthyroidism.

Simple goitre is one of the types of hypothyroidism. It is generally endemic in nature and essentially a response to iodine deficiency. The gland enlarges in size due to

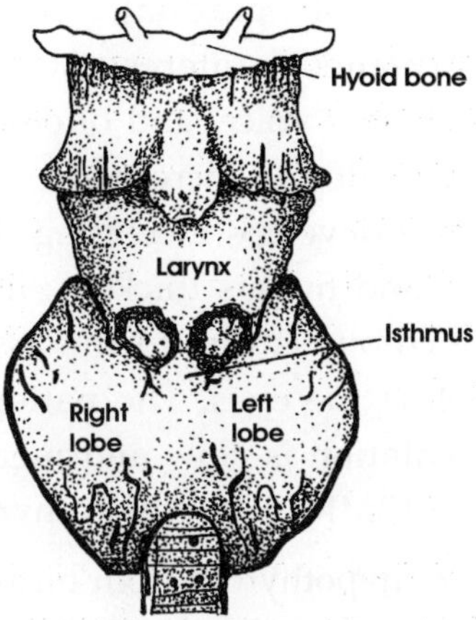


*fig.* **3.11 The human thyroid gland**

compensatory hypertrophy. Iodine is a constituent of thyroxine. In iodine deficiency, less thyroxine is produced by the gland. The lowered concentration of thyroxine in blood exerts feedback effect on the pituitary that secretes more thyroid-stimulating hormone (TSH). This hormone stimulates hyperplasia (multiplication of the thyroid cells, resulting in more number of cells) of the thyroid gland and hence the gland is enlarged.

Hypothyroidism may be due to causes other than dietary deficiency of iodine. It may be the end result of a number of diseases of the thyroid gland, or it may be secondary to pituitary failure.

The following clinical symptoms may be observed in the syndrome of adult hypothyroidism: In the initial stage, the thyroids are diffusely enlarged due to hyperplastic changes. Later nodular goitre develops with local areas of excessive colloid accumulation. The deposition of an excess of mucoprotein in the skin, usually in the forearms and often in the legs and feet, occurs. This condition is known as myxedema. Although myxedema is a synonym for adult hypothyroidism, its gross changes in the limbs are observed only in severe cases. The onset is usally gradual. The patient develops progressive lethargy and disinterest. He may have slurred speech, a husky and slow voice, and often deafness. He loses appetite. He gets a moderate increase in weight due largely to water retention. He develops increasing intolerance to cold. The skin of the lips and fingers thickens; it becomes dry and yellowish; its pale colour is due to the associated anaemia. There is edema below the eyes. The patient's hair is brittle and scanty. His mentation is slow and memory is poor. The basal metabolic rate (BMR) of the hypothyroid patient falls.

Children who are hypothyroid from birth are called cretins. They are dwarfed and mentally retarded. They have enlarged, protruding tongues and pot bellies. Puffiness of the face and limbs may occur later.

There is hyper-function of the thyroid gland in hyperthyroidism. It is otherwise known as Graves' disease or thyrotoxicosis. An excessive supply of thyroxine (the thyroid hormone) to the peripheral tissues is the basis of this condition. Hyperthyroidism may result from overmedication with potent thyroid materials or from hyperactivity of the thyroid. The latter condition may be due to traumatic stress of the mind, or toxic adenoma (tumour). In both the conditions of stress and adenoma, there is diffuse and/or focal glandular hyperplasia.

The physiological consequences of hyperthyroidism are opposite to those seen in hypothyroidism. The symptoms are: nervousenss, rapid loss of weight, enlargement of the thyroid gland, protrusion of the eyes (exophthalmic goitre), hyperphagia (abnormally increased appetite), heat-intolerance, increased pulse pressure, pulse rate and blood flow, a fine tremor of the outstretched fingers and a warm, soft skin. Despite the increased appetite, a persistent weight loss occurs due to increased heat production. The basal metabolic rate is elevated. The thyroxine concentration in blood increases. The protein-bound iodine (PBI) usually rises.

The exact etiology of thyrotoxicosis is so far unknown. In this connection, we would refer to the work of K.N. Udupa.[28] We accept his theory and accordingly recommend our meditational therapy.

Stress causes increased activity of the cerebral cortex. The prefrontal area is activated by the other cerebral centres. It stimulates the limbic system of the brain, which in turn stimulates the posterior hypothalamus. Next the autonomic nervous system is activated by the hypothalamus. The cholinergic nerves (nerves of the parasympathetic division) secrete excess of acetylcholine. Subsequently, the adrenergic nerves (nerves of the sympathetic division) and the adrenal medulla secrete excess of catecholamines (adrenaline and noradrenaline). These neurohumours are gradually neutralised by the local liberation of histamine in the thyroid gland. Ultimately, the process may end in resolution or healing by fibrosis.

Dr. Udupa's *in vitro* and *in vivo* experimental work showed that excess of acetylcholine produced marked hypertrophy and hyperplasia of the thyroid cells, rapidly enhanced the thyroid activity and showed symptoms of neurosis. When he subsequently increased the blood-level of catecholamine, the hypertrophy and hyperplasia of the thyroid gland could be maintained for a longer period and cardiovascular symptoms could be observed. In the last phase of his experiments, he injected histamine which produced a severe autoimmune reaction in the thyroid gland.

Dr. Udupa made therapeutic studies. In the early stage of Graves' disease, tranquillizers along with antithyroid drugs

---

28. Udupa, K.N., 1985, pp., 278-304.

produced good results. In the second stage with excess of catecholamine turnover, beta adrenergic blockers produced expected results. In the late stage in which autoimmune reactions were exhibited, prednisolone (cortisone) treatment gave beneficial results albeit slowly.

It is a fact that many persons are subjected to stress sometime or other. But most of them do not suffer from thyrotoxicosis. Secondly, familial susceptibility to this disease has been observed. Probably genetic predisposition may explain it. Some of the neutralising enzymes of the neurohumours (such as cholinesterase, monoamine oxidase, histaminase) may be deficient in the thyroid glands of some persons with specific genotypes.

With this knowledge on the physiopathology of the thyroid gland, we now switch over to its *yoga*-therapy. *Āsana*s (for example, *sarvāṅgāsana*), *mudrā*s (for example, *kaṇṭha-mudrā*) and *bandha*s (for example, *jālandhara-bandha*) improve the thyroid health. If goitre is due to iodine deficiency in the diet, the treatment should be dietary supplementation. The prognosis of cretinism treated by meditational therapy is not good. Meditational therapy would certainly be the best if the disease is due to mental stress or pituitary malfunctioning.

*Saṁyama* on the *ājñā-cakra* has profound influence on the prefrontal area. Thereby the excess of the secretion of acetylcholine will be reduced to normal. If this is successful, the limbic system and the hypothalamus would not be activated by the prefrontal area and the over-stimulation of the autonomic nervous system would be avoided.

*Saṅkalpāyana* on the pituitary gland should be practised twice or preferably thrice daily. The appropriate *saṅkalpa* (resolve) may be like this: 'My pituitary, secrete normal quantity of TSH, not less, not more'. *Samādhi* should follow after mentally repeating the resolve about ten times.

In the second phase of the meditation, *dhāraṇā* and *dhyāna* should be practised on the thyroid gland itself. This is to be followed by *saṅkalpāyana.* The *saṅkalpa* for hypothyroidism may be like this: 'My thyroid, secrete more thyroxine, enough for my good health. Normalise your size'. The *saṅkalpa* for hyperthyroidism may be like this: 'My thyroid, secrete less thyroxine, enough for my good health. Normalise your size'.

The *viśuddha cakra* at the throat level regulates the thyroid. The anatomy of this *cakra* should be well comprehended. Meditation on this *cakra* helps a great deal in maintaining normal thyroid health.

Meditational therapy, without medicinal and surgical therapy, may be successful in preventing and curing both hypothyroidism and hyperthyroidism (exceptions already stated). But most patients do not attain that high level of perfection in meditation which is likely to give a spectacular success. *Yoga* is not contradictory to medical therapy. It is always advisable to be treated by a competent doctor and use meditation as a complementary therapy. The question of a *siddha yogī* is different. Generally, he does not get the diseases of hormonal deficiencies and imbalances. If he gets due to some unavoidable reasons, he can cure himself by *yoga* practice only.

### High cholesterol level and atherosclerosis

Cholesterol is a lipid, a kind of fatty substance with a complex structure. Some types of diets such as meat, fish, prawns and eggs (egg-yolk) are rich in cholesterol. Any food of animal origin, with high content of saturated fat, is not good for health and, for this purpose, cholesterol is the incriminating factor.

In addition to the intake of dietary cholesterol, the body gets endogenous cholesterol too. The body cells synthesise cholesterol out of a simple substance known as acetyl-CoA.

Carbohydrates, fats and proteins must ultimately enter into the TCA (tricarboxylic acid cycle) for catabolism and, in that process, they must be converted into acetyl-CoA. The body synthesises cholesterol out of acetyl-CoA. It is a usual phenomenon that persons with adiposity (obesity) have higher levels of serum cholesterol. A genetic predisposition for cholesterolaemia is generally observed. Many diabetic persons have higher levels of cholesterol in their serum. The higher level of low-density-lipoprotien (LDL) in the serum indicates danger from the source of cholesterol, whereas high-density-lipoprotein (HDL) is not so harmful.

Cholesterol is a necessary biochemical in the body. It plays important role in the structure and functions of brain cells. It is a precursor of steroid hormones and sex hormones. In normal situations, it is not an unwanted substance. However, when its level becomes too high, it poses problems of health-hazards. The intake of an excess of saturated fats in the diet and the danger from high level of cholesterol in the body generally bear a positive correlation. The plant kingdom is free from cholesterol. A vegetarian diet, if well balanced, is better than a non-vegetarian diet. However, an intake of an excess of calories coupled with a sedentary life, an intake of an excess of saturated fats like butter and ghee and a genotype favourable for obesity are very likely to pose the problem of cholesterol for health even if a person is a vegetarian.

Cholesterol, being an alcohol, combines with fatty acids to form esters that are deposited on the internal wall of arteries and arterioles. As a result, the lumen of the blood vessels in the heart and the brain becomes narrower and the wall becomes harder. The cerebral vessels become more fragile and may break due to higher arterial pressure. This condition is known as stroke. Cerebral haemorrhage, if excessive and unchecked, may lead to coma and death. It may end in paralysis.

Atherosclerosis in the heart may lead to ischaemic heart disease due to the narrowing of the cardiac blood vessels and the consequent inadequate supply of blood to the cardiac musculature. There may be complete blockage at some point. In that case, the area distal to the point of blockage may degenerate and die, finally ending in an infarction.

Some heart patients avail the opportunity of bypass surgery and live. But the risk of further blocking of the coronary artery and its branches after the operation cannot be ruled out. For such patients, diet-control, stress management and practice of *yoga-nidrā* and meditation are dependable preventives.

The prevention and treatment of cholesterolaemia by *yoga* have been established through the ages. The yogic diet is a good preventive. His mental peace is a favourable factor for prevention. *Āsanas, bandhas* and *mudrās* are also preventive and curative.

The whole body (*sarvāṅga*) is the focus of meditation for curing atherosclerosis. *Dhāraṇā* is done on the whole body from the head to the feet and from the feet to the head, to be repeated. *Dhyāna* is done on the idea of lowering the synthesis of cholesterol in the body. The *saṅkalpa* is appropriately phrased. It may be like this: 'I order my body to synthesise less cholesterol to maintain the normal level'. The *saṅkalpāyana* is to be followed by *samādhi* and preceded by *dhāraṇā* at the *ājñā-cakra* and *dhyāna* on the idea of the lowering of cholesterol.

## Viral hepatitis

Jaundice is the symptomatic name of viral hepatitis. It is an infectious disease caused by a pathogen which is a virus. The virus invades the liver tissue and causes inflammation in the tissue. The question may arise: 'How can meditation kill the virus which multiplies in the host cell by millions and billions?' Meditation does not directly kill the micro-organism. It activates the immune system of the body. The infective agent is inactivated by cellular as well as humoral immunity.

Reference may be made to section 3.4 on the subject of meditation and psychoimmunology. Viral hepatitis is simply an example. Any infectious disease caused by viruses, bacteria and protozoa evokes the same immunological response as viral hepatitis, with, of course, suitable changes specific to the nature of the pathogen.

*Saṁyama* should be practised on the whole body (*sarvāṅga*) in a sequential manner. The focal point of *dhāraṇā* sequentially shifts from head to feet, from feet to head, from head to feet, and so on. The *saṅkalpa* (resolve) may be like this: 'My immune system, kill the invading pathogen'. While *saṅkalpāyana* is performed, about five seconds may be allowed at each shifting focal point. After *saṅkalpāyana,* the meditator should merge in *samādhi.*

The *sarvāṅga saṅkalpāyana* is the first phase of meditation in the treatment of an infectious disease. In the second phase, the meditator does *saṅkalpāyana* on the actual site of the disease. In this case, the liver is affected and hence the focus is the upper, right abdomen. The *saṅkalpa* may be like this: 'My liver, be healthy'. As usual, the *saṅkalpa,* repeated for not less than about five minutes, should be followed by *samādhi.*

In this case, there is a third phase too. *Saṁyama* should be performed on the *maṇipūra-cakra* (navel area). The petals of the *cakra,* the colours of the petals, the *yantra* of the *cakra* and its colour, the seed (*bīja*) *mantra* and *mātṛkā* on the petals should be meditated upon.

Here we may mention the territorial jurisdiction of each *cakra.* The *mūlādhāra-cakra* controls the nose, the organs of defecation, urination and discharge of sexual fluids and the adjacent area. The *svādhiṣṭhāna-cakra* exercises its regulatory power on the tongue and mouth, the ovaries, the uterus, the vagina, the testes, the penis, the accessory sex glands and the area adjacent to the *cakra*. The *maṇipūra-cakra* regulates the eyes, the legs and feet and the upper abdominal organs (stomach, pancreas, liver, spleen, small intestine and the proximal large intestine). The *anāhata-cakra* controls the skin, the hands, the heart, the lungs and the bronchi. The *viśuddhi* controls the ears, the pharynx and larynx, the tonsils, the immune system of the body, the thymus, the thyroids, the parathyroids and the adjacent area in the neck region. For meditation to exert influence on the pituitary gland, the pineal gland, the prefrontal area of the cerebral cortex and the sinuses, the *ājñā-cakra* is the selected site. This is the site of *manas, buddhi* and *ahaṅkāra.* This *cakra* is to be meditated upon for improving and stabilising the mental power and the power of concentration. The *ājñā-cakra* is the third eye. Meditation is to be done on this *cakra* for attaining intuitional ability. For the treatment of any disease of the head and the brain, *jyotirliṅga* meditation is to be practised on the *sahasrāra* area (the *jyotirliṅga* is located at the *brahmarandhra,* the apex point of the *suṣumṇā*). To get rid of mental stress and anxiety, meditation on this seventh *cakra* and also on the *ājñā-cakra* is recommended. The *cakra* for meditation is to be selected, depending upon the organ which has been diseased. Meditation may also be done on the *bindu* at a level equidistant from the *ājñā* and the *sahasrāra.*

## Cancer

Normally every cell of the body obeys the dictates of the *ahaṅkāra* (Egoity) that holistically controls the body. Every cell, tissue and organ work in harmony for the overall benefit of the body. This harmony and holism, however, are not maintained if the genetic (DNA) constitution of a cell is altered. Such an altered cell declares autonomy and becomes rebellious.

It multiplies and grows without caring for the interest of the body. It becomes malignant. This is our concept of oncogenesis.

Physical agents like X-ray and ultraviolet rays may be mutagenic. Prolonged irritation may be a causal factor. Some chemical agents may induce mutation too. Hereditary predisposition to genetic mutation may be running in some families. Hormonal imbalance is one of the incriminating factors. Imbalance (excess or deficiency) of any neuro-humour may also cause mutagenesis. Severe mental trauma, anxiety and tension, working for a long period, may be carcinogenic. Some benign growths like brain-tumour may be caused by sustained anxiety.

A perfected *yogī* does not suffer from cancer. Not a single cell of his body has the power to declare autonomy. A *yogī* who has not attained perfection due to reasons beyond his control (a houeholder, a businessman, a service-holder, or a politician may be practising *yoga,* but may not be able to guard off extraneous influences) may sometimes be affected with cancer. If the disease is diagnosed at an early stage and if the patient sincerely practises *yoga,* he can get the regress of the disease and finally a complete cure. The *yoga*-treatment may be complementary to medical therapy or it may be the sole treatment, depending upon the degree of attainment of the *yogī.* A cancer-patient has very little chance of getting the utmost benefit from *yoga* by newly learning it and applying it for the treatment. For such cases, another perfected *yogī* may treat the patient by *mantra*-therapy, prāṇic healing and other advanced yogic techniques.

One of the aphorisms of Patañjali on *bhūtajaya* has already been referred to.[29] For sure success in getting a cure, the *yogī* must have attained victory over the *bhūta*s. In that case, the

29. *PYD,* III.44.

cancer cells stop proliferation and the existing cells wither away.

The *yogī* performs *saṁyama* and *saṅkalpāyana* on the area affected with cancer. The *saṅkalpa* may be like this: 'My immune system, kill all the cancer cells'. The *saṅkalpa* should be followed by *samādhi*.

In order to activate the immune system, *saṁyama* and *saṅkalpāyana* should be practised on the whole body (*sarvāṅga*). The sequence should start from the head, progress in sequence, go down up to the feet and ascend in the reverse sequence, up to the head. This completes a cycle. A minimum of eight cycles should be repeated in a single sitting. The *saṅkalpa* may be like this: 'My immune system, fortify my body's defence against cancer cells'.

For the fortification of the immune system, *saṁyama* and *saṅkalpāyana* should be practised on the *viśuddhi* at the throat. This is the *cakra* that purifies the whole body, activates the immune system to produce more cellular as well as humoral antibodies and gears up the body in the act of detoxification.

It takes some longer time to get a complete cure. Meditation for a longer time is also recommended to take care of any possible metastasis and the persistence of any cancer cell hiding somewhere in the body.

## Bone-fracture

It may be mentioned at the outset that there is practically no medicine for the healing of a fracture, or, to speak generally, for the repair and healing of any organ or tissue in the body. The limb or organ or tissue heals itself, not passively, but by active participation in the repairing and healing process. If the damaged tissue does not heal itself, the doctor becomes helpless.

What does the doctor do then ? He prescribes drugs like antibiotics to check the invading micro-organisms. He prescribes replacement therapy as insulin in the treatment of diabetes. He prescribes drugs to correct physiological disorders as in the case of hyperacidity. He treats the patient in many ways. He helps the patient's system help itself. In the special case of bone-fracture, the doctor makes the fractured pieces stay in correct alignment and close contact. He makes the affected limb immobile. If there is an open wound or any chance of infection, he prescribes antibiotics and other drugs for the healing of the wound. The doctor practically does nothing for the *actual* repair and healing of the fractured bone. The bone has the necessary *intelligence,* ability and dexterity to repair and heal itself.

Some tissues repair themselves in their own image. The replaced cells are of the same type as were the damaged cells. The more specialised a tissue, the less ability it has to regenerate. To cite an example, the neurons in the brain, if damaged, cannot regenerate. When the power of regeneration is lost, the damaged tissue is repaired by the formation of white connective tissue (collagen fibres). This is akin to the repair of a brick wall by cement mortar.

The more young a patient, the greater ability he has to repair his damaged tissue and organ. In older patients, this ability to repair is reduced and sometimes markedly reduced. This happens especially in the healing of fractured bones.

To accelerate the healing process of fractured bones, meditational therapy may be an alternative one. It should be complementary to usual medical or surgical therapy, done by a competent doctor.

The meditator should perform *saṁyama* and *saṅkalpāyana* on the fracture-site. The *saṅkalpa* may be like this: 'My fractured bone, repair and heal up quickly'.

*Saṁyama* and *saṅkalpāyana* should also be performed on the whole body (*sarvāṅga*). The technique has already been given. The resolve may be suitably paraphrased. It may be like this: 'My body, gear up all forces to quickly heal my fractured bone'.

What has been said on the meditational therapy of the repair and healing of fractured bones may be applied, *mutatis mutandis,* to the repair and healing of any organ or tissue in any disease-condition. This is especially useful in the convalescent period. For example, a patient, in the recovery stage of pulmonary tuberculosis or broncho-pneumonia, may speed up the repairing process of the lungs by this meditational technique.

# 3.6

# Meditation for the Retardation of Geriatric Processes

THE Sanskrit word *jarā* and the Greek word *geras* are almost synonymous. The English word 'geriatrics' has been derived from the Greek word *geras.* The Sanskrit language has a number of words in connection with old age and the late stage of old age. These words are: *vārddhakya* (adjective form = *vṛddha*), *jarā, sthavira, atharva.* A person becomes old usually at the age of sixty years. Most of the physiological processes of geriatrics begin at the age of 60 to 65 years. Marked reduction of sexual libido takes place at this age. Cataract is an old-age disease that affects some persons, both male and female. The enlargement of the prostate gland in some males, with consequent difficulty in micturition, is a senile occurrence. Although Alzheimer's disease, with serious loss of memory, affects a low percentage of people at the age of 65 or after, the reduction in memory is a general feature of senility which starts at the age of about 65. Vision and hearing capacities are also reduced in old age. Individual, racial and climatic differences do exist. Both nature and nurture do influence the onset of old age. Notwithstanding these differences, it may not be incorrect to say that the age of about 65 years is the time of the old-age signal for most people in the world.

An old person becomes *sthavira* or *atharva* at a very late age. In the Western, cold climate, this stage corresponds to the age of 90 or more. In the tropics, this stage comes about one decade earlier, although individual differences do exist.

This is the age of *jarā*, not of old-age (*vārddhakya*).

A number of traits are inherited. The genes (that is, the DNA-constitution of the body) are inherited from the parents, and through them, many of the old-age diseases and other characteristics are programmed. Nature is supported and greatly influenced by nurture. The physical conditions in which a person lives, the financial security or insecurity he has, the food and drinks he takes, his living styles, the stress and strain to which he is subjected in life, the way he manages the stress and strain and the personal philosophy of life decide the early or late onset of senility and the severity thereof.

## Retardation of ageing

Some philosophy cherishes the utopia that man would finally declare his victory over old-age and death and that he would be an immortal god, converting this earth into heaven. The death-rate can be reduced and has been reduced. Old-age can be delayed and, in this regard, the ancient *yogīs* did achieve success. Even in the modern world, some amount of success has already been achieved, although through different means. Old age (*jarā*) and death (*mṛtyu*) can be delayed, but cannot be prevented. Death is a necessity for the smooth running of the creation. A deathless human species on the earth, without complete stoppage of birth, cannot be practically thought of. If death is a necessity, decay, old-age and disease are also necessities. If we think of the prevention of the necessities, we speculate impossibilities. Hence our efforts should be to delay old-age and death with simultaneous planning for the reduction of birth rates.

The physiological functions of many organs of the body become less efficient in old-age. Senility atrophy and degeneration take place in some organs. The micro-anatomy of the tissues undergoes senile changes. For example, there is a drastic reduction in the number of brain cells; the yellow, elastic fibres are replaced with the white, collagen fibres, with the reduction in the elasticity of the walls of the blood vessels; the tendons and ligaments become tougher and hardened; the cartilages at the joints become degenerated, ossified, decayed or eroded; the lubricant synovial fluid in the joints dries up; the bones become decalcified, porous and fragile. The immune system of old persons loses its efficiency.

### How does yoga retard ageing ?

*Yoga* has techniques to delay the onset of senility and to retard the senile processes. *Yama* and *niyama* markedly help the maintenance of a healthy life and the delaying of old-age. *Āsana*s and *prāṇāyāma* have positive roles to play. *Bandha*s and *mudrā*s do help too.

Here we would specifically stress the importance of meditation in the retardation of senility. How does meditation play its role ? Meditation retards the death-rate of cerebral neurons. It calms the mind and prevents the agitation in the nervous system. It maintains a balance in the secretion of neuro-humours. Through the favourable influence of the cerebral cortex in general and the prefrontal area in particular on the limbic system and the hypothalamus, it prevents or minimises the effects of worries, anxieties and mental traumas. As a fact, it does not allow the onset of worries, anxieties and tension. The hypothalamus is favourably influenced to modulate the pituitary gland for maintaining an ideal hormonal balance by suitably activating the endocrine system of the body. The hypothalamus is also influenced to regulate the autonomic nervous system, both parasympathetic and sympathetic, for a normal functioning, and for maintaining a sympathetic-parasympathetic balance. Meditation strengthens the immune system of the body that exercises vigilance and fights against invading micro-organisms. The neuro-humoral balance and the hormonal balance retard the ageing processes.

What has been said here refers to the gross body. In addition to its effects on the gross body, meditation has favourable influence on the subtle body too. All the seven *cakra*s of the body are normalised by meditation. All the *nāḍī*s (psychic channels) and especially the three major *nāḍī*s, namely, *suṣumṇā, iḍā* and *piṅgalā,* function normally and efficiently due to the meditational influence. The *antaḥkaraṇa* (internal instrument) and especially its three principal components, namely, the *buddhi,* the *ahaṅkāra* and the *manas* are rendered purified and transparent by meditation, and thereby their efficiency is improved.

## Meditational technique for delaying senility

The general meditation may be practised. *Dhāraṇā* may be done on the *ājñā-cakra. Dhyāna* may be done on the *praṇava,* (*AUṀ*). *Samādhi* may be *sabīja* (with seeds) in the initial state of the practice. The perfected *yogī* should remain in *nirbīja* (seedless) *samādhi* for a period as long as possible.

In addition to the *ājñā-cakra* meditation, *saṁyama* on the other *cakra*s may be done individually. *Jyotirliṅga* meditation may also be done. In addition to *saṁyama, japa* and *ajapā japa,* if practised sincerely and regularly, would give added benefits.

# 3.7

# Meditation for the Promotion of Mental and Spiritual Health

So far we have dealt with physical health to a major extent and mental health to a minor extent. But mental health is not less important than physical health and both are interdependent. Spiritual health concerns the spirit (self or *ātman*). It is the path of ascension to the final goal of liberation. In this section, we propose to take up some important features of mental health and spiritual health.

## Mental health

### CALMNESS OF MIND

By nature, mind is wavering and unsteady.[30] It constantly produces waves of varying frequencies and wavelengths. Calmness and steadiness are alien to it. Mental labour, worries and tension lead to a mental state (*jāgrata*) in which beta waves with a frequency of 14 to 28 cycles per second are produced. Meditation calms the mind, prevents its wavering and makes it steady. Mind is ordinarily restless; it is accustomed to act on impulse. But it can be controlled by dispassionateness (*vairāgya*) and practice (*abhyāsa*).[31-32] Passion is a potent cause of the restlessness of mind. It must be given up in order that mind is to be controlled and calmed.

30. *BG*, VI.26; 33-34.

31. *PYD*, I.12 (*abhyāsavairāgyābhyāṁ tannirodhaḥ*).

32. *BG*, VI.35 (*asaṁśayaṁ mahābāho manodurnigrahaṁ calam. abhyāsena tu kaunteya vairāgyeṇa ca gṛhyate*).

The meditative state is an alert state devoid of concrete visual imagery. It is characterised by a feeling of tranquillity and lack of tension and anxiety. Alpha waves with a frequency of 8 to 13 cycles per second and an amplitude of microvolts up to 40 are produced by the brain in the meditative state. This state is associated with a feeling of passivity. This is a state in which mind is neither active nor drowsy; it is a neutral state.

When an individual is asleep or unconscious, his brain produces delta waves with a frequency of 2 to 3 cycles per second (below 4 cycles per second). Delta waves are emitted in deep, dreamless sleep (*suṣupti*), in which there is great receptivity to learning. This is the state which is very conducive to getting knowledge, directly absorbed into the unconscious mind, bypassing the sense-organs.

Theta waves have a frequency of 4 to 7 cycles per second. They are profusely emitted during sleep (*svapna*) with dreams. When *saṁskāra*s or *vāsanā*s bubble up from the unconscious to the surface of the mind, theta waves are emitted by the brain. Many children emit theta waves during their waking state (*jāgrata*); this is, of course, rare in adults. The brains of *yogī*s emit theta waves during their deep state of meditation. Some mediums emit theta waves during their receptivity of extrasensory perception. Yogic ecstasy and emission of theta waves go together.

An adept *yogī,* in the higher *samādhi* state, can completely curb the rising of the impulses of the mind (*yogaścittavṛttinirodhaḥ*).[33] In that state, the brain-waves completely cease to rise. If a meditator can attain this state and regularly practices meditation, he can control his mind and harness it for useful and creative work.

---

33. *PYD,* I.2.

## CONCENTRATION

It is a hard job for many persons to concentrate on a particular topic. Their mind wavers and wanders from topic to topic. They fail to focus their attention on anything especially where concentration is to be sustained for a prolonged period. Such unsteady mind can be rendered steady by meditation. In *dhāraṇā* and *dhyāna,* attention is fixed on a particular location and a particular idea. In *samādhi,* consciousness is withdrawn from location and idea and a state of thoughtlessness prevails. Regular practice of meditation promotes the concentration of the mind. Once this is achieved, the mind becomes more productive and creative.

## MEMORY

Information are stored in the mind (not in the brain). The mind-store is not confined to the data of the present life only. Data of past lives have also been stored in the mind.

The recall of the stored information from the mind-store is known as memory.[34] To recall some stored information from the memory of the computer is easier and more dependable than that from the mind. We know very little about the mind, its store of information, the exact location of the store and the mechanism of storing. Hence it is not clear for us why recall of information from the mind is sometimes not easy. The information has been stored. It is not recalled at times when we want to do so, whereas it automatically comes to the surface when do not try for it. Very often stored information are buried in the mind and too intricately trapped and bound to be hardly released.

Meditation cannot be said to be the open sesame for recalling all information from the store of the mind, as and when we desire. However, it is a fact that meditation

---

34. *PYD,* I.11 (*anubhūtaviṣayāsampramoṣaḥ smṛtiḥ*)

facilitates the improvement of memory. How exactly it does is not known. But it is known that it does.

### Senile dementia

Loss of memory is a natural phenomenon among old persons. With some, it is less; with some others, it is more. By the age of twenty, neurons of a person usually die by the thousands, most probably never to be replaced. A person's brain, at the time of birth, contains about 100 billion ($10^{11}$) neurons. If 5,000 of them die a day, 99,983,585,000 are still left at the age of 90. Due to the loss of neurons, cognitive processes (the acts of knowing and perceiving things) slow down as we grow older. This, however, widely varies from person to person.

About 15 per cent of people over 65 suffer from some form of dementia. In addtion to the death of neurons due to ageing, other changes are responsible for the senile dementia. Arteriosclerosis or hardening of the cerebral arteries and multiple small strokes reduce the flow of blood to the brain and hence reduce memory. Huntington's chorea, a disorder, characterised by jerky involuntary movements, affecting the shoulders, hips and face, is accompanied by a progressive dementia. Alzheimer's disease (German neurologist Alois Alzheimer first discovered the disease in 1907) is a serious disorder of the brain manifesting itself in premature senility. Both these diseases are so far incurable. Alzheimer's disease is responsible for more than 50 per cent of the dementia cases of senility in the over-65 population.

Meditation cannot cure these incurable diseases, especially after their onset. We have no experimental data to claim that meditation can prevent their onset. This much can be said that the loss of memory due to the death of neurons in the natural process of ageing can be arrested or postponed, partly at least, by regular practice of meditation.

PROMOTERS OF MENTAL HEALTH

In the second part of this book, *yama*s and *niyama*s have been briefly described. In the total *aṣṭāṅga-yoga,* these two are the prerequisite limbs. *Dhāraṇā, dhyāna* and *samādhi,* combinedly known as *saṁyama,* constitute the apex in which the first five limbs culminate. The preparatory stages condition the mind for better health. These conditions are the promoters, some of which are listed below:

***Altruism*:** A *yogī* is not a self-centred person. If he is a theist, he dedicates himself to the service of the creation of God. He completely surrenders to God.[35] He does not live for himself alone; he lives for all. He rejects the idea — one for one, the seed of individualism. He fosters the idea — one for all and all for one.[36] He may be an agnostic or an atheist. Irrespective of his belief, he should live an altruistic life. Altruism promotes love, curbs hatred, reduces enmity, purifies mind and promotes mental health.

***Equality in vision*:** *Samadarśana* (equality in vision) is a quality of the *yogī*. If he is a theist, he sees God in everything and sees everything in God.[37] He feels that he is not different from *Brahman* and there is nothing which is different from *Brahman*.[38] The atheist or agnostic *yogī* may not accept the idea of *Brahman* and God. But he should realise that all living and non-living creatures have their own rights to exist and exist with dignity. No atheism and agnosticism should shun the maxim — live and let live. The *Gītā*'s moral maxim[39] should be practised by

35. *BG*, XI.55; XVIII. 66; YV, 40.1; IU, 1.
36. *BG*, V.25; XII.4; XII.13.
37. *BG*, VI.30; VII.19.
38. *BU*, I.4.10; II.5.19; IV.4.19; *CU*, VI.8.7; VI.9.4-VI.14.3; III.14.1; IV.11.1; *KTU*, II.1.11.
39. *BG*, VI.32.

any type of *yogī* — theist, atheist and agnostic. Equality of others with oneself is the central idea of this moral principle. If circumstances are equal, the *yogī* sees that whatever is pleasant to himself is pleasant to all creatures, and that whatever is painful to himself is painful to all beings.

***Action without attachment***: The Sanskrit word for attachment is *āsakti*. One should not relinquish action; but one should give up attachment to the fruits of action.[40] It may not be misunderstood that the *Gītā* teaches the abandonment of the fruits of action. Any action may bear good fruits, bad fruits or no fruits, all of which are not under our control. In case of the second or the third alternative (bad fruit or no fruit), attachment to the fruit of action brings agony to a person. Unattached action is free from *tāmasika* or *rājasika* pleasure and agony.

***Equanimity of mind***: The *yogī* always maintains equanimity (*samatvam*) of mind.[41] A life may meet with success or failure, profit or loss, victory or defeat. The *yogī* is not perturbed nor perplexed in one of the paired conditions. The *yogī* is a *buddhiyogī*.[42] His *buddhi* (intellect) is constantly in communion with the Universal Spirit. In *buddhiyoga,* the mind is neutral to pairs such as pleasure and pain, profit and loss, success and failure, victory and defeat, etc. This equanimity of mind is *yoga* which is the skill in actions.[43] An atheist or an agnostic may not recognise the Universal Spirit or his individual spirit. Nevertheless, he should maintain equanimity of mind in order that he gets peace in life. And peace in life is the most valuable asset.

---

40. *BG*, II. 47.

41. *BG*, II. 48.

42. *BG*, II. 49-50.

43. *BG*, II. 50.

***The six foes are to be given up*:** Every person has six foes (*ripus*), intrinsically present in himself. These six are: lustful and craving desire (*kāma*), anger (*krodha*), covetousness (*lobha*), delusion (*moha*), arrogance (*mada*) and envy (*mātsarya*).[44] A person's mental health can never be good when these foes work with full force. The more are they attenuated, the better is the mental health. The best state of mental health is attained when they are completely subdued. When the *yogī* yokes his self to the Universal Self, he becomes an unfathomable steady ocean into which the rivers of desires enter. As the ocean is not affected by the entry of the water of rivers, so does the *yogī* in whom desires merge without producing any response at all[45]. The atheist or agnostic may take a secular attitude. None the less, he cannot get a good mental health as long as he falls a victim to these six foes which are not extrinsic, but are intrinsic.

***Be humane*:** The *yogī* should cherish compassion (*karuṇā*) and give up cruelty and violence. He should promote universal friendship and brotherhood (*maitrī*) and give up hatred. He should be happy over the happiness of others (*muditā*). He should forgive others and ignore the defects and deficiencies in others (*upekṣā*).[46]

***Satisfaction*:** The Sanskrit word for satisfaction is *santoṣa*. It is the property of a healthy mind and no person can be a *yogī* without a healthy mind. The *yogī* is satisfied with whatever he gets.[47] This may be misunderstood as inertia, inaction, lack of perseverence and laziness. Modern life is rat-race for more

---

44. *BG*, I.38; II.43; II.52; II.55; II.62-63; II.70-71; III.2; III.37; IV.16; IV.19; IV.22; IV.35; VII.11; XI.1; XIV.12-13; XIV.17; XVI.4; XVI.8; XVI.10; XVI.16; XVI.18; XVI.21; XVIII.35; XVIII.53; XVIII.73.

45. *BG*, II.70.

46. *PYD*, I.33.

47. *PYD*, II.32; *BG*, III.17; XII.14; XII.19.

and more. Dissatisfaction and desire with sky as the limit provide the basic stimulus to hard work, competition and progress. This modern trend in behaviour seems to be antagonistic to yogic satisfaction. This seeming anomaly is, however, a misinterpretation. Any *sāttvika* effort should aim at maximum benefit to humankind. Intertial laziness is fought against by *yoga.* What it emphasises is this: In spite of your best efforts to improve and progress, you get something which may not be a peak achievement. The best pragmatism would say: 'Be satisfied with whatever you get by your *maximum* effort'.

***Peace.*** The Sanskirt word for peace is *śānti.* The Vedic seers were concluding their daily prayer with a peace-invocation. They were praying for peace in the universe, peace in the human society, peace in the plant as well as animal kingdom and peace in the five primary, material beings — solids, liquids, gases, energy and *ākāśa* (space).[48] Today materialistic affluence and peace are negatively correlated in many societies of the world. Everything other than peace may be in plenty. There is a severe dearth of peace even in affluence. Every *yogī* should try to get peace for himself; at the same time he should try to promote peace in the universe.

The salient promoters of mental health, briefly described in the foregoing paragraphs, are to be acquired by practice of *yama* and *niyama* and also by practical meditation for auto-improvement. Sustained auto-suggestion throughout the life is the best method for self-improvement and this is a type of meditation. An unhealthy mind is too sickly and morbid for the practice of meditation. Hence every meditator should take active steps to improve his mental health. Mental health is a prerequisite for spiritual health. The next concluding portion deals with spiritual health.

48. *YV,* 30.3; 36.17.

## Spiritual health

Yoga uses the word *citta*. We would interchange the two words *citta* and *antaḥkaraṇa* for the discussion on spiritual health. The latter means internal instrument. It has three main constituents, namely, *buddhi* (intellect), *ahaṅkāra* (ego) and *manas* (mind). In a strict sense, the *citta* of *yoga* is the thinking substance of *buddhi*. The *citta*, when unbridled and uncontrolled, is turbid and unsteady.

### THE PURIFICATION OF THE CITTA

Meditation purifies the *citta* (*cittaśuddhi*). The *citta* of the non-*yogī* may be opaque or translucent. But the *yogī*'s *citta* becomes transparent (*svaccha*). The *citta* gets rid of all external tinges and remains in its own form. This is the *ṛtambharā* state.[49] *Ṛtambharā prajñā* generates its own *saṁskāras;* but these *saṁskāras* erase the already printed *saṁskāras*, which were debasing in nature and which could bind the self.[50]

Patañjali uses the term *karmāśaya* for the reservoir of *saṁskāras* in the *antaḥkaraṇa* of the subtle body.[51] This is really the Unconscious of modern psychology. Sigmund Freud's Id, Ego and Super-Ego and the Unconscious are descriptive terms only without any anatomical reference. This is, however, not the case in the psychology of *Yoga* and *Tantra*. The subtle body (*sūkṣma śarīra*), the causal body (*kāraṇa śarīra*) and the *antaḥkaraṇa* in the subtle body are anatomical subtle structures. No liberation of the self is possible as long as the *karmāśaya* exists and functions.[52] In the first stage, the good *saṁskāras* generated by the *ṛtambharā prajñā* occupy the place of the already stored

---

49. *PYD*, I.48 (*ṛtambharā tatra prajñā*); III.5 (*tajjayātprajñālokaḥ*).

50. *PYD*, I.50.

51. *PYD*, II.12 (*kleśamūlaḥ karmāśayo dṛṣṭādṛṣṭajanmavedanīyaḥ*).

52. *PYD*, II.13.

debasing *saṁskāra*s which are thereby uprooted from the *karmāśaya*. This is the first step leading to liberation, but not the final step.

Here we are not going into the details of the different types of *samādhi*. Both *nirvitarka* and *nirvicāra samādhi*s are *nirvikalpa*. Nevertheless, they are still with seed (*sabīja*) since the modifications of the *citta* (*cittavṛtti*s) do not fully subside. When *ṛtambharā prajñā* is attained, the *yogī* gets the true nature of things with full comprehension. *Ṛtambharā prajñā* also produces *saṁskāra*s which are stored in the *karmāśaya*. But these *saṁskāra*s are benign in type and they uproot the already stored harmful, binding *saṁskāra*s, generated out of passion (*rāga*) and aversion (*dveṣa*). With the removal of the harmful *saṁskāra*s from the *karmāśaya*, the *yogī* comes nearer the released state. Finally, the *saṁskāra*s born out of *ṛtambharā prajñā* are erased. This is the stage of *saṁskāra*lessness, the seedless (*nirbīja*) *samādhi*. This is the released state.

## KAIVALYA, THE LIBRATION OF THE SĀṄKHYA-YOGA

The Sanskrit word *kaivalya* has been derived from the word *kevala* meaning 'only'. *Kaivalya* means 'isolation'. The *apparent* binding of the *puruṣa* (self) and *prakṛti* (primordial matter) is the state of bondage. The isolation of the self from *prakṛti* is liberation in the Sāṅkhya and the *Yoga* systems.

According to the Sāṅkhya, the multiple *puruṣa*s (sentient selves), by nature, are eternal, eternally pure, enlightened and unconfined.[53] In reality, the *puruṣa* is never bound and eternally free.[54] In contrast, the *prakṛti* (primordial matter, which is an evolvent and not an evolute; not the evolved matter of the manifest universe) is insentient and single. The conjunction of a *puruṣa* with the *prakṛti* makes the former apparently bound

53. *SPS*, I.19.

54. *SPS*, I.162 (*nityamuktatvam*).

and the disjunction makes it apparently released. Nescience (*avidyā*) is the cause of the conjunction (*saṁyoga*).[55] The doctrine of reflection is an important one in the Sāṅkhya philosophy. As a white crystal gets coloured through its proximity to a *Hibiscus* flower or a coloured gem, so does the *prakṛti* get sentience from the *puruṣa*.[56] The same doctrine of proximity and reflection also explains the seeming agency of the *puruṣa*,[57] although *prakṛti* is the real doer of actions. The doctrine explains the seeming bondage and release of the *puruṣa*.[58] The Sāṅkhya holds that creation results from passion (*rāga*) and release from dispassion (*vairāgya*).[59] The *citta-vṛtti*s (the modifications of the *citta*) are fivefold, both painful (*kliṣṭa*) and non-painful (*akliṣṭa*).[60] The *kleśa-vṛtti*s are five, namely, ignorance (*avidyā*), egoity (*asmitā*), passion (*rāga*), aversion (*dveṣa*) and clinging to life (*abhiniveśa*). They are reflected on the *puruṣa* which is tinged (*uparāga*) thereby. On the cessation of these modifications, the reflections of the *vṛtti*s cease to function, resulting in the recovery of the intrinsic form (*svarūpa*) of the *puruṣa*.

It has already been said that dispassion (*vairāgya*) is one of the means for release. The direct means of release is knowledge.[61] By implication, bondage results from ignorance.[62] What is knowledge and what is ignorance ? For the present purpose, discrimination between *prakṛti* and *puruṣa* and

---

55. *PYD*, II.24 (*tasya heturavidyā*).
56. *SPS*, I.96.
57. *SPS*, I.164.
58. *SPS*, II.35 (*kusumavacca maṇiḥ*).
59. *SPS*, II.9.
60. *SPS*, II. 33; *PYD*, I.6-7.
61. *SPS*, III. 23; *PYD*, II.25-27.
62. *SPS*, III.24.

realisation of the intrinsic nature of *puruṣa* is knowledge, and the lack of this knowledge is ignorance. Meditation (*dhāraṇā, dhyāna, samādhi*) removes passion and causes the cessation of the action of *rajas* (*rāgopahatiḥ*).[63] From *rāga,* comes restlessness. Steadiness is achieved due to the cessation of *rāga*. Meditation causes the removal of the taint of the *citta,* generated by external objects. This taint is an obstruction to knowledge. Since meditation removes this obstruction, it opens the door to knowledge. Meditation accomplishes this act through inhibition of modifications (*vṛttinirodhaḥ*). The five *vṛtti*s have been enumerated by the Sāṅkhya and the Yoga.[64]

Meditation generates some types of modifications in the *citta*. But these modifications are not stored in the *karmāśaya*.[65] Hence they cannot bind the self. Meditation with seed (*sabīja*) attenuates *kleśa*s, but does not remove the attenuated last traces. These last traces can be fully erased only by seedless *samādhi* (*nirbīja samādhi*)[66] by which the effect (*citta*) is dissolved in its cause. Even before the dissolution of the *citta* in its cause, the attenuated *kleśa*s behave like burnt seeds that do not germinate. These attenduated *kleśas,* being burnt by discriminative knowledge, cannot generate new *saṁskāra*s.[67]

The rise of discriminative knowledge, resulting from meditation, imparts transparency to the *citta*.[68] The *yogī,* with a clear and transparent *citta,* becomes omniscient.[69] The *yogī*

---

63. *SPS,* III.30.

64. *SPS,* II.33; *PYD,* I.6.

65. *PYD,* IV.6 (*tatra dhyānajamanāśayam*).

66. *PYD,* II.10.

67. *PYD,* IV.28.

68. *PYD,* IV.29.

69. *PYD,* III.49.

should not mis-utilise his power of omniscience to which he should not be attached too. The power of omniscience does not stand as a hindrance to a detached *yogī*. Such a *yogī* attains to *dharmamegha samādhi*. This state is the summit of spirituality (*dharma*) which showers like torrential rains (*megha*).

Once the *dharmamegha samādhi* is attained, the five *kleśas*[70] (*avidyā, asmitā, rāga, dveṣa, abhiniveśa*) and the three types of *karma*[71] (*śukla:* white or virtuous; *kṛṣṇa:* black or sinful; *śukla-kṛṣṇa:* black and white or mixed) with their roots are destroyed.[72]

A *yogī*, after attaining *dharmamegha samādhi* and after ridding *kleśa*s and *karma*s, is liberated even though he lives with his body. This is the *jīvanmukta* (liberated even though living) state. The *jīvanmukta* still supports his body and continues living. As long as the least trace of *saṁskāra*s persists, the body is retained like the whirling of the potter's wheel.[73] When the *jīvanmukta* leaves the body due to natural death, he gets *videha mukti* (body-less liberation). There is no rebirth of his self after this.

For the released self, the *guṇa*s (*sattva, rajas, tamas*) cease to function. They dissolve in their cause. This dissolution of the effect in its cause is known as *pratiprasavaḥ* (involution). With this, the individual self (*puruṣa*) becomes isolated from the *prakṛti*. It stays in its own form (*svarūpapratiṣṭhā*). This is *kaivalya*.[74]

---

70. *PYD*, II.3.
71. *PYD*, IV.7.
72. *PYD*, IV.30.
73. *SPS*, III.82-83.
74. *PYD*, IV.34.

MOKṢA OF THE NON-DUALISTIC VEDĀNTA

The Sāṅkhya and the Yoga philosophies are almost the same. Both accept two classes of realities, namely, the single *prakṛti* (primordial matter) and the multiple *puruṣa*s (sentient beings). The former, without being reflected by the *puruṣa* and without the proximity of the *puruṣa,* is insentient. Sāṅkhya is atheistic[75] whereas Yoga recognises God (*Īśvara*).[76] But the *Īśvara* of Yoga is not Creator God. He is one of the many *puruṣa*s with the difference that He is a Special *Puruṣa*.[77] His speciality lies in being unconnected with the five *kleśas*.[78] the four types of *karmas*,[79] *vipāka*[80] or the fruition of *karma* and *āśaya*[81] (the reservoir of *karmas*). Both the Sāṅkhya and the Yoga philosophies hold the doctrine of transformation (*pariṇāmavāda*). Their liberation is *kaivalya* or the isolation of the *puruṣa* from the *prakṛti.*

We do not accept the metaphysics of *Yoga* even though we accept the *Yoga* techniques and the theories thereof. We adhere to the non-dualistic (Advaita) Vedānta which recognises one *Puruṣa* only instead of multiple *puruṣas.* The individual selves are not different from the Universal Self (*Brahman* in the attributeless aspect and *Īśvara* in the aspect with attributes). The *Mūla* (primordial) *Prakṛti* is *Mahāmāyā* which is the Power (*Śakti*) of *Brahman* or *Īśvara.* Both the possessor of Power (*Śaktimān*) and Power (*Śakti*) are not separable. The universe of matter and energy (*jagat*) may be called *prakṛti,* but it is not

---

75. *SPS*, I.92 (*īśvarāsiddheḥ*).

76. *PYD*, I.23.

77. *PYD*, I.24 (*kleśakarmavipākāśayairaparāmṛṣṭaḥ puruṣaviśeṣa īśvaraḥ*).

78. *PYD*, II.3.

79. *PYD*, IV.7.

80. *PYD*, II.13.

81. *PYD*, II.12.

the *Mūla-Prakṛti* or *Māyā*. The *jagat* is not a transformed product of *Māyā*. By virtue of the projecting (*vikṣepa*) and the concealing (*āvaraṇa*) power of *Māyā*, *Brahman* appears as the *jagat*, and this process is known as *adhyāsa*. Due to *adhyāsa*, B appears as non-B (*atasmiṁstadbuddhiḥ*).[82] The *jagat* (universe) of multiplicity is not non-existent.[83] *Brahman* is absolute Truth (*Pāramārthika satya*) whereas the *jagat* is an empirical truth (*vyāvahārika satya*). It is *mithyā* by virtue of its being changeable and modifiable. It cannot independently exist; its existence is *Brahman*-dependent.

With this much metaphysics, we would like to dilate the concept of *mokṣa* (liberation) in the Advaita Vedānta. As in the Yoga, the bondage of the individual self in the Vedānta is also empirical. The apparent bondage is through reflection (*pratibimba*) or *upādhi* (limiting adjunct). The apparent bondage is due to ignorance (*avidyā*). Discriminative knowledge (*viveka*) which distinguishes the self from the non-self and the realisation of the identity of the self and *Brahman* give *mokṣa* (release from bondage).

Self-purification is the preliminary step to spiritual ascension. Dirty water is to be filtered, sterilised, distilled and re-distilled to become pure water; so does the self purify itself. This is *ātma-śuddhi*. The methods of *ātma-śuddhi* have already been described.

Meditation helps in the realisation of 'He is I (*so'ham*)', 'That thou art (*tat-tvam-asi*)', 'I am *Brahman* (*ahaṁ brahmāsmi*)'. The removal of ignorance and the dawning of enlightenment on *brahmavidyā* (the knowledge on *Brahman*) lead to the final goal of *mokṣa* (liberation). According to the Advaita Vedānta,

---

82. *BSŚB*, Introduction.

83. *BS*, II.2.28.

a liberated self becomes *Brahman*. It is a full merger with the loss of individual identity.

## SUPERNORMAL PHENOMENA (VIBHŪTIS) AND PERFECTIONS (SIDDHIS)

The third chapter of *Pātañjala Yoga-Darśana* is known as *Vibhūti-Pāda*. The word *vibhūti* is very often translated as 'miracle'. We do not accept the concept that there is anything like a miracle. When some event is not a commonplace, and the why and the how of the event are not known, it is a miracle. Once facts about the event are explored, it ceases to be a miracle. We use the expression 'supernormal phenomena' for such events. We avoid the term 'paranormal', since the prefix 'para' means 'beside' or 'beyond' and not 'super'. We would mention some salient supernormal phenomena pertaining to *Yoga*.

*Dhāraṇā, dhyāna* and *samādhi*, done together, is known as *saṁyama*.[84] When the *saṁyama* of a *yogī* becomes mature, he gets supernormal knowledge and wisdom (*prajñālokaḥ*).[85]

Whatever work a person does and whatever he experiences through his senses, mind and intellect are recorded in his *antaḥkaraṇa*. These micro-prints are technically known as *saṁskāras*. There are two types of *saṁskāras* — *vāsanā-saṁskāra* and *dharmādharma-saṁskāra*.[86] *Saṁskāra*s are cumulatively recorded through past lives and the present life. *Saṁyama* should be gradually practised on gross, subtle and subtler things. At the subtlest state, *saṁyama* can be practised on the *saṁskāras*. By direct perception of the *saṁskāra*s (*saṁskārasākṣātkaraṇa*), one can get knowledge on one's previous

---

84. *PYD*, III.4.

85. *PYD*, III.5.

86. *PYD*, II.12; IV.8-11.

births.[87] By the same technique, applied on the *saṁskāras* of another person, the *yogī* can also get knowledge on the previous births of the other person.

The *yogī*, by doing *saṁyama* on the *citta* (*antaḥkaraṇa*) of another person, can know what the other person is thinking at that time and what data have been stored in his *antaḥkaraṇa*.[88]

Through *saṁyama* on the form of his own body (*kāyārūpa-saṁyama*), the *yogī* becomes invisible to others (*antardhānam*).[89] He does not go anywhere else; he stays there in the proximity of the other person; in spite of this fact, the other person cannot see him. How does it happen? The other person's subtle visual organ is to make contact with the *yogī*'s body in order that the former can see the latter. Due to the *saṁyama* of the *yogī* on the form of his body, this contact is lost. Hence the *yogī* becomes invisible.

What has been said with reference to the visual perception also holds good for the auditory, olfactory, gustatory and tactile perceptions.

For loving all and making friendship with all, the *yogī* should do *saṁyama* on the idea of love and friendship (*maitrī*). For generating compassion for the suffering humanity, the *yogī* should perform *saṁyama* on the idea of compassion (*karuṇā*). For feeling happy with the happiness of others and for getting rid of envy, the *yogī* should perform *saṁyama* on the idea of congratulation (*muditā*).[90]

The solar channel in the subtle body is the *piṅgalā* or *sūrya nāḍī*, right of the central *suṣumṇā*. By performing *saṁyama* on

87. *PYD*, III.18.

88. *PYD*, III.19.

89. *PYD*, III.21.

90. *PYD*, III.23.

the *sūrya-nāḍī,* the *yogī* gets knowledge on the fourteen worlds (*bhuvana*) of the universe.[91]

The lunar channel in the subtle body is the *iḍā* or *candranāḍī,* left of the central *suṣumṇā.* By performing *saṁyama* on the *candranāḍī,* the *yogī* gets knowledge on all the galaxies (*tārāvyūha*).[92]

*Dhruva* is in the summit of the subtle body. It is in the thousand-petalled *cakra* (*sahasrāra*) where Lord Śiva sits. God Śiva is unmodifiable and constant and the controller of all. The Sanskrit word for 'constant' is *dhruva.* By *saṁyama* on the *dhruva,* the *yogī* gets knowledge on all the stars of the universe.[93]

The umbilical *cakra* (*nābhi-cakra*) of *Yoga* is the same as the *maṇipūra-cakra* of *Tantra.* By doing *saṁyama* on the *nābhi-cakra,* the *yogī* gets knowledge on the macro- and the micro-anatomy of his gross, subtle and causal bodies.[94]

The *kaṇṭhakūpa* (throat-pit) of the *Yoga* is the same as the *viśuddha-cakra* of the *Tantra.* By performing *saṁyama* on the throat-centre, the *yogī* can restrain his appetite and thirst.[95]

Below the *kaṇṭhakūpa* and above the heart-centre (*anāhata-cakra*), there is a minor subtle centre inside the thoracic cavity. It is known as *kūrmanāḍī* (the tortoise channel). By performing *saṁyama* on the *kūrmanāḍī,* the *yogī* renders his body and mind calm and stable (*sthira*).[96]

---

91. *PYD,* III.26 (*bhuvanajñānaṁ sūrye saṁyamāt*).

92. *PYD,* III.27.

93. *PYD,* III.28.

94. *PYD,* III.29.

95. *PYD,* III.30.

96. *PYD,* III.31.

At the top of the *brahmarandhra* is a subtle spot known as *mūrdhajyotis* (the top light). It is the place where God Śiva dwells in the form of a phallus with a light-point at the top. This is the *jyotirliṅga.* By doing *saṁyama* on this *mūrdhajyotis,* the *yogī* can have divine vision (*siddhadarśanam* or *divya-dṛṣṭi*)[97].

The *yogī,* through sustained practice of meditation, may develop *prātibha* (intuitional insight) by which he may know everything without *saṁyama* on any spot.[98]

In the proximity of the *anāhata* (the heart-centre) is a subtle spot known as *hṛdaya* or *hṛdaya-puṇḍarīkam.* It is lotus-shaped. By doing *saṁyama* on this *hṛdaya,* the *yogī* can know the *citta* with its *vṛttis.*[90]

The seat of *udāna* is the throat-centre (*viśuddha-cakra*) in the subtle body. By performing *saṁyama* on it, the *yogī* can get victory over the *udāna,* and thereby his body becomes too light. He can walk on water, mud, thorns, etc. At the time of death, his subtle body, with the help of *udāna,* leaves the *brahmarandhra* to pass upwards.[100]

*Samāna* is one of the five *prāṇa*s whose seat is the *maṇipūra-cakra* at the level of the umbilicus. By doing *saṁyama* on the *samāna,* the *yogī* can get victory over it, and thereby he shines like fire.[101]

*Karmasaṁskāra*s are the causes of the bondage of the *citta.* Through the practice of *samādhi,* the *yogī* relaxes this bondage. Simultaneously, he gets the knowledge on the movement of the *citta.* Such a *yogī*'s *citta,* with the subtle *indriya*s, can leave

97. PYD, III.32

98. *PYD,* III.33

99. *PYD,* III.34.

100. *PYD,* III.39.

101. *PYD,* III.40.

his own body and enter into the body of a living or a dead person (*paraśarīrāveśaḥ*).[102]

By performing *saṁyama* on the connection between *ākāśa* (Space) and the subtle auditory organ (*śrotra*), the *yogī* can get clairaudience (*divya-śravaṇam*). He can hear sounds, ordinarily inaudible to others, and sounds from any distant source in the universe.[103]

By doing *saṁyama* on the relation of the body and *ākāśa* (Space), and *saṁyama* on very light substances, the *yogī* can move in Space.[104] *Ākāśa* is the source of all the matter in the body. Solids, liquids, gases and energy are the products of *Ākāśa* and these products can be converted back into *Ākāśa*. This is the relation between the body and *ākāśa*. By *saṁyama* on this relation, the *yogī*'s body becomes *ākāśa* and moves in *ākāśa*.

*Pṛthvī* (solid matter), *jalam* (liquid matter), *agni* (matter as energy like heat, light, etc.) *vāyu* (matter in gaseous form) and *ākāśa* (Space) are the five *bhūta*s (states of matter). Each of these *bhūta*s is in five states. The states are: (a) *sthūlāvasthā* (gross state), (b) *svarūpāvasthā* (the state of own form), (c) *sūkṣmāvasthā* (subtle state), (d) *anvayāvasthā* (the state of internal relation) and (e) *arthavattvāvasthā* (the state of significance). The *yogī* does *saṁyama* on the five *bhūta*s and all the five states of each *bhūta*. Thereby he gains victory over them (*bhūtajaya*).[105]

The five subtle organs of perceptions (*indriya*s) have five states each. These five states are: (a) *grahaṇāvasthā* (the state at the time of perception), (b) *svarūpāvasthā* (the state of own

---

102. *PYD*, III.38.

103. *PYD*, III.41

104. *PYD*, III.42.

105. *PYD*, III.44.

form), (c) *asmitāvasthā* (subtle state), (d) *anvayāvasthā* (the state of internal relation) and (e) *arthavattvāvasthā* (the state of significance). The *yogī* does *saṁyama* on each of these states and thereby he gains victory over the five *indriyas*.[106]

Resulting from the *indriya-jaya*, the *yogī* gets three gains. The first one is *manojavitvam*. The *yogī*'s body and *indriyas* can travel long distances in the analogy of the mind. This is the result of *saṁyama* on the *grahaṇa* state (the state at the time of perception) of the *indriyas*. The *yogī* does *saṁyama* on the *svarūpa* (own form) state of the *indriyas* and thereby can perceive things at distant places even though his body does not travel. This is called *vikaraṇabhāvaḥ*. The *yogī* does *saṁyama* on the other three states (*asmitā, anvaya, arthavattva*) of the *indriyas*. Thereby he gains control over *pradhāna* or *prakṛti* (*pradhānajayaḥ*).[107] *Pradhāna* is the Primordial Nature constituted of the three strands (*guṇas*) — *sattva, rajas* and *tamas*.

*Ṛṣi* Patañjali gives an aphorism on 'out-of-body travel'.[108] He uses the term *mahāvideha*. The *yogī* does *saṁyama* on the *svarūpa* state of the *manas* and the *indriyas* and thereby he gets out of the body. By this, the cover on knowledge is destroyed.

Next we would briefly describe the eight *siddhis*. The Saṅkhya mentions eight *siddhis*.[109] These are, of course, major. In addition to the major ones, there are many minor *siddhis* too. Before we go into the details, we would like to define *siddhi*. There is no exact English equivalent of this word. It may be literally translated as 'perfection', which does not convey the exact meaning. Instead of giving a verbal definition, we would like to clarify the concept. *Siddhi* is that ability which

106. *PYD*, III.47.

107. *PYD*, III.48.

108. *PYD*, III.43.

109. *SPS*, III.40 (*siddhiraṣṭadhā*).

a perfected *yogī* attains. It is not a normal phenomenon occurring in common people. Hence it is *alaukika* (uncommon). It is supernormal. It is apparently a miracle, a supernatural phenomenon, but really a natural phenomenon which can be sceintifically expalined if and when we get detailed knowledge on it. Only some trained *yogīs* can perform it and the layman (non-*yogī*) cannot do it.

An aphorism of *Pātañjala Yoga Darśanam* enlists six *siddhis*.[110] These are *prātibha, śravaṇa, vedana, ādarśa, ākhāda,* and *vārtā.* Through the *prātibha siddhi,* the *yogī* gets direct knowledge on the past, present and future, and he gets knowledge on micro-objects, concealed objects and distant objects. *Śravaṇa* is clairaudience (*divya śravaṇa*) through which the *yogī* can hear from any place of the universe. *Vedana* is *divya sparśa* (divine touch) through which the *yogī* can get tactile sensation from a long distance. *Ādarśa* is *divya darśana* or clairvoyance. The *yogī* can see things at a distance from which light-stimulus does not reach his eyes. *Ākhāda* is divine gustation through which the *yogī* can taste an object without physically tasting it. *Vārtā* is divine olfaction through which the *yogī* can experience an odour without physically smelling it.

Reference has been made by Patañjali to eight *siddhis* in another aphorism.[111] These eight are listed here: (1) *Aṇimā* is the process of making oneself atomic. (2) The *yogī,* by the *siddhi* of *laghimā,* makes himself light. He can walk on water, mud and thorns and move in Space. (3) The *yogī* can enlarge his body or any part of it. It is called *mahimā.* (4) *Garimā* is the action of making one's body heavy. (5) The *yogī* can get any material object at his hand whenever he desires it. It is called *prāpti.* (6) *Prākāmya* is the freedom of will of a *yogī* through

---

110. *PYD,* III.36.

111. *PYD,* III.45.

which he attains things without any obstruction and obstalces. The *yogī* achieves it by his *saṁyama* on the five *bhūtas*. (7) *Vaśitva* is the *siddhi* by which the *yogī* brings animals and human beings under subjugation. (8) *Īśitva* is the power of mastering, controlling and ruling inanimate objects and animate beings.

The *yogī* should not be attached to the *siddhi*s that hinder his spiritual progress and attainment.[112] In spite of *ṛṣi* Patañjali's proscription, many *sādhaka*s spend their yogic career in exhibiting *siddhi*s only. *Siddhi*s come and go. The *yogī* does not bother at all when *siddhi*s come and when they go.

## MODUS OPERANDI LOST

We have mentioned a number of *vibhūti*s and *siddhi*s of *yoga*. The exact mechanism of achieving success has not been given. *Ṛṣi* Patañjali has written some aphorisms only. The techniques were passed down from the preceptor to the disciple. It is a challenge to modern science to discover the techniques. It would be unproductive and self-deceiving to suppose that the *ṛṣi* was speculating and day-dreaming. A perfected seer like Patañjali whose other yogic concepts have been tested and restested to be true is not expected to state things which are not facts. Further investigations are necessary to uncover the cover on our knowledge.

## HIGHEST OPTIMISM IN YOGA

In Part III of this book, we have dealt with a number of benefits that can be obtained by the practice of *yoga*. One can have a strong physique and a strong mind. One can enjoy good health, both physical and mental. One can prevent and cure one's diseases. One can be free from tension and anxiety. One's life can be spiritual. Yoga can give a holistic, healthy and creative life.

---

112. *PYD*, III.37.

The most important optimistic aspect of *yoga* is the fact that one can liberate oneself by one's own efforts. One can be liberated while still living (*jīvanmukta*).

We uphold the *mokṣa* theory of liberation instead of the *kaivalya* theory. The yogic practices for both *mokṣa* and *kaivalya* are the same. There is a conceptual difference, however. Our goal is to become *Brahman*. Everyone of us is not essentially different from *Brahman;* but we are alienated. Through the practice of *yoga,* it is possible for everybody to distil and redistil himself finally to become Pure Existence, Pure Consciousness and Pure Bliss.

# Glossary

*abhiniveśa:* Clinging urge to live; clinging to life.

*ābhyantara vṛtti:* Inhalation.

*abhyāsa*: Practice.

*ādarśa*: Clairvoyance.

*adhiṣṭhāna*: Substratum; the underlying reality which is responsbile for the appearance of the surface entity.

*adhyakṣa:* Chairperson.

*adhyāsa:* When some substratum, S, appears as non-S, something other than S, the phenomenon is known as *adhyāsa*.

*adhyāsavāda:* The doctrine of *adhyāsa;* the doctrine of B (*Brahman*) appearing as non-B.

*adhyāya:* Study.

*advaita:* Non-dualistic.

*āgama:* Knowledge obtained directly without any mediation; revealed knowledge.

*āgāmī:* Future.

*agni:* 1. Fire. 2. God as the substratum of fire. 3. Heat. 4. Matter in the form of energy.

*agocara:* Beyond the cognisance of the senses.

*agocarī-mudrā:* A yogic, symbolic gesture in which gazing is done at the tip of the nose.

*aham:* I.

*Ahaṅkāra/ahaṅkāra:* Ego or egoity, the evolute of *Buddhi* (*buddhi*).

*ahiṁsā:* Non-violence in thought, speech and action.

*ajapā:* The unconscious repetition of a *mantra,* done without the movement of the lips; the spontaneous repetition of the *mantra* — *so'ham* (He is I).

*ājñā:* 1. Command, Order. 2. The eyebrow centre in the subtle body.

*ājñā-cakra:* The psychic centre in the subtle body, located between the two eyebrows.

*ajñānam:* Ignorance; nescience.

*ākāśa:* Space; the fifth and the subtlest form of material existence.

*ākāśī:* Pertaining to *ākāśa* or Space.

*ākhāda:* Divine gustation; a yogic *siddhi* by which an object is tasted without any physical contact.

*akliṣṭa/akliṣṭā:* Non-productive of hindrances to *yoga.*

*akṣara:* 1. A syllable. 2. That which never decays and perishes. 3. *Brahman.*

*ālamba:* Support.

*alaukika:* Uncommon.

*amātra:* Devoid of any of the three syllables, *a, u, ṁ,* of *AUṀ.*

*anāhata:* 1. Unbeaten. 2. The psychic centre in the subtle body at the level of the heart.

*anāhata-cakra:* The psychic centre in the subtle body at the level of the heart.

*anāhata dhvani:* Unbeaten sound; mystical, divine sound produced at the *anāhata-cakra;* the sound *'AUṀ'* which is produced without anything being beaten.

*Ānanda:* Bliss.

*ānanda-bhuk:* One that experiences bliss.

*ānandamaya kośa:* The blissful sheath.

*anāsakta:* Detached.

*anāsakti:* Non-attachment; detachment.

*aṇimā:* A yogic *siddhi* by which one makes oneself atomic.

*annamaya kośa:* The material sheath.

*anṛta:* Disorder; disorderliness associated with entropy.

*antaḥkaraṇa:* Internal instrument located in the subtle body, its three principal components being *buddhi, ahaṅkāra* and *manas.*

*antaḥprajña*: That which cognizes the internal mental impressions.

*antara*: Internal.

*antara kumbhaka*: The holding of breath during the interval between complete inhalation and the start of exhalation.

*antaraṅga*: Inner limb; close.

*antardhānam*: Becoming invisible to others.

*antardṛṣṭi*: Inner vision.

*antaryāmī*: The inner controller.

*anumāma*: Inference.

*anvaya*: Internal relation.

*anvayāvasthā*: The state of interal relation.

*Āpaḥ*: The primordial cosmic fluid or plasma, evolved from *Mahat* or *Virāḍ*.

*apāna*: 1. The *Prāṇa* that dwells in the *mūlādhāra* and functions in the expulsion of faeces, urine, semen and uterine-*cum*-vaginal discharges. 2. The outgoing breath.

*aparigraha*: Non-accumulation of wealth; non-acceptance of kind or cash, if such acceptance is immoral.

*āpekṣika satya*: Relative reality; relative truth.

*aprakaṭa*: Unmanifested.

*apraketaṁ salilam:* Un-differentiated cosmic micro-fluid.

*aprameya:* Immeasurable.

*arthavattva:* Significance.

*Arthavattvāvasthā:* The state of significance.

*āsakti:* Attachment.

*āsana:* 1. A yogic posture. 2. Something on which one sits.

*asaṅgaḥ:* Detachment.

*āśaya:* Reservoir; a storing place; the reservoir of karmic impressions.

*asiddhi:* Failure.

*aśiva:* Bad; harmful; malignant; pernicious, malevolent.

*asmitā:* 1. Egocentricity. 2. Subtlety.

*asmitāvasthā:* Subtle state.

*āśrama:* 1. Hermitage; a hermit's dwelling place. 2. A quarter of one hundred years — the expected lifetime of a human being.

*aṣṭāṅga:* The eight limbs; the eight components.

*asteya:* Non-stealing.

*asundara:* Ugly.

*āsura:* Demoniac.

*aśvinī-mudrā:* One type of yogic gesture in which the two anal sphincters make rhythmic movements simulating what the horse does.

*atharva:* An old person with physical and mental incapability resulting from senility.

*Ātmā:* The Great Self; the Universal Self; *Brahman.*

*ātmā:* The individual self.

*ātmajñāna:* Knowledge on the self or Self.

*ātmakrīḍā:* One who plays with one's self.

*ātman:* The same as *Ātmā* or *ātmā;* Self; self.

*ātmārāma:* One who finds delight in one's self.

*ātmaśuddhi:* Self-purification.

*AUṀ:* The verbal symbol that designates *Brahman.*

*āvaraṇa śakti:* Veiling or concealing power.

*avidyā:* Ignorance; nescience.

*Avyakta:* The Unmanifest.

*āyāma:* 1. Restraining. 2. Expansion in all directions.

*bahiraṅga:* Outer; outer limb.

*bahirdṛṣṭi:* Outer vision.

*bāhya:* External.

*bāhya kumbhaka:* The interval between complete exhalation and the start of inhalation.

*bāhyavṛtti:* Exhalation.

*bandha:* Binding, bonding or locking.

*bandhana:* Bondage.

*bandha-traya:* The triple locks.

*basti:* The yogic method of cleansing the intestines.

*bhairava-mudrā:* A kind of yogic *mudrā* in which the palms are placed on the lap, both facing upward, the dorsal surface of the right hand touching the left palm.

*bhakti:* Devotion.

*bhāṅga:* Leaves and flower-tops of Indian hemp.

*bhāvātīta:* That which transcends any *bhāva* (thought or idea).

*bhrū:* Eyebrow.

*bhrūmadhya:* Between the eyebrows.

*bhūta:* 1. Any of the five states of material existence — solids, liquids, gases, energy and *ākāśa* (space). 2. Any created entity, either living or non-living.

*bhūtajaya:* Victory over matter (*bhūtas*).

*bhūtātmā:* The self in a non-living entity.

*bhuvana:* 1. World. 2. One out of the 14 parts of the universe.

*bīja:* 1. Literally means 'seed'. 2. The residual whirl of mind, still persisting in the *savikalpa* and *nirvikalpa samādhi,* on the awareness of the *yogī*'s identification with the *dhyeya,* is the seed (*bīja*).

*bindu:* 1. A point. 2. A minor psychic centre in the head in between the *ājñā* and the *sahasrāra.*

*bindu-visarga:* A psychic centre in the subtle body, located above the *lalana-cakra* and in between the *ājñā-cakra* and the *sahasrāra.*

*brāhma:* Pertaining to *Brahma* or God.

*brahmacarya:* Abstinence from sexual indulgence.

*brahmagranthi:* A psychic knot formed by the *suṣumṇā, iḍā* and *piṅgalā* at the *mūlādhāra.*

*brāhma-muhūrta:* Auspicious time, 4 a.m. to 5 a.m.

*Brahman:* The formless, attributeless, actionless, unmodifiable, timeless, spaceless, immaterial Reality that is pure Existence, Consciousness and Bliss.

*brahma-nirvāṇa:* A complete merger of the individual self in the Great Self.

*brahmarandhra:* The orifice in the *suṣumṇā* at the summit of the head.

*brahmavidyā:* Knowledge on *Brahman.*

*brāhmī sthitiḥ:* Stay in *Brahman.*

*brahmopāsanā:* The worshipping of God.

*Buddhi/buddhi:* 1. Intellect. 2. *Buddhi* for an individual corresponds to *Virāḍ* or *Mahat* for the entire cosmos.

*buddhiyoga:* *Karmayoga* with constant fixation of intellect on God, with equanimity of mind in both success and failure.

*buddhiyogī:* One who practises *buddhiyoga.*

*caitanyādhyāsa:* The superimposition of consciousness.

*cakra:* 1. The wheel; the circle; the vortex; the disc; the discus. 2. Any one of the psychic centres in the subtle body.

*candra:* Moon

*candrabhedī prāṇāyāma:* A type of *prāṇāyāma* in which the *prāṇa* pierces the *candranāḍī.*

*candranāḍī:* The psychic channel located on the left side of the *suṣumṇā;* otherwise known as the *iḍā.*

*catuṣpāt* : Four quarters.

*Cetas:* Consciousness; *Brahman.*

*cetomukhaḥ:* One who heads towards the pure, fundamental Consciousness.

*cidāveśa:* The induction of consciousness in an insentient entity due to reflection of *brahma*-consciousness.

*cinmudrā:* The yogic seal made by the index finger and the thumb for the promotion of consciousness.

*Cit:* The fundamental Consciousness; *Brahman.*

*cit:* Consciousness; empirical or induced consciousness.

*citchāyāpatti:* The falling of the shadow of consciousness; the reflection of consciousness.

*citta:* The yogic term for the thinking faculty.

*cittaśuddhi:* The purification of the *citta.*

*cittavṛtti:* The whirls of mind.

*daiva:* Divine.

*darśanendriya:* The subtle organ of visual perception.

*devatā:* Deity: A god.

*dhāraṇā:* A yogic process in which concentration is focussed on a spot.

*dharma:* Meritorious action; virtuous action; spirituality; doing actions that should be done.

*dharmādharma saṁskāra:* Mental prints generated out of virtuous and sinful actions.

*dharmamegha samādhi:* The yogic state of *samādhi* in which spirituality showers like torrential rains.

*dharma-saṅkaṭa:* Crisis in the judgement of good and bad.

*dhauti:* The yogic method of cleansing the upper alimentary canal.

*dhotī:* A long cloth that Hindu males wear on the loin.

*dhruva:* 1. Constant, 2. Lord Śiva seated in the *sahasrāra*.

*dhvani:* Sound.

*dhyāna:* Focussing the attention on a single idea that flows in the mind continuously without interruption.

*dhyeya*: That which is meditated on; the idea or notion on which *dhyāna* is done.

*dīpa:* A lamp.

*divya darśana:* Divine vision; clairvoyance.

*divya-dṛṣṭi:* Divine vision; clairvoyance.

*divya sparśa:* Divine touch.

*divya śravaṇam:* Clairaudience.

*draṣṭā:* Seer.

*draṣṭuḥ:* Of the seer.

*dṛṣṭi:* Gazing; vision.

*duḥkha:* Suffering.

*Durgā:* Mother Goddess who destroys evil forces and protects against misfortunes.

*dvandva:* A pair of opposites.

*dvandvātīta:* Pairs of opposites transcended.

*dveṣa:* Aversion.

*ekākṣara:* Monosyllable; it usually refers to *AUṀ in yoga*.

*ekībhūtaḥ:* Unified.

*Gaṇeśa:* God who controls all, His symbolic representation being elephant-headed, pot-bellied and short-statured.

*gāñjā:* Marijuana.

*gārhasthya:* The life of a householder.

*garimā:* The yogic *siddhi* by which the body becomes heavy.

*gāyatrī:* 1. A Vedic metre. 2. The celebrated Vedic *mantra* in *gāyatrī* metre. 3. Mother Goddess Sarasvatī, the consort of Brahmā.

*ghrāṇendriya:* The subtle organ of olfactory perception.

*grahaṇāvasthā:* The state at the time of perception.

*grāhya:* Perceivable or cognisable object.

*gṛhastha:* Householder.

*guṇa:* 1. Strand or string. 2. Attribute, property or quality.

*guru:* Preceptor; spiritual preceptor; art-preceptor.

*haṭha-yoga:* The branch of *yoga* that is primarily concerned with physical exercises and body-purificatory practices.

*hṛdaya:* Same as *hṛdaya-puṇḍarīkam.*

*hṛdaya-puṇḍarīkam:* A minor psychic centre in the chest in between the *anāhata* and the *viśuddhi,* but in the proximity of the *anāhata.*

*icchā:* Wish; desire.

*iḍā:* The tubular, psychic channel in the subtle body located on the left side of the *suṣumṇā.* It is also called the *candranāḍī.*

*indriya:* The sensory and motor subtle organs.

*īśitva:* A yogic *siddhi* by which objects, both animate and inanimate, are controlled.

*iṣṭa-devatā:* Chosen tutelary deity.

*Īśvara:* God; the Lord who rules and controls.

*īśvara-praṇidhāna:* Surrender to God; stay in God.

*jāgarita:* Waking.

*jagat:* The changeable, modifiable and impermanent universe which is in constant motion.

*jāgrata:* Waking.

*jala/jalam:* 1. Water. 2. Matter in fluid state.

*jāla:* Net or web.

*jālandhara bandha:* A type of yogic *bandha* with chin-lock.

*japa:* The repetition of a *mantra.*

*jarā:* Late old age, at or beyond the age of 65.

*jaya:* Victory.

*jīvana:* Life.

*jīvanmukta:* Liberated, although still living.

*jīvātmā:* The individual self in a living being.

*jñāna:* Knowledge.

*jñāna-mudrā:* A type of yogic seal made by the index finger and the thumb.

*jñānayoga:* The *yoga* of knowledge; the realisation of the non-duality of *Brahman* and one's identity with *Brahman.*

*jñānayogī:* One who practises *jñānayoga.*

*jñānendriya:* Subtle sonsory organs; the five subtle organs of perception.

*jyoti:* Light.

*jyotirliṅga:* The phallus-shaped light in the subtle body at the apex of the head; Lord Śiva in the *sahasrāra* in the form of light.

*Kaḥ:* *Āpaḥ* or the primordial cosmic Plasma, evolved from *Mahat* or *Virāḍ.*

*kaivalya:* The isolated state of the self in the Yoga concept of liberation; the state of the self completely separated and detached from the Primordial Nature or *Prakṛti.*

*kākī:* Pertaining to *kāka* or the crow.

*kākī-mudrā:* A yogic symbolic gesture in which the lips are pursed so as to resemble a crow's beak.

Kālī: Power or consort of God Rudra (Śiva); Mother Goddess pertaining to *Kāla* or Time.

*Kāma:* Lustful desire; desire.

*kāmanā:* Desire.

*kanda:* Bulb.

*kaṇṭhakūpa:* Throat-pit; the same as the *viśuddha-cakra.*

*kaṇṭha-mudrā:* Throat-seal; a kind of yogic *mudrā* in which both the lateral sides of the throat are pressed by the dorsal surfaces of the fingers of the hands (from the knuckles to the tips of the fingers).

*kapālabhāti:* A type of *prāṇāyāma,* by which the frontal portion of the head is purified.

*kāraṇa:* Cause.

*kāraṇa-śarīra:* Causal body.

*karma:* 1. Mental impressions produced by an individual's actions are imprinted in the *buddhi* of the *antaḥkaraṇa.* These are *karma*s in the Vedānta and the Yoga. 2. Action.

*karma-saṁskāra:* Karmic impressions recorded in the mind.

*karmāśaya:* The reservoir of *karmas,* located in the subtle body.

*karma-vipāka:* The fructification of the karmic impressions.

*karmayoga:* The *yoga* of action without attachment to the fruits thereof.

*karmayogī:* One who practises *karmayoga.*

*karmendriya:* The five subtle organs of action.

*karuṇā:* Compassion.

*kāyārūpa:* The form of one's own body.

*kevala:* Only

*khecarī:* One who moves in *kha* or *ākāśa* or Space.

*khecarī-mudrā:* One type of yogic gesture with tongue-lock.

*kīrtana:* The loud singing of devotional songs with or without instrumental music; the loud repetition of a *mantra* with instrumental music.

*kleśa:* A hindrance or impediment to *yoga.*

*kleśamūla:* Rooted in *kleśa.*

*kliṣṭa/kliṣṭā:* Productive of hindrances.

*kośa:* Sheath.

*kriyā:* 1. A yogic process. 2. Action.

*kriyāyogaḥ:* The collective name for austerities (*tapaḥ*), studies of spiritual scriptures (*svādhyāya*) and surrender to God (*īśvara-praṇidhāna*).

*krodha:* Anger.

Kṛṣṇa: The full incarnation of Viṣṇu, God of love and righteousness who sustains the universe; God who attracts everybody and everything; God who cultivates divinity in everybody.

*kṛṣṇa:* Black in colour; sinful.

*kṣamā:* Forgiveness.

*kṣetra/Kṣetra:* 1. Field. 2. Cosmic Field.

*kumbhaka:* Retention of breath in

the yogic *prāṇāyāma.*

*kumbhaka-rahita: Prāṇāyāma* without retention of breath.

*kumbhaka-sahita: Prāṇāyāma* with retention of breath.

Kuṇḍalinī: The Divine Mother of the universe who pervades the Cosmos and, at the same time, dwells in the *mūlādhāra-cakra* in a coiled form.

Kuṇḍalinī Yoga: The *yoga* that deals with the arousal of the serpent power and the related ascent and descent.

*kūrmanāḍī:* The tortoise-shaped subtle channel, located in the chest below the *viśuddhi* and above the *anāhata-cakra.*

*laghimā:* A yogic *siddhi* by which one makes oneself light.

Lakṣmī: The Power or Consort of Viṣṇu; Mother Goddess who nourishes the universe; the Goddess of wealth.

*lalana-cakra:* A small psychic centre situated in the back of the nasopharynx between the *bindu* and the *viśuddhi.*

*līlā:* Sportive play.

*liṅga:* 1. It literally means 'phallus'. It is the symbol for God Śiva, the benevolent and auspicious; the symbol for the Father of the universe. 2. A suggestive sign or symptom. 3. Subtle. 4. Gender.

*liṅga-śarīra:* Subtle body.

*lobha:* Greed; covetousness.

*loṭā:* Traditional Indian mug with an almost sperical shape.

*mada:* Pride mixed with arrogance.

*mahā:* Great.

*mahā-bandha:* The perineum retraction lock.

*mahākāśa:* Great Space.

*Mahāmāyā:* The Great *Māyā;* the Power of *Brahman* or *Īśvara* (God); *Mūlaprakṛti* or the Primordial Nature.

*mahā-mudrā:* A yogic gesture that has the utmost importance among the *mudrās.*

*maharṣi* : A great saint; a great seer.

*Mahat:* The Great; the first evolute evolved from *Prakṛti* or the Primordial Nature; the Cosmic Intellect; the Cosmic Mind; the Sāṅkhya word equivalent to the Vedic *Virāḍ.*

*mahāvedha:* A yogic process with some resemblance to *mahā-mudrā* and *mahā-bandha.*

*mahāvrata:* Great vow.

*mahimā:* The yogic *siddhi* by which the body or part of it can be enlarged.

*maitrī:* Friendship and love.

*manas:* Mind.

*mānasika:* Mental. The *mānasika japa* is a kind of *japa* in which the *mantra* is mentally repeated.

*maṇḍala:* A kind of mystical diagram used in invoking a diety.

*maṇipūra-cakra:* A psychic centre in the navel region of the subtle body.

*manojavitvam:* Travelling ability of the body and senses like that of the mind.

*manomaya kośa:* The mental sheath.

*mantra:* A mystic syllable or syllables uttered for concentrated attention on a thought.

*maraṇa-trāsa:* The fear of death.

*mātṛkā:* Each character of the Sanskrit alphabet placed in a *maṇḍala* or *yantra,* to which some magical power is ascribed.

*mātsara:* One who is envious, jealous or malicious.

*mātsarya:* Jealousy, malice or envy.

*Māyā:* The Power of *Brahman* or God; Primordial Nature; the Mother of Nature made up of matter and energy; the Mother of the universe.

*Megha:* Clouds; rains.

*mithyā:* One that is changeable, modifiable, impermanent and dependently existent.

*moha:* Delusion.

*mokṣa:* The Vedāntic liberation; the re-establishment of the identity of the individual self and the Universal Self.

*mṛtyu:* Death.

*mṛtyubhaya:* Fear of death.

*muditā:* Joy over the success and happiness of others.

*mudrā:* 1. A seal. 2. A symbolic gesture used in *yoga.* 3. Mystical gestures shown in Yoga, Tantra and Hindu worshipping rituals.

*muhūrta:* Time; moment.

*mukta:* Liberated; free.

*mūla:* Root or base; primordial.

*mūla-bandha:* A type of yogic *bandha* in which the muscles of the lower abdomen are contracted and pulled upward and backward.

*mūlādhāra-cakra:* The psychic centre which is the base or foundation; the lowest psychic centre of the subtle body, located two fingers above the anus and two fingers below the genital organ.

*mūlaprakṛti:* The Primordial Nature; the Mother of Nature made up of matter and energy; the mother of the universe; Māyā.

*mūrdhajyotis:* The top light; Lord Śiva seated at the summit in the *sahasrāra* as a light point.

*nābhi-cakra:* The umbilical psychic centre, same as the *maṇipūra-cakra.*

*nāda:* 1. Vigorous sound. 2. The

vibrations of the Primordial Nature.

*nāda-yoga:* A kind of *yoga* in which sound is meditated upon.

*nāḍī:* 1. The psychic channel in the subtle body through which *Prāṇa* flows. 2. A tubular, hollow structure.

*nāḍi-śodhana-prāṇāyāma:* The *prāṇāyāma* which purifies the *nāḍīs*; the kind of *prāṇāyāma* in which breathing is done through alternate nostrils.

*Nāra: Āpaḥ* or the Primordial Cosmic Plasma, evolved from *Mahat* or *Virāḍ.*

*nāsā:* Nose.

*nāsikāgra:* The tip of the nose.

*nāsikāgra-dṛṣṭi:* The nosetip gazing.

*nauli:* The yogic practice of the contraction and control of the abdominal muscles.

*nauli-kriyā:* The action or the practice of *nauli.*

*neti:* 1. The yogic method of nasal cleansing. 2. Not this.

*neti-loṭā:* A small water-vessel with a side outlet (spout), used for nasal cleansing in *Haṭha-Yoga.*

*nidrā:* sleep.

*niraham:* I-less; ego-less.

*nirbīja:* Seedless; *samādhi,* without *saṁskāra* traces.

*nirdvandva:* A state neutral to pairs of opposites.

*nirguṇa:* Attributeless; devoid of qualities or properties.

*nirmama:* My-less.

*nirodha:* Prevention: preventing the generation of.

*nirvaira:* One who gets rid of enmity; one who has no enmity with anybody.

*nirvicāra samādhi:* Super-reflective *samādhi* in which the *dhyeya* is subtle rather than gross. In this *samāpatti,* the *citta* does not maintain distinctions of the place, the time and the cause of the *dhyeya* and is fully absorbed in the *dhyeya* only. The space-time as well as the cuase-effect relation-ships of the subtle *dhyeya* are completely emptied.

*nirvikalpa samādhi: Samādhi* without *vikalpa* or without alternative manifoldness; the super-deliberative and the super-reflective types with reference to gross and subtle objects, respectively; both are with seed.

*nirvitarka samādhi:* Super-deliberative, on gross object, without *vikalpa* and with seed. In this yogic state, no distinction is maintained among the word used for the object (*nāma*), the intended object itself (*rūpa*) and the act of knowing. The *citta* is completely absorbed in the *dhyeya* only.

*niṣkāma karma:* Desireless action.

*niṣṭhā:* Steadfast adherence.

*nistraiguṇyaḥ:* Free from the three *guṇas* — *sattva, rajas* and *tamas.*

*niyama:* 1. The performance of actions prescriptive in *yoga.* 2. Rules.

*OṀ/AUṀ:* The mono-syllable, verbal or written, that designates *Brahman; praṇava.*

*oṅkāra:* The sound of *OṀ/AUṀ*

*padma:* Lotus.

*padmāsana:* A kind of yogic posture; the lotus-pose.

*pañca:* Five.

*pāramārthika satya:* 1. Absolute Reality. 2. Absolute truth.

*Paramātmā:* The Great Self; *Brahman; Īśvara* or God.

*paraśarīrāveśaḥ:* Leaving one's own body and entering the body of another living or dead person.

*parigraha:* Accumulation of wealth; immoral acceptance of cash or kind.

*pariṇāmavāda:* The doctrine of transformation.

*Pātañjala:* Pertaining to Patañjali.

*piṅgalā:* The psychic channel in the subtle body, located on the right side of the *suṣumṇā.* It is also called the *sūrya-nāḍī.*

*prajñā:* Wisdom: refined intellect.

*Prājña:* One of the four states of *Brahman* in which the individual is in deep sleep, does not desire anything, and does not experience and dream. The Self as *Prājña* is *Īśvara* (God).

*prajñālokaḥ:* Supernormal knowledge and wisdom.

*prajñānaghanaḥ:* One that has been condensed into a mass of consciousness.

*prākāmya:* A yogic *siddhi* by which things are attained without obstructions and obstacles.

*prakaṭa:* Manifestation.

*Prakṛti:* 1. Manifested Nature of matter and energy. 2. The unmanifested Power of *Brahman* which is the Mother of the manifested Nature.

*pramāṇa:* 1. Proof. 2. Means of getting valid knowledge.

*Prāṇa:* An all-pervasive subtle substance that is the mother of all forms of forces and energy; the fundamental, activating or energising principle; an evolute of *Āpaḥ.*

*prāṇa:* 1. The *Prāṇa* that dwells in the *anāhata-cakra* and functions in the chest area in inhalation. 2. The incoming breath.

*prāṇamaya kośa:* The vital sheath.

*praṇava:* The monosyllable *AUṀ/OṀ* that stands for *Brahman.*

*prāṇāyāma:* The yogic process of breath-control through which *prāṇa* is collected, stored and restrained.

*praṇidhāna:* Surrender; stay in.

*prapañcopaśama:* The universe ceases to be (in the fourth or the *Turīya* state).

*prapatti:* Surrender.

*prāpti:* The yogic *siddhi* by which any material object comes to the hand, whenever desired.

*prārabdha:* Already initiated.

*praśāntātmā:* One with a serene and tranquil self.

*praśānti:* Perfect Peace.

*praśvāsa:* Exhalation.

*prātibha:* Intuitional insight. Through *prātibha,* a *yogī* gets direct knowledge on the past, present and future, and also on micro-objects, concealed objects and distant objects.

*pratibimba:* Reflected image.

*pratiprasavaḥ:* Involution.

*pratyāhāra:* Withdrawal; the yogic process in which the senses are withdrawn.

*pratyakṣa:* Mediate knowledge obtained through sense-perception.

*pratyaya:* Conception, notion or idea.

*pravivikta-bhuk:* One that experiences objects isolated and stored in the mind.

*pravṛtti:* Potent urges and desires of life; clinging to sensual enjoyment and indulgence.

*prema:* Intense Love.

*pṛthvī;* 1. Earth. 2. Solid matter.

*pūraka:* Inhalation in the yogic *prāṇāyāma.*

*Pūrṇa*: Full; *Brahman.*

*Puruṣa:* The primordial Cosmic Person; God.

*puruṣa:* The individual self which is sentient and immortal; the sentient spirit.

*rāga:* Passion.

*rāgopahatiḥ:* The cessation of the action of passion.

*rajas*: The string or strand of activity and motility.

*rājasika:* Pertaining to the attribute of *rajas* or activity.

*rasanendriya:* The subtle organ of gustatory perception.

*recaka:* Exhalation in the yogic *prāṇāyāma.*

*ripu:* Enemy.

*ṛṣi:* Seer, a saint; a monk.

*ṛta*: Perfect order.

*ṛtambharā:* Productive of orderliness, calmness and serenity.

*rudragranthi:* The psychic knot formed by the *suṣumṇā*, the *iḍā* and the *piṅgalā* at the *ājñā.*

*sabīja:* With seed; *samādhi* with *saṁskāra* traces as the seed.

*Saccidānanda:* Existence, Consciousness and Bliss; *Brahman.*

*sādhaka:* A person who sincerely and arduously practises something with perseverence.

*sāḍī:* A long, decorated cloth put on by Indian ladies.

*saguṇa:* With attributes.

*Saḥ*: He.

*sahasrāra:* The thousand-petalled lotus in the summit or crown of the head; the seventh psychic centre in the subtle body, located at the cerebral apex.

*sakāma karma:* Action with thirsty desires.

*Śakti:* Power, Consort; the Power of *Brahman;* the consort of God; Divine Mother.

*Śaktimān:* The possessor of Power.

*samadarśana:* Equality in vision.

*samadarśī:* One who has equality in vision.

*samādhi:* This is the supreme yogic state devoid of thoughts, forms, attributes, functions and material existence in the mind; complete union or complete identification with *Brahman;* the yogic state in which the *buddhi* is completely absorbed in the self or Self.

*samāna: Prāṇa,* stored in the *maṇipūra-cakra* that functions in the production of energy, in the equalisation of *prāṇa* and *apāna* and in balancing anabolism and catabolism.

*samāpatti:* Literally means 'to become like that'. It is the yogic state of the *buddhi* of transparency, devoid of *rājasika* and *tāmasika* whirls, to become one with the knower, the act of knowing and the object-to-be-known, both gross and subtle.

*samaṣṭi:* Totality; collectivity.

*samatvam:* Equality; equanimity.

*śāmbhavī:* The adjective form of 'Śambhu' (God) in feminine gender.

*śāmbhavī-mudrā:* The symbolic gesutre in *yoga,* in which gazing is done at the eyebrow centre at the top of the nose.

*saṁskāra:* Mental impressions imprinted in the internal instrument of the subtle body; imprints on the *antaḥkaraṇa.*

*saṁskāra-piṇḍa:* The totality of the mental impressions stored in the subtle body.

*saṁskāra-sākṣātkaraṇa:* Direct perception of the *saṁskāras.*

*samyak caritra:* Good conduct.

*saṁyama: Dhāraṇā, dhyāna* and *samādhi* done together.

*sāmyāvasthā:* The equipoised state.

*sañcita:* Cumulatively added and stored.

*sandhyā:* Junction; the junction of any two periods of the four periods of the day of 24 hours, each period having the duration of six hours.

*saṅga/saṅgaḥ:* Attachment.

*saṅkalpa:* Resolve: a strong autosuggestion; a strong determination.

*saṅkalpāyana:* A yogic technique through which a resolve is introduced to the Unconscious; a yogic technique of autosuggestion in a state of yogic trance.

Sāṅkhya: An Indian School of philosophy founded by Kapila; it adheres to dualism, the insentient Primordial Nature being one category and the innumerable sentient spirits belonging to a second category.

*saṇmukhī-mudrā:* A kind of yogic *mudrā*, also called the *yonimudrā*.

*saṁnyāsī:* one who has renounced the world.

*śānti:* Peace.

*santoṣa:* Contentment.

*sarala:* Simple.

*śaraṇa:* shelter; refuge.

*śaraṇāgati:* surrender.

Sarasvatī: The Power or Consort of Brahmā, the creator God of the Hindus; Mother Creatrix; the Goddess of knowledge.

*śarīra:* Body.

*sarvabhūtahite ratāḥ:* Dedicated to the welfare of all beings.

*sarvāṅga:* The whole body; all the limbs and parts of the body.

*sarvāṅgāsana:* A type of yogic *āsana* in which the body below the head is raised upward; the shoulder-stand pose.

*Sat:* Existence.

*ṣaṭkarma:* Six yogic purificatory exercises.

*sattva:* The string or strand of goodness and purity.

*sāttvika:* Pertaining to the attribute of *sattva* or goodness and purity.

*Satya/satya:* 1. That which exists; Existence. 2. Truth.

*śauca:* Cleanliness of mind, speech and body and also cleanliness of the environment.

*śava:* Corpse; dead body.

*śavāsana:* The corpse-pose in *yoga*.

*savicāra:* The *samāpatti* which is *savicāra* is reflective, concerned with subtle objects rather than gross and associated with the place, the time and the cause of the *dhyeya*. The *citta*, while being absorbed in the *dhyeya*, maintains these distinctions.

*savikalpa:* With *vikalpa* or awareness of alternatives out of more than one; *savikalpa samādhi* includes *savitarka* and *savicāra* types, the former on a gross and the latter on a subtle object.

*savitarka:* In *savitarka samāpatti*, the *yogī*'s *citta* is absorbed in gross matter with reference to the word used for the object (*nāma* or name), the meaning of the word (*rūpa* or the form of the intended object) and the act of knowing (*jñāna*). The distinction among these three is maintained in the *savitarka* state.

*siddha:* Accomplished; perfected.

*siddhadarśanam:* 1. Divine vision; clairvoyance. 2. The sight of liberated, perfected persons (*siddha puruṣa*s).

*siddhāsana:* A kind of yogic posture recommended for meditation; accomplished pose.

*siddha-yoni-āsana:* The accomplished pose, specially modified for women.

*siddhi:* Success; perfection; supernormal phenomena exhibited by a perfected *yogī*.

Śiva: 1. Literally means 'the auspicious, the benign and the benevolent'. 2. The Sanskrit word for God. 3. One of the Hindu Trinity: God who annihilates and dissolves.

*smṛti:* Memory.

*śodhana:* Purification.

*so'ham:* He is I.

*sparśanendriya:* The subtle organ of tactile perception.

*śraddhā:* Faith, trust, confidence, truthfulenss and belief in; unwavering faith.

*śravaṇa:* 1. The act of hearing. 2. Clairaudience.

*śravaṇendriya:* The subtle organ of auditory perception.

*śrotra:* The subtle auditory organ.

*sṛṣṭi:* Creation; emanation from the self; manifestation from the Unmanifest.

*stambha-vṛtti:* Retention.

*sthavira:* Advanced old-age in which the limbs and the whole body are unable to function normally.

*sthira:* Firm; stable; steady; unmoving.

*sthitaprajña:* One whose wisdom is firmly established in the concept that one is the Supreme *Brahman*.

*sthūlabhuk:* That which experiences the gross material objects.

*sthūla-śarīra:* Gross body.

*sthūlāvasthā:* Gross state.

*sukha:* Comfort, happiness.

*sukhāsana:* A kind of yogic posture; the comfortable pose.

*śukla:* White; virtuous.

*śukla-kṛṣṇa:* A mixutre of black and white; a mixture of good and bad.

*sūkṣma-śarīra:* Subtle body.

*sūkṣmāvasthā:* Subtle state.

*sūkta:* Hymn.

*sundara:* Beautiful.

*sūrya:* Sun.

*sūryabhedī prāṇāyāma:* The type of *prāṇāyāma* in which *prāṇa* pierces the *sūryanāḍī.*

*sūryanāḍī:* The psychic solar channel, otherwise known as *piṅgalā.*

*suṣumṇā:* The central subtle channel in the body, flowing vertically inside the spinal cord.

*suṣupti:* The state of deep sleep.

*sūtram:* 1. Aphorism. 2. A thread.

*sva:* Own.

*svabhāva:* Own nature; the sum total of one's *saṁskāras.*

*svaccha:* Transparent.

*svādhiṣṭhāna cakra:* The psychic centre in the subtle body, located two fingers above the root of the genital organ.

*svādhyāya:* The study of spiritual scriptures; *praṇava-japa.*

*svapna:* Dream.

*svarūpa:* Own form.

*svarūpapratiṣṭhā:* Stay in one's own form.

*svarūpāvasthā:* The state of own form.

*svarūpe:* In the own form.

*śvāsa:* Inhalation.

*svastika:* 1. Auspicious. 2. A kind of mystical cross or mark with the extremities of the four arms bent round in the same direction.

*svastikāsana:* A kind of yogic posture; the auspicious pose.

*Taijasa:* One of the four states of *Brahman* in which the Self cognises the internal, mental impressions and experiences objects isolated and stored in the mind.

*tamas*: The string or strand of inertia, impurity and darkness.

*tāmasika:* Pertaining to the attribute of *tamas.*

*tanhā:* A Pāli word for 'thirst'.

*tanmātra:* Literally means 'that only'. Five types of subtle fields in the Sāṅkhya cosmogony, each field giving rise to one state of matter (*bhūta*).

Tantra: Hindu/Bauddha religio-philosphical system in which Mother-worship is a dominant feature; the body is deified and sanctified for the rituals; *mantra*s and *yantra*s are made use of; and Kuṇḍalinī is aroused.

*tapaḥ:* Austerity.

*tārāvyūha:* Galaxy.

*trāṭaka:* Steady gazing at a particular point without winking.

*tri:* Three.

*triśūla:* Trident.

*tṛṣṇā:* Thirst.

*Turīya:* The fourth state of *Brahman;* the absolute state.

*turīya:* Literally means 'fourth'. It is the terminal *samādhi* state in *yoga.*

*udāna: Prāṇa,* stored in the *viśuddhi,* that acts in the upward movement in processes such as vomiting and hiccup is *udāna.*

*uḍḍiyāna:* To fly up.

*uḍḍiyāna bandha:* The abdominal retraction-lock in which *prāṇa* flies up through the *suṣumṇā nāḍī.*

*ujjayī prāṇāyāma:* A type of *prāṇāyāma* in which inhalations and exhalations are done through both nostrils without retention of breath.

*upādhi:* Limiting adjunct. An adventitious entity is the *upādhi* of a real entity when the former confines the latter, both being apparently but closely associated.

*upāṁśu:* A kind of *japa* in which the *mantra* is repeated in a whisper or humming, without being made audible to others.

*uparāga:* Tingeing.

*upāsanā:* Worshipping.

*upekṣā:* The action of ignoring the defects in others.

*uttarīya:* A piece of cloth that traditional Hindu males wear on the shoulders.

*vācaka:* That by which one is designated.

*vaikharī:* A kind of *japa* in which the *mantra* is verbally and audibly repeated.

*vairāgī:* One who has given up passion.

*vairāgya:* Freedom from worldly passion; dispassion; dispassionateness.

*Vaiśvānara:* One of the four states of *Brahman* in which the Self cognises the external world and experiences the gross material objects.

*vajra:* Thunderbolt; the name of a subtle prāṇic channel — *vajranāḍī.*

*vajrāsana:* A kind of yogic posture; the thunderbolt pose.

*vārddhakya:* Old-age.

*vārtā:* Divine olfaction; experiencing an odour without physically smelling it. It is a yogic *siddhi.*

*vāsanā:* A special type of *saṁskāra* that is more deeply buried in the Unconscious and more forcibly binding in nature.

*vāsanā-saṁskāra:* Mental prints of *saṁskāras* of *vāsanā* type.

*vāsanāśaya:* The reservoir of *vāsanās*, buried in the deep layers of the Unconscious in the subtle body.

*vaśitva:* A yogic *siddhi* by which human beings and animals are subjugated.

*vastu:* Material objects.

Vāsudeva: Kṛṣṇa, the son of Vasudeva; God.

*vāyu:* 1. Wind. 2. The prāṇic energy called *Prāṇa*. 3. That which makes something work. 4. Matter in gaseous form. 5. All-pervasive God as the substratum of gaseous matter.

*vedana:* A yogic *siddhi* by which one gets tactile sensation without physically touching; divine touch.

Vedānta: A number of allied philosophical systems of India, based on the Upaniṣads, the *Brahmasūtra* and the *Bhagavad-Gītā*.

*vibhūti:* Supernormal phenomena.

*videha-mukti:* Liberation after leaving the body on death.

*vidyā:* Knowledge.

*vijñānamaya kośa:* Intellectual sheath.

*vikalpa:* A verbal knowledge on something which is devoid of existence; hallucinatory perception, resulting from mental projection out of the store in memory; alternative choice out of more than one.

*vikaraṇabhāvaḥ:* The perception of things present at distant places without getting physical stimulus from the perceived objects.

*vikṣepa śakti:* Projecting power.

*vīṇā:* A classical, musical string instrument of India.

*vināśa:* Annihilation.

*vipāka:* The fruition of *karma*.

*viparīta:* Reverse; opposite.

*viparītakaraṇī:* Reversing.

*viparītakaraṇī-mudrā:* A yogic gesture in which the sun dwelling in the navel is brought upward to the throat, and the moon dwelling in the *bindu-visarga* is carried downward to the throat.

*viparyaya:* False knowledge due to the process of B mistakenly known as non-B.

*Virāḍ:* The Great; the Cosmic Mind; the Supermind; the Vedic word equivalent to the Sāṅkhya *Mahat*.

*viṣāda:* Agony.

*viṣādayoga:* The mental state of languor, lassitude, dejection, depression or despondency.

Viṣṇu: 1. God who pervades all. 2. God who sustains the universe

*viṣṇugranthi:* The psychic knot formed by the *suṣumṇā*, the *iḍā* and the *piṅgalā* at the *anāhata-cakra*.

*viśuddha:* Pure.

*viśuddha-cakra:* The psychic centre at the level of the throat in the subtle body.

*viśuddhi:* The same as the *viśuddha-cakra.*

*vivartavāda:* The doctrine that the universe which is a mere illusion is the phenomenal appearance of *Brahman* which is the sole real entity.

*viveka:* Knowledge that discriminates good from bad, right from wrong.

*vrata:* The observance of vows.

*vṛtti:* Whirl.

*vṛttinirodha:* The inhibition of the modifications on the mind.

*vyakta:* Manifested.

*vyāna:* *Prāṇa,* stored in the *svādhiṣṭhāna-cakra,* that works in movements in all directions as is the case in the circulation of blood and lymph and in the transmission of nerve impulses.

*vyaṣṭi:* Individual.

*vyāvahārika satya:* 1. Empirical reality. 2. Empirical truth.

*yama:* Restraint; self-control; non-performance of actions proscriptive in *yoga.*

*yantra:* Mystic geometrical figures used in Tāntric worshipping.

Yoga: An Indian system of philosophy that also prescribes physical and mental practices for the well-being of the individual and his spiritual liberation.

*yoga:* Etymologically derived from the Sanskrit verb-root *yuj* which means 'to unite'. The word *yoga* means 'the union of the individual self with the Universal Self' and also 'the isolation of the spirit (*puruṣa*) from the Primordial Nature (*prakṛti*).

*yoga-mudrā:* A type of yogic gesture, which is really an *āsana,* but which can give the benefits of a *mudrā.*

*yoga-nidrā:* Yogic sleep; a self-induced yogic trance in which auto-suggestions are made.

*yogāsana:* Yogic pose or posture.

*yogastha:* While united with God; while the mind is fixed on God.

*yogī:* One who has practised and mastered Y*oga.*

*yoni:* 1. The female generative organ: womb; uterus; vagina; vulva. 2. Source, origin.

*yoni-mudrā:* A kind of yogic *mudrā,* also called the *saṇmukhī-mudrā.*

# Bibliography


Allen, R.J., 1983, *Human Stress: Its Nature and Control*, Minneapolis, MN: Burgess Publishing Company.

Bammer, K. and Newberry, B.H., 1983, *Stress and Cancer*, Toronto: C.J. Hogrefe.

Benson, H., 1974, 'Decreased blood pressure in borderline hypertension subjects who practised meditation', *Journal of Chronic Diseases*, 27: 163.

Benson, H., 1975, *The Relaxation Response*, New York: Morrow.

Benson, H., Greenwood, M.M. and Klemchuk, H., 1977, 'The relaxation response: Psychophysiologic aspects and clinical applications'. In: Lipowski, Z.J., *et al.*, *Psychosomatic Medicine*, New York: Oxford University Press.

Benson, H. and Klipper, M.Z., 1975, *The Relaxation Response*. New York: Avon Publishers.

Benson, H., Kotch, J.B., Crassweller, K.D. and Greenwood, M.M., 1977, 'Historical and clinical considerations of the relaxation response', *American Scientist*, *65* (July): 441-43.

Best, C.H and Taylor, N.B., 1966 (1st publ.1937), *The Physiological Basis of Medical Practice* (8th edn.), Baltimore: The Williams and Wilkins.

*Brahmasūtra Śāṅkarabhāṣya, The* (vol.1 & 2 ) 1982 (1st publ. 1981), Delhi: Parimal Publications.

Calder, N., 1971, *The Mind of Man*, New York: Viking.

Cella, J.H. and Watson, J., 1991, *Manual of Laboratory Tests*, Philadelphia: F.A. Davis Company.

Charanpuri, G.S. (Sanskrit Text & Hindi Trans.) 1984, *Śiva Saṁhitā*, Mumbai: Khemaraj Shrikrishnadas.

Danielou, A., 1973 (1st publ.1949), *Yoga*, London: Johnson Publications.

Datey, K.K., Deshmukh, S.N., Dalvi, C.P. and Vinekar, S.L., 1969, 'Shavasan: a yogic exercise in the management of hypertension', *Angiology*, 20: 325.

Dean, S.R., 1970, 'Is there an ultraconscious beyond the unconscious?', *Canadian Psychiatric Association Journal, 15:* 57-61.

Gopal, K.S., Anantharaman, V., Nishith, S.D. and Bhatnagar, O.P., 1975, 'The effects of yogasanas on muscular tone and cardiorespiratory adjustments', *Yoga Life,* (May): 3-11.

Gorakṣanātha, Yogī, *Gorakṣa-Saṁhitā.*

Guinness, A.E. (ed.), 1990, *ABC's of the Human Mind,* New York: Reader's Digest.

Guyton, A.C., 1966, *Textbook of Medical Physiology,* Philadelphia: W.B. Saunders.

Hilgard, E.R., 1973a, 'A neodissociation interpretation of pain reaction in hypnosis', *Psychological Review, 80:* 396-411.

Hilgard, E.R., 1977, *Divided Consciousness: Multiple Controls in Human Thought and Action,* New York: Wiley Interscience.

Hilgard, E.R., Atkinson, R.L. and Atkinson, R.C., 1979 (1st publ. 1953), *Introduction to Psychology* (7th edn.), New York: Harcourt Brace Jovanovich Inc.

Iyengar, B.K.S, 1997 (1st publ. 1966 by George Allen & Unwin, London), *Light on Yoga,* New Delhi: HarperCollins.

Iyengar, B.K.S., 1981, *Light on Prāṇāyāma* (*Prāṇāyāma Dīpikā*), London: George Allen & Unwin.

Jaggi, O.P. (M.D.), 1974, *Mental Tension and its Cure,* Delhi: Orient Paperbacks.

Jaggi, O.P. (M.D.), 1982, (1st publ.1975), *You Can Prevent Heart Attack,* Delhi: Orient Paperbacks.

Joshi, K.S., 1983, *Yogic Prāṇāyāma,* Delhi: Vision Books.

Lidell, L., 1983, *The Book of Yoga,* London: Ebury Press.

Lipowski, Z.J., *et al.*, 1977, *Psychosomatic Medicine,* New York: Oxford University Press.

Lysebeth, A.V., 1988 (1st publ. 1979), *Prāṇāyāma: The Yoga of Breathing,* London: Unwin Paperbacks.

Mahāyogīndra, Śrīnivāsabhaṭṭa, *Haṭharatnāvalī.*

Morgan, C.T., King, R.A., Weisz, J.R. and Schopler, J, 1986 (1st publ. 1956), *Introduction to Psychology* (7th edn.), New York: McGraw-Hill Book.

Ostrander, S. and Schroeder, L. 1973, *Psi-Psychic Discoveries behind the Iron Curtain*, UK: Abacus.

Panda, N.C., 1996, *Mind and Supermind* (Vol.I & II), New Delhi: D.K.Printworld.

Pandit, Shambhu Nath, 1992, *Stress Management through Yoga and Meditation*, New Delhi: Sterling Publishers.

Patel, C.H., 1973, 'Yoga and biofeedback, management of hypertension', *Lancet, 2:* 1053.

Patel, C.H., 1975, 'Twelve-month follow up of yoga and biofeedback', *Lancet, 1:* 62.

Radhakrishnan, S., 1960, *The Brahma-sūtra,* London: George Allen & Unwin.

Radhakrishnan, S. 1967 (1st publ. 1948), *The Bhagavadgītā,* London: George Allen & Unwin.

Radhakrishnan, S. 1969 (1st publ.1953), *The Principal Upaniṣads,* London: George Allen & Unwin.

Rodriguez, T. and Ram, K. (ed. & trans.), 1992, *Pure Yoga (The Gheraṇḍa-Saṁhitā),* Delhi: Motilal Banarsidass.

Sachdeva, I.P., 1978, *Yoga and Depth Psychology,* Delhi: Motilal Banarsidass.

Saraswati, Swami Muktibodhananda and Saraswati, Swami Satyananda (trans. & ed.), 1985, *Haṭhayoga Pradīpikā* (by Yogīndra Svātmārāma), Munger (Bihar, India): Bihar School of Yoga.

Saraswati, Swami Satyananda, 1983 (1st publ. 1969), *Asana Pranayama Mudra Bandha* (6th edn.), Munger (Bihar, India): Bihar School of Yoga.

Saraswati, Swami Satyananda, 2000 (1st publ.1974; 2nd end. 1983), *Meditations from the Tantras,* Munger (Bihar, India): Bihar School of Yoga.

Schwarz, M.S. and Associates, 1995, *Biofeedback: A Practitioner's Guide,* 2nd edn., New York: The Guilford Press.

Selye, H. 1976, (1st publ. 1956), *The Stress of Life* (rev.edn.), New York: McGraw-Hill).

Shastri, G.D., (ed.), 1990, *Sāṅkhya Yoga-Darśanam* (*The Yoga-Darśanam of Patañjali*), Varanasi: Chaukhamba Saṅskrit Sansthan.

Shrivastava, S.C. (ed.) 1988, *Pātañjala Yoga-Darśana* (with Vyāsa Bhāṣya), 2nd edn., Varanasi: Chaukhamba Surbharati Prakashan.

Sinha, N., 1979 (1st publ. 1915 by Panini Office, Allahabad), *The Sāṅkhya Philosophy* (2nd edn.), New Delhi: Oriental Books Reprint Corpn.

Śivānanda, Svāmī, 1971 (1st publ.1935), *Kuṇḍalinī Yoga* (6th edn.). Sivanandanagar (India): The Divine Life Society.

Śivānanda, Svāmī, 1972. *Japa-Yoga* (7th edn.), Sivanandanagar (India): The Divine Life Society.

Udupa, K.N. (M.D.), 1985 (1st publ.1978), *Stress and its Management by Yoga*, 2nd edn., Delhi: Motilal Banarsidass.

Vinekar, Kuvalayananda, 1963, *Yogic Therapy — Its Basic Principles and Methods*, New Delhi: Ministry of Health, Govt. of India.

Wallace, R.K. and Benson, H., 1972, 'Physiology of meditation', *Scientific American, 226(2)*: 84-90.

Wallace, R.K., Benson, H., Wilson, A.F. and Garret, M., 1971, 'Decreased lactate during transcendental meditation', *Proceedings of the Federation of American Society for Experimental Biology, 30(2)*: 376.

Warrier, A.G. Krishna (tr.), 1983, *Śrīmad Bhagavad Gītā Bhāṣya of Śrī Śaṅkarācārya*, Chennai: Sri Ramakrishna Math.

Wenger, M., and Bagchi, B., 1961, 'Studies of autonomic function in practitioners of *yoga* in India', *Behavioral Science, 6*: 312-23.

Wenger, M., Bagchi, B. and Anand, B., 1961, 'Experiments in India on 'voluntary' control of the heart and pulse', *Circulation, 24:* 1319-25.

Woods, J.H., 1983 (1st publ. 1914 by Harvard University Press), *The Yoga-System of Patañjali*, Delhi: Motilal Banarsidass.

Yogi, Maharishi Mahesh, 1975 (1st publ. 1963 by George Allen & Unwin, London), *Transcendental Meditation*, New York: The New American Library.

# Index